PENGUIN BOOKS

CHINAPHOBIA—A WASTED OPPORTUNITY

Dr Karim Alwadi is an entrepreneur/political scientist based in Beijing since 2001. Started up and founded several companies in China spanning sectors from machinery manufacturing, infrastructure investment and development, to the travel industry.

He received his Bachelor's and Master's Degrees in International Relations, focusing on Sino–Arab Relations, at China RenMin University. obtained his PhD degree in International Politics from China Foreign Affairs University. He is also an active member of the Chinese Academic society.

Karim currently holds the following positions:

- Fellow of Ren Min University Middle East and African Studies Institute.
- Senior Fellow at the Institute of Global Governance and Development at Tong Ji University in Shanghai.
- China-Arab State Expo Advisory Board Member
- Co-Founder of the Saving Syrian Children Program, a charity program initiated in 2017, with a focus on providing aid to Syrian families affected by war.
- Fellow of the Aspen Institute—Global Leaders Program.
- YPO (Young President Organization) Beijing Chapter member.
- Recipient of the 2019 McNulty Prize Catalyst Fund.

Dr Mohammed Kheir Alwadi was born in 1948. He studied Media and Publicity in Moscow State University from 1968 to 1974, from where he received his master's degree.

He received an Honorary Doctorate from the Russian Academy of Sciences in St Petersburg, of which he became an integral member. He served as a Director for foreign radio stations in Radio Damascus in 1975, then as a General Director of Syrian Radio in 1977. In the period 1978–1980, he was Director of Syrian National Television.

He became Chief Editor, General Director General of Alwahda Foundation for Press and Publishing, and Chief Editor of *Al-Thawra* newspaper in Syria from 1980 to 1990.

In 1990, he became Director General for Tishreen Foundation for Press and Publishing, and the Chief Editor for *Tishreen* newspaper.

In 2000, he became an Ambassador Extraordinary and Plenipotentiary for the Syrian Arab Republic in the People's Republic of China, until the end of 2008.

In 2002, he became a Non-Resident Ambassador for Syria in both Vietnam and Mongolia.

In 2009, he founded the China and Asia Research Centre, which to date he still heads. In 2013, he became an integral member of the Russian Peter the Great Academy of Sciences and Arts. He is a member of International, Arab, and Syrian Federations of Journalists. He has written many political articles and studies about international affairs and Chinese–Arab relations as well as a large number of books on politics and mass media, including:

The Most Important Media Bodies in the World British Broadcasting Corporation – the Arabic Section Studies about Psychological War and Propaganda Chinese Foreign Policy China's Experiences from Extremism to Moderation Chinese-Israeli Relations – Cold Considerations Meetings with Leaders from Countries of Asia *The Chinese Community: A View from the Inside* (under publication). He has also published a number of literary works, including the novel *The Flaming Frost* and a collection of short stories.

ChinaPhobia—A Wasted Opportunity

KARIM ALWADI & MOHAMMAD
KHEIR ALWADI

PENGUIN BOOKS

An imprint of Penguin Random House

PENGUIN BOOKS

USA | Canada | UK | Ireland | Australia
New Zealand | India | South Africa | China | Southeast Asia

Penguin Books is part of the Penguin Random House group of companies
whose addresses can be found at global.penguinrandomhouse.com

Published by Penguin Random House SEA Pte Ltd
9, Changi South Street 3, Level 08-01,
Singapore 486361

First published in Penguin Books by Penguin Random House SEA 2022

Copyright © Karim Alwadi and Mohammad Kheir Alwadi 2022

ISBN 9789815017717

Typeset in Garamond by MAP Systems, Bangalore, India

www.penguin.sg

Contents

Preface

ChinaPhobia has become one of the most striking phenomena in international politics today. Opinion polls and surveys in many countries monitor the rise in anti-China sentiment. The US China confrontation became one of the main headlines of news outlets around the world. Western media focus on anti-Chinese actions and activities taking place in different parts of the world. The topic of ChinaPhobia occupies a leading position in the activities of many research centres, conferences, and political symposia.

Raising the issue of ChinaPhobia and clarifying the reasons for its emergence and the possibility of it becoming a constant phenomenon in international life is the first step towards a solution, because diagnosing the disease is halfway to the cure. Our work is not an attempt to widen the gap or further inflame feelings of hatred between China and America, but rather to raise awareness and warn against the detrimental cost of the spread of ChinaPhobia. We also hope that rational people will play their part in limiting this phenomenon.

The authors of this book address this theme and their views about the causes and costs of its emergence. They forewarn of the dangers in escalating ChinaPhobia, not only to the economy and trade, but also to international relations on a global scale. Given China's growth and opportunities for prosperity and stability, exacerbating ChinaPhobia could cost the world dearly. The authors address primary factors driving this phenomenon including China's view of the development of these relations, and how the Chinese think and plan to promote the growth of their country in coming decades. Their hope is to decrease some of the current tensions.

The authors of the book are not originally from China or America, but both have decades of experience as active Chinese observers, and residents of China, with colleagues in all levels of Chinese government and society. The authors' Arab and Russian backgrounds offer a fresh third-party perspective about this book in both form and content. The content is presented by father and son in a conversational style, with the aim of making the subject accessible as a topic for ordinary discussions that benefit from the distinct perspectives of multiple generations and cultures. Family conversations are often what influence people's political perspectives and decision making; voices of tradition and innovation in dialogue can reshape present actions. Though their views are not so different towards this topic, their background and life experience has led to a different procedure of processing China's role in the world, both took two different ways to reach the conclusions of the book.

The father, Dr Mohamed Kheir Al-Wadi is a writer, journalist, politician, and diplomat, who has followed the situation in China for more than thirty years and toured all regions of China. He served as Ambassador to China and Dean of the Arab Diplomatic Corp in Beijing from 2000 until early 2009—the ruling era of Presidents Jiang Zemin and Hu Jintao. Prior to that, he made three press visits to China, in 1992, 1996 and 1998, where he met with several Chinese leaders and wrote articles on the economic and social development of the country during that period. Since the completion of his diplomatic duties in China, he has travelled to Beijing almost every year, writing hundreds of articles and five books about China. Two of them were translated into Chinese and published in Hong Kong—tackling Chinese foreign policy, China's economic and social development, China's relations with Middle Eastern countries, and developments within Chinese society. His fifty-year career as a writer also provided him many opportunities

to communicate with influential Southeast Asian leaders about what
was happening in China. His latest book, published in 2019, recounts
how China benefited from the opinions and experiences of Asian
leaders to bring about the 'Chinese Renaissance'.

He now heads the Centre for China and Asia Strategic Studies, which
he founded ten years ago. He admits that much about China remains
a mystery even after thirty years of study. His lack of fluency in the
Chinese language limits his understanding and direct communication
with a culture of intense interest to him and importance to the world.

The second author of this book, his son, Dr Karim Alwadi, has
lived in China for twenty years, speaks fluent Chinese, Arabic, Russian
and English, and is raising two children in Beijing with his Chinese
wife. Karim is a graduate of China Ren Min University. He serves as
a fellow of several Chinese think tanks and is an active participant in
Chinese and international academic activities around China, particularly
surrounding the Belt and Road Initiative. A successful businessman,
Karim's mastery of the Chinese language, intimate experience with
Chinese culture, and energetic and broad involvements offer insightful
observations into Chinese thinking, priorities, and actions. Karim
has achieved a remarkable presence in cultural and political arenas,
including writing a book in Chinese, published in China, discussing the
situation in the Middle East and the role of Hezbollah. He is an active
participant in talk shows broadcast by Chinese-language television
channels and has a significant presence at intellectual conferences and
events inside and outside China. He is a fellow of the Aspen Institute
and a member of Young Presidents' Organization (YPO).

This father and son team are both eager students of politics and
culture, and active communicators. They have personal experience of
the devastating mistrust, fear, hatred and bloodshed resulting from
growing 'Islamophobia' in the West. They share their insights about
growing ChinaPhobia in the hopes of helping reduce the terrible
human costs that growing animosities inevitably bring.

Introduction

Why have we written this book?

As Syrians, we have been living through the devastating costs of war firsthand. That is why we hope the US and China can avoid escalating their current tensions, and respect can replace growing ChinaPhobia.

Father: Humanity has suffered enough from division and war. I witnessed with horror the suffering of the Cold War which hostility to communism produced. It plunged the world into bloody proxy wars—the Korean War starting in the summer of 1950, the Soviet intervention in Hungary in 1956, and the Cuban missile crisis of 1962 which put the world on the brink of a devastating nuclear clash between the Soviet Union and the United States. I lived through the Vietnam War (1965–1975) which claimed the lives of some 60,000 American soldiers and more than four million Vietnamese; the entry of Soviet tanks into Czechoslovakia in 1968 and the June 1967 war between Arabs and Israelis. Ten years of the Afghan War (1979–1989) in Afghanistan killed 30,000 Soviet soldiers and hundreds of thousands of Afghans, followed by the October War in the Middle East in 1973. These wars cost the world millions of victims and tens of millions of displaced persons, as well as the destruction of the areas where these wars took place.

I also experienced, by virtue of my studies in the Soviet Union and my subsequent stay in Russia, the fallout of the Cold War and its implications for the Soviet people, as well as the consequences of the tragic fall of the Soviet Empire and its states. When the Soviet economy collapsed, tens of millions of people were plunged into poverty, instability, and chaos. Crime and organized crime spread, and wars broke out between Armenia and Azerbaijan, and in Georgia. Moldova cracked. The Latin Wars exploded in Tajikistan and elsewhere, and hostility between Baltic and Russian nations warmed up. CommunismPhobia opened the gates of hell for many peoples and countries. Even the United States, which considered itself victorious at the time, was not spared losses.

Son: I would add that hostility to communism and the subsequent Cold War also diverted huge amounts of global resources for military purposes and caused an arms race which threatened global security and stability and left poverty and famine in many parts of the globe.

As you mentioned, the United States considered itself the winner of the Cold War. The American author Fukuyama came up with his famous theory that the victory of Western capitalism over communism meant 'the end of history as such,' the end of wars and tragedies and the beginning of a new era for the world free of threats.

The history that followed disproved his theory, as more wars and regional conflicts exploded, threatening international peace and security. Surprisingly little has been said about the huge price of the USA's claimed victory in the Cold War!

Father: The main reason to start with this Cold War history is that we do not want hostility toward China to plunge the world into a similar era of suffering and war. Currently the growing tensions are evident mainly in trade, cyber and media arenas between China and the United States, but they could again ignite a significant arms race, and exacerbate tensions in Southeast Asia.

Son: Let me point out two additional dimensions of this that seem important to raise. The first is that hostility to communism and the

Cold War was based on ideology between countries mostly of one race and continent, namely Europe; ChinaPhobia adds ethnic tensions that can magnify these ideological tensions.

My second concerns the deeply held, though not often voiced in public, conviction of many Western scholars and politicians that the West is and must remain the centre of present-day human civilization. Many believe that the centre of gravity should not and will not move back to Asia. Though it's not politically correct to speak of it aloud, this mentality—especially within the elites of the Western hemisphere—clearly surfaces behind closed doors. While the advocates of keeping the status quo openly express their admiration for China and its incredible rise, their anxiety and jealousy at China's rise seems to manifest colonial historical prejudices and their deep belief that modernity is a product of Western civilization.

In the traditional World Board of Directors, the Chinese giant stands out as an ethnic outsider. Furthermore, this new ambitious member doesn't play by the rules! After China's rise became a reality, the established insiders began to publicly cast doubt on the possibility of China's continued progress, claiming that this was a temporary boom, a soap bubble that would burst, as it did in Japan. The persistence of these negative sentiments became fertile ground for subsequent anti-China actions and the politically motivated magnification of perceived threats. As ChinaPhobia escalates, it is not surprising that the current trade wars are prompting military tensions or proxy wars. As an example, during the last week of August 2020, the USA sent a U-2 spy plane into a no-fly zone over the PLA army military exercise, followed by China's launching of two missiles in the South China Sea with a message on Twitter: *'Nice aircraft carriers you have there, shame if they hit one of our missiles!'* The tense atmosphere now characterizing US–China relations does little to absorb tensions and reduce friction, diminishing the trust between the Chinese and US leaderships, and allowing for an increased influence by anti-American and anti-Chinese actors.

Both America and China believe the next decade will be crucial in defining the contours of this century. America is likely to make extraordinary efforts to curb China during this period. Beijing believes that this decade will be like a bottleneck; if it can negotiate it safely, its leadership role in the world will be assured—a role which everyone will have to recognize and accept. This suggests that the confrontation between the two giants currently has era-defining high stakes suggesting ChinaPhobia will likely intensify. So let us begin by trying to shed light on the key factors that influence its growth.

Chapter 1

The Growth of ChinaPhobia

Many factors have led to the growth of ChinaPhobia in the United States and other areas of the world. This part of the book focuses on the most important of them.

1: China's Fast and Furious Economic Growth

China's rapid growth in both economic and world status terms is one of the most important reasons for the campaign against it. China has moved from providing the basic needs of the Chinese people, to a stage where it is now competing with America and the entire West. China's surprisingly rapid rise has fueled great resistance.

Father: When the country was in its early-stage growth phase, many Western politicians and media outlets discussed the importance of partnership with China. But as China began to bloom, these politicians started throwing stones, and the media which once praised China, began to propagate China as a threat.

I am convinced that the Chinese were never intoxicated by the praise of the West; neither are they trembling now from the vilification directed at them. Rather, they have been focusing their efforts on breaking free from the shackles of underdevelopment and dependency, and healing the deep wounds left by external intervention, mostly Western, over the last two centuries of humiliation and enslavement. They have been doing their best to mobilize nationalist sentiments so that China can regain its historic place in today's world.

Son: The Chinese will never forget the insulting phrases which were written at the entrances to Shanghai's western concession areas, which said: 'No Chinese and no dogs allowed!' The fact that Beijing has been occupied and exploited multiple times by foreign invaders will never be erased from China's memory. These bitter feelings are one of the main reasons driving the Chinese to work hard and take advantage of every opportunity to raise the status of their nation.

Father: The Chinese are skilled at reading history and events, taking advantage of opportunities and benefiting from the advice of others. At a side meeting at the 2003 Boao China Economic Conference, Lee Kuan Yew, former Prime Minister of Singapore, told me that the father of Chinese reform, Deng Xiao Ping had visited Singapore in 1978 and was impressed by the growth experienced in Singapore at the time. He asked the Prime Minister what he advised China to do to start similar economic processes. Lee told me: 'I advised Deng two things: the first was to improve relations to the fullest extent with the United States, as it is the only country that can supply China with the money and technology it needs, and the second was to start experimenting with special economic zones on the coastline.'

Fortunately for China at the time, the political situation in the world was conducive to rapprochement with the United States, as both countries were joined by a common animosity towards the Soviet Union. The Americans believed that they could bring China into the West's democratic camp, through the creation of a new Marshall Plan for China. So America opened its financial and technical vaults to China, and Washington provided China with weapons to fight its arch enemy Vietnam. The USA allowed military cooperation between Israel and China at the end of the 1970's. During the forty years of reform and opening-up, hundreds of billions of Western dollars poured into China, and thousands of Western companies brought advanced technology into China's economy. America and Europe opened their markets to Chinese goods and products, becoming China's number one trading partners.

This Western and American openness, particularly towards China, raised a big question in American circles as to why the West was funding economic progress in Communist China.

Son: Some in America say that the USA contributed to the development of the Chinese dragon, and now that it has grown up, it is threatening the USA and breathing fire in America's face.

Father: This is part of the truth, but not all of it. The West helped China primarily for its own interests. In the 1990s, I visited China several times and saw the clouds of toxic smoke emitting from factories, which caused terrible pollution to the environment. Foreign companies have eliminated labour-intensive environmentally polluting industries from their shores, and instead sent them to China and other countries in the developing world. Western markets fulfill their needs for cheap goods produced by these factories, without having to bear their terrible environmental and humanitarian consequences.

Moreover, Western companies setting up in China were driven by the normal desire to profit from, and capitalize on, the vast Chinese market. For example, China was making around $10 for every iPhone produced by an American company in China, which sold for $1,000!

In addition, most of the money China has made from US companies has been invested in US Treasury Bonds, and these funds are now feeding the US economy. This does not mean that China has not benefited technologically and economically from the presence of foreign companies. Without the foreign mobile phone industry in China, Chinese companies such as ZTE or Huawei would not be able to become world leaders in the telecommunications industry. The economic benefit was mutual, and the presence of foreign capital in China enabled it to train technicians and develop technology and modern management systems. Nobody can deny these benefits.

During this time, the Chinese failed to intervene effectively in international policy issues. I once asked President Jiang Zemin at the beginning of the third millennium about the situation in the Middle East and China's contribution to peace there. He surprised me by saying: 'The Middle East is a region far away from China!' I wanted to comment that America is geographically farther from China than the Middle East, yet the Chinese leadership was giving its full attention to its relationship with America. But out of respect for the Chinese presidency, I did not! Of course, things changed later, and the Middle East became more interesting to Chinese politics once it became the main supplier of oil to China.

China's leadership and people worked incessantly and did not want to involve themselves in foreign problems that would cause them to deviate from their main goal. The task of foreign policy was to provide a peaceful environment for China's development. I think that was, in fact, China's stated primary goal at the end of the second millennium and the beginning of the third. Therefore, Henry Kissinger's statement in his memoirs, that China was hiding its objectives and making others speculate, is not true. The Chinese leadership was clear and firm about one thing, and that was to lift China out of poverty and build the country under the leadership of the Chinese communist party

Son: Without a doubt, Western investments contributed to the growth of the Chinese industry. However, the main reason China was able to compete economically with America was due to precise, practical, and ambitious Chinese plans, with leadership and a political will that knew what it wanted and where it was going. This leadership mobilized the Chinese and the potential of the entire nation to the demands of rapid development. Since 1978, Deng's reforms and opening-up policy provided the framework and locomotion that led China's economic development over three decades.

A quick look at Deng Xiaoping's reforms will explain how this happened. Deng was convinced that maintaining the communist regimes and rules that governed China's economy since 1949 would disrupt any possibility of moving forward. Therefore, Deng introduced economic and partly political reforms along the following four axes:

Firstly, to restrict the term of leadership positions in China, Deng introduced a compulsory retirement system for senior officials, and moved away from Mao Zedong's style of personal worship. These measures ensured continued renewal within the Chinese leadership, limited the possibility of individual mistakes, and gave the West the impression of some democracy in China, as each new presidency brought different leadership styles.

Secondly, the old principle of selecting teams, which was based on absolute loyalty to the Communist Party, was replaced by the principle of evaluating the extent of the success and tangible economic results achieved by a person in his or her job. In order to meet the economic growth targets, the party had to take a liberal approach toward the business community. This weakened the Communist Party's grip on economic life.

Thirdly, the adoption of a competitive system in all economic enterprises in China, both between companies and regions, and between cities and rural areas launched individual initiatives and sparked enthusiasm in Chinese institutions. Not only entrepreneurs, but local governments were also competing fiercely to attract business opportunities; Chinese officials were, in many aspects, much better in business management than even the businessmen.

Fourthly, Deng raised the slogan 'get rich' and ignited a great competition for the accumulation of wealth in government and private sectors. Wealthy segments emerged in the private sector as the leadership allowed unbalanced economic growth which created great income disparity between individuals and between some of the developed and poorer areas. Deng believed that the accumulation of wealth would allow wealthy enterprises and individuals to lead the country's economic progress, the idea being that those regions, entities and individuals would eventually take the lead to help develop other areas in China. This did happen, but at a high social cost.

Thus, Deng undertook radical economic reforms, namely, the arbitration of market laws in supply and demand and an opening up to the West. Deng also implemented some limited political reforms in the government sphere, partially affecting the Communist Party of China. These reforms were considered a partial return to capitalism in China. The West and America welcomed and supported these reforms, considering them a valid step toward China's return to liberalism and its approach towards the Western camp.

Subsequently, the slow reversal of this approach began, justified by its inappropriateness to China's circumstances. The slogan of the market economy was replaced with another slogan: that of the socialist market economy or a guided market economy, combining the advantages of both capitalism and communism. But these reforms did not radically change the role of the ruling Communist Party; they did not adopt the electoral system, nor Western democracy, nor freedom of the Press, nor the possibility of holding accountable leadership at the highest level. Despite this partial liberal openness, the state-led market economy continued to dominate and had the final say on all issues.

As of 2013—under President Xi Jinping—the West noticed the beginning of the decline of the Deng era and the gradual retreat from the liberal approach, along with the continued self-congratulating concept within China. After revising the following fact sheet, the USA began to feel the brunt of the Chinese challenge.

- China's annual growth rate from 1979 to 2018 was 9.5 per cent, while Western economies were at 2.9 per cent. In 1978, China's economy was 1.75 per cent of the world's economy, rising to 16 per cent in 2019.
- Today, China is the world's largest trading country and has the largest consumer market.
- Over 130 Chinese companies are on the Fortune Global 500 list.
- China's annual per capita income was about $300 in 1978, rising today to more than $10,000.
- China invests in over 45 per cent of the renewable and sustainable energy market.

Father: The Chinese challenge to America manifests itself not only in economic development figures, but also in the innovative strengths and creative mentality that are now driving development in China. Perhaps the most important element of China's push forward is that Chinese leadership can turn the country's weaknesses into strengths. There are those who say that China is a country of limited resources, that there is not enough oil and gas to fuel the arteries of the gigantic Chinese economy. There is a shortage of all basic raw materials, while arable land comprises only one-fifth of the area of China. The huge population, which amounts to about 1.4 billion, has an insufficient number of young workers, and aging is beginning to seep into the joints of Chinese society. China's weaknesses can continue to be counted indefinitely, but Chinese leaders—from Deng Xiaoping to the present—have miraculously managed to turn these weaknesses into strengths. I will discuss this in a little bit more detail for the benefit of those who want to see China's image as it is in real life, and not just the picture provided by non-objective research centres and the media.

To start with, it is not true that there is a lack of resources in China. But developmental strategists took advantage of this myth to fill the Chinese with enthusiasm, pushing them to devote themselves to double their efforts at work. at the beginning of the reform and opening-up phase, Chinese leaders began to speak about the results awaiting the Chinese people which would alleviate their sufferings and raise their standard of living. Therefore, Chinese citizens worked hard and devotedly to attain the promised paradise.

In the early 1990s, I had the opportunity to visit the city of Shenzhen, opposite Hong Kong, before the latter returned to China. I visited the construction sites in that city which was a small fishermen's village at the time. Our guide was a young engineer who showed us the work on the largest building there and explained that construction continued twenty-four hours a day, seven days a week, and that every day one floor of the skyscraper was completed in the city. The young man then pointed his hand at Hong Kong's tallest skyscraper, saying with pride and enthusiasm: 'In two months, that skyscraper will no longer be the highest.'

This was repeated when I visited the work sites of the Three Gorges Dam, one of the miracles of modern construction in China. Tens of thousands of workers and engineers were building the dam without a weekend off. I have seen the same image in the construction of the sports buildings when China hosted the 2008 Olympic Games, particularly the Bird's Nest stadium. Some accompanying colleagues rightly criticized the difficult working conditions, but the pride these workers have in knowing that they are building the Chinese dream causes them to overlook these difficult conditions.

Son: The culture of hard work continues to this day in China. Indeed, dedication to work is considered a good moral in Chinese society. For example, a Chinese wife begins to worry when she sees her husband busy with things that are not work-related. Most of my friends, employees of government or academic institutions, work overtime every day. Most conferences and events are organized on weekends, lest time be wasted. So I always joke with my friends in Europe that they should refrain from complaining about Chinese competition, because those who work seventy to eighty hours a week cannot equate with those who work forty hours or less in Europe. Chinese workers cannot be compared with citizens of countries in the Arab world, Africa and Latin America, where one third of the population suffers from direct unemployment, and another third suffers from disguised unemployment.

The scarcity of raw materials and the modest economic background of most of the older generation in China today has prompted the Chinese to reduce waste of materials and energy, and to research and design accordingly.

China is convinced that it cannot plunder the wealth of other countries, as the Western colonial states have done, and cannot print banknotes and sell them as hard currency like the US dollar. There are no enormous natural resources in China, and the Chinese have lived with the undeniable fact that they make up 20 per cent of the world's population, while their country contains less than 3 per cent of the world's natural resources. Just for the sake of comparison, Russia's population accounts for about 2 per cent of the world's population, while Russia is sitting on 14 per cent of the world's resources! China has therefore brought about its renaissance at the expense of the well-being of its people by focusing solely on work and production, so that the value of each person in China is measured primarily by his or her professional success. These factors have had a profound impact on the Chinese revival that the world is witnessing today.

Of course there are big problems and difficulties in China; this model has produced severe side effects especially on the mental and spiritual side and the people there are not mere puppets, but I am talking about an exciting social and economic experience that has achieved a miracle in this country.

Moreover, having studied at the Ren Min University in Beijing, I appreciate the difficult, intense, and ruthless competition that my Chinese colleagues had to enroll in the university; out of over ten million students, only 2,541 were accepted into the university in 2020. Before that, all these students had to take difficult examinations to finish school. It is true that not all university students, who now number about 50 million, are talented, but if we consider that 1 per cent of the 8 million Chinese university graduates each year are extremely talented, it means that there are 80,000 extremely talented graduates annually from Chinese universities, with 60 per cent from scientific disciplines. In addition, there are about 1 million Chinese students studying each year in foreign countries, including around 400,000 in America and hundreds of thousands in Europe, Canada and Australia.

China's budgets for scientific research and invention are now at the forefront, as announced by China's National Bureau of Statistics (NBS) on 27 August 2020. China's spending on research and development hit a record high at 2.23 per cent of its GDP in 2019, up by 0.09 per cent from the previous year. China's total expenditure on R&D, for which it annually allocates billions of dollars, exceeded $322 billion, up 12 per cent from 2018. I know from living in China that top Chinese technological companies like Huawei pay the world's top engineers' annual salaries of $5–10 million each. An executive of a leading Taiwanese tech company told me that he was unable to match this salary figure and could not compete with Huawei in this regard.

Father: I want to add that, on average, the typical Chinese family is considered the highest spender on education worldwide. The Chinese family focuses on teaching their children not only sciences, math and literature but the recent economic boom has enabled most Chinese families to invest heavily in language, music and sports tuition. The term 'tiger mother' was invented by the Chinese to describe a mother who has devoted all her efforts and mobilized the entire family, especially grandparents, to serve the upbringing of her children. Each child must be raised and educated according to a general rule of 不要让孩子输在起跑线上 which means that parents' mission is to get the children as fit and ready as an Olympic champion at the starting line of the competition, i.e., their life after graduation. The general mentality in China is that life is the Olympics and only the best can get into the competition. My daughter-in-law Joanna Cui is one such tiger mother; my son's family is the perfect example of the status quo. My son Karim decided when he had children, that he would try to avoid that Chinese education trend common today, where children can be seen studying daily until 10 p.m., with only few days of rest a year. Most of the holidays are occupied with extra classes so the children can keep up with the fierce competition between the students. So, when Dalia and Daniel were born, they chose to enroll them in international schools so they could have a more diverse environment in China.

However, within a few years the general surroundings and culture of bringing up children has taken effect; besides their busy academic life, my grandchildren in Beijing have at least two extra daily activities between art, sports, music etc. This is now the basic standard in China spanning all economic levels; it's a common fact that most children in China are much busier than adults. This unprecedented Chinese family interest in educating their children, and having the financial capacity to do so, is combined with the government's continued investment in the education system. Today, schools in rural China are built and equipped to the same level as any school in Beijing and Shanghai. The strong technological infrastructure is used to enhance the quality of teaching in rural areas, which is still a challenge in China. Virtual classes now allow teachers in developed cities to teach rural students online. This trend will change the current status quo and build creative generations, leading to the emergence of ambitious new graduates with knowledge and culture, with whom it will be difficult for the rest of the world to compete. We must prepare ourselves to see Chinese occupying the pinnacles of art, sport and science over the next twenty years. It is only a matter of time.

Another point I would like to mention is that the current generation living in China, and spreading throughout the world, are those who were raised under the umbrella of a poor country. Those Chinese families struggled for a living, with no possibility of educating their children and equipping them with skills that would make them universal citizens. This era produced a generation with many downsides, as is evident from the behaviour of some Chinese tourists around the world. This causes resentment, because they represent a generation that has leaped from poverty to extreme wealth in a very short time, but in the next twenty years this will inevitably change. The world must then begin to deal with the new generation of Chinese, who speak several languages fluently and have excellent scientific and social skills—a generation that is confident in itself and its future. Surveys indicate that the Chinese are among the most optimistic people in the world about the future, with an optimism ratio of about 82 per cent compared to 35 per cent in America and even less in Europe.

Son: China realized early on that the road to global glory requires the world's best minds and talents. On 27 September 2021 Chinese president Xi Jinping held together with all top six leaders of the Chinese Communist Party (CCP) an unprecedented meeting on attracting and cultivating top global talents, a sign of the importance of this issue. In November 2019, I participated in a conference on the topic of 'Importing Knowledge' at a Chinese university. One Chinese expert stated that China buys minds, not just the world's goods and services. He referred in this regard to Italy, which is currently experiencing a large migration of its scientists, whose new destination is China. During his lecture in Beijing University in late October 2019, a Russian academic noted that Russia is already worrying about the migration to China of Russian minds, especially in the technical field. China has become their preferred destination, after the Western world closed its doors to them.

Father: China's great successes over the past forty years are now one of the causes of ChinaPhobia in the United States. As we have pointed out earlier, these concerns about China in US leadership circles have doubled, following the profound change in the Chinese leadership when President Xi Jinping came to power. His ambitious program seeks to shift his country from advancing and accumulating wealth to the stage of gathering strength. America never expected to get into a confrontation with the Chinese giant that it had helped during the 1970s and 1980s.

US leadership was thinking of repeating with China what they did with Japan and Germany. America provided technical, economic and financial assistance to its former enemies Germany and Japan, resulting in Japan becoming an economic giant leading Asia, while Germany became another gigantic force leading Europe, while both countries continued revolving around America's orbit.

As I pointed out, this experience enticed America to do the same with China, but the results were disappointingly opposite to expectations. Japan and Germany have not dared to compete with America for global leadership, but China is doing so with self-confidence. This is evidenced by the economic realities on the ground, whereas the size of China's economy today has reached the critical point America fears, which is 68 per cent of the US economy mass. China, with its own independent national political decision, differs from Japan and Germany. It scares America that China has accumulated the strength of all the USA's ex-competitors: Japanese economic power, the Soviet military power, and German industrial might, along with an independent political will and strong sense of sovereignty.

2: Shifting the Centre of Gravity to Asia

A second factor prompting ChinaPhobia is the West's fear of shifting the centre of gravity in global development to Asian countries, to parties that do not belong to the Western system of values and beliefs.

Father: From the outset, it must be acknowledged that the Asian continent has long been the centre of gravity in human history, the origin of the oldest human civilizations, Indian, Arabic, Persian and Chinese, and the cradle of religions such as Islam, Christianity, Buddhism and Judaism. If the states of this continent have gone through a period of stagnation and regression, they are now gathering strength to re-launch and occupy pioneering positions in human civilization.

Home to 60 per cent of the world's population, Asia has all the necessary ingredients: its land contains more than 60 per cent of the world's gas and oil, especially in the west, and its biggest consumers from the east comprise the fastest-growing economies. Asian countries were able to establish active regional organizations—like the Shanghai Cooperation Organization and Association of Southeast Asian Nations (ASEAN)—which played important role in maintaining the stability of the region. An example of this success is demonstrated in the case of Myanmar, whereby the international community condemned and launched a series of sanctions against this ASEAN member country considering the Rohingya crisis and the military coup which followed. It would be fair to say that the ASEAN organization has played an important role in stabilizing the crisis by protecting the country from foreign intervention and trying to find a solution domestically with regional support.

Meanwhile other regional organizations such as the Arab league failed completely in their missions and today Syria, Libya, Yemen are obvious examples of the failure of these regional institutions.

Father: Russia is also a good example. After the collapse of the Soviet Union, Russia, of which half is in Asia, has counted itself as a European country and Russian people looked upon themselves as Europeans. Most of the focus of the Russian state policy and strategy was built on full integration with the western hemisphere, but we can see today that Russia has in the last five years started turning towards Asia and in particular to east Asia, where strategic partnerships are strengthening day-by-day with China, India, Vietnam and even Japan!

That proud member of the Western community, Australia, is economically dependent upon its Asian partners. After realizing that it will never be part of EU, NATO member Turkey has turned strategically to its Asian hemisphere by strengthening its footprint in the Muslim world and its neighbourhood as well as opening its doors wide to deep strategic economic integration with rising Asian economies by positioning itself now as the 'Gate to the West' instead of the old moniker of the 'Gate to the East'.

Gulf countries are in fierce competition with each other to win the East Asian clients, as they send their best staff to their newly opened regional offices in Shanghai and Beijing. A good friend of mine told me that a major Gulf oil company offered him deals where they deliver to China, with payment for the crude oil being made only after selling this commodity in the Chinese market—something unthinkable just three years ago! Asian countries are now leading the way in scientific inventions, the majority of high-tech industries and their markets are based in Asia. That is not to say that Asia is paving the road towards prosperity and that there are no serious obstacles or disputes between those countries, but we believe that this unprecedented interconnecting and economic integration will prevail over any obstacle.

One only needs to look at what is happening today between China and India. The economic factor that did not exist when the two countries entered a war in the 1960's has played an important role in containing the disputes between the two Asian giants. The integration between economies in Asia has achieved great success as today Asian countries trade with each other, more so than in any other part of the world. This kind of integration has fundamentally changed how Asian countries look at each other and stabilized the peace of the continent which was a paramount factor in the rise of Asia commencing at the start of the twenty-first century.

China's story is the most important component of this rise. Of course China doesn't represent the entire Asian ascent but it has played an important role. China stands out as the greatest rising power, ambitious to regain its important position in human civilization, as has happened several times in history.

China has long been an important global trading centre, through the land and sea network of the Silk Road. In the fifteenth century, China regained its international commercial position when it started importing silver from the Spanish empire and returned to play a major role in world trade through the tea trade in the eighteenth century, with a population of 400 million at the time. Throughout its long history, China has frequently been the centre of gravity in the commercial world, and this has not led to wars with its neighbours.

History is not over, as Fukuyama predicted, but new powers such as China, Russia, India, Japan and South Korea have stepped up, and they are writing their own pages in human story. Western-style liberty is not the final solution for governess of humanity.

Although more than a quarter of a century has passed since Samuel Huntington's theory, *The Clash of Civilizations,* it is still being circulated by many forces in the western hemisphere to justify hostility to China and fuel the phobia against what it represents, just as it did with Islam. Huntington says: 'The future conflict in the world will be between Western civilization on the one hand, and the Chinese and Islamic civilizations on the other, because these two civilizations have global ambitions, and they seek to update and modernize, compete with America, and reject the Western model, and this represents a sufficient reason for the conflict between them and West.' Huntington also adds, and here lies the theoretical basis for ChinaPhobia and hostility to Islam, 'Nations need enemies!'

Charles Krauthammer commented on the end of the Cold War: 'One is over and we will find another war,' and he stressed that 'America's next ideal enemy will be different, it will be an ideological and cultural enemy, a racist, and strong enough to pose a credible threat to American security.' These descriptions perceived to apply to China.

Considering the unprecedented escalation of the ChinaPhobia theory, which is taking effect today in mainstream American media, economics and politics, proponents of this theory have found a new intellectual supporter in the articles and lectures of another American thinker, John Mearsheimer, who has written several books and delivered many lectures, including one on 12 August 2019 at the Australian Centre for Independent Studies.[1]

Given the fact that Mearsheimer represents the realist line and is famously outspoken on how US hegemony thinks, and given the seriousness of what this thinker put forward in that lecture, we will focus on him in some detail. Mearsheimer says: 'The United States will not allow anyone to take the world's top spot from it. It has been and will remain the leader of the world.' And he adds: 'The American people are a special nation, a civilization maker and the creator of the most progressive inventions in history, and it will remain so.'

He emphasizes: 'We believe that China's growth is not peaceful, and it is quietly seeking to displace the United States as it begins to grow stronger than all its neighbours in Asia, and this will result in their fear and therefore their compliance with its will, and this will lead to China's hegemony over the Pacific Ocean America's lifeline. We will not allow this and we will not allow China to become a serious competitor to us. We have the strength and determination to do so, and America is a formidable force with no limits for its multiple methods of breaking its competitors. We will absorb the Chinese

[1] John Mearsheimer, 'China debate: John Mearsheimer | Hugh White | Tom Switzer' [video], YouTube. Available at: https://youtu.be/oRlt1vbnXhQ. Accessed May 2022.

onslaught and turn China back. We have brought down a number of empires in history, brought down the Bismarck Empire, destroyed the Nazi-Hitler Empire, destroyed the rise of Japan, and under our pressure the Soviet Empire collapsed.'

As the lecture took place in Australia, the lecturer issued a stern warning to the nation for its great openness towards China: 'Australia should choose two approaches: either to help the Chinese genie enemy and to evolve in its orbit, so Australia becomes an enemy of America, or friendship with America. It has to choose between the formal and temporary prosperity provided by China, and the security and independence provided by America.'

Remarkably, after these strong words, Mearsheimer said that he is not anti-China, does not wish China ill, and does not fully agree with America's actions, but is simply describing the reality of the American machine and its operating system!

Other American thinkers have taken relatively more flexible positions toward China, including Banning Garrett, a former US National Security Bureau official and current professor at Singularity University, who worked on the China file for a long time. In a private conversation with Karim on 25 September 2019, he expressed his opinion on Sino–US relations, saying: 'The mutual suspicion between China and America will turn into hostile and potentially dangerous acts of confrontation, and such a confrontation is not promising.'

As for ChinaPhobia, Garrett noted that: 'If hostility to Islam is a war against religion, then the hostility to China is a war against the Chinese government and the Communist Party, and it will be passed on to Chinese citizens if the Chinese leadership continues to direct them and push them to do anti-Western things and disrupt the possibility of constructive dialogue between the two sides.' In this regard, he said: 'At every meeting, the Chinese negotiating delegation merely accused America of being responsible for everything. The problem is that the Chinese negotiators are not used to self-criticism and the review of mistakes, so the dialogue with them has been futile.'

Asked about the possibility of China being able to displace America, the American scholar replied: 'The current century will remain

American, and China will not be able to lead the world and will not be able to make any Chinese century, because it lacks the basic stability of its acceptance globally. Communist ideology fell with the demise of the Soviet Union, and China has no soft powers to attract others, except for Chinese history and cuisine, even Confucius institutes adopted by the Chinese government to spread Chinese culture have fallen because these institutes deviated from their original mission.' The thinker added: 'China's first problem is now that Beijing has presented the Chinese Dream Project as a race to achieve scientific and technical leadership in the West, and this has frightened Western companies and made them run away from China.'

In order to complete the image of US intellectual attitudes toward China, we will present the views of some writers and politicians calling for a change to the current US strategy towards China by keeping the engagement policy and communication channels open between the United States and China. These American scholars stress that deepening cooperation between China and America serves the development of all humanity. Among them is Thomas Friedman, a well-known American writer and journalist who once wrote: 'I think the Chinese and American economies have become largely intertwined, and China and America have become Siamese twins from an economic perspective, of course, given the interlocking economic interests between the two countries.' But, as Friedman added: 'America must stand up to Chinese arrogance and its disregard for America's ability, and Beijing must act responsibly and change its policy toward the others.'

Unfortunately, China has few friends among American thinkers, and they do not constitute the current general intellectual thinking and research in America, which is hostile to China and supports the hawks of the US administration. A review of American intellectuals' sayings indicates that most of them are concerned about China's rapid growth and have a fear of China competing with the United States for world leadership. These discourses confirm their insistence on America's determination to counter China's growing influence in the world and prevent it from approaching the positions of the US leadership. The words of these thinkers lead us to believe that although ChinaPhobia has not acquired racist characteristics, there are American currents and voices that do not want the world's centre of gravity to move to Asia and non-white nations.

Son: There are dozens of Western writers and philosophers who have extolled the principles of coexistence between races and civilizations and have called for international collective action to achieve prosperity and stability in the world by focusing on education, culture, science and health.

Unfortunately, these calls of a humanitarian nature have been neglected, and instead racist theories have upheld that call for conflict, clashing of civilizations, spreading of hatred, increasing of arms expenditures and the inevitability of wars among civilizations. When you look at most of those voices on both sides, I have observed one common similarity between them which is grey hair! Millennials care less about race, cultural background or religions. Just ask the advocates of a new cold war and superpower confrontation and they will agree that their children think differently and that they face difficulties in understanding them. The young generation has a different view of the world and refuses to inherit the old establishment's heavy heritage and pay its outstanding debts.

Father: Unfortunately, some still live in the dark caves of the Cold War.

To return to our subject, the sayings of these American thinkers are still in circulation in different forms and versions. For instance, Kiron Skinner, the State Department's Director of Policy Planning said, at the Future Security Forum in May 2019, that: 'Challenging "the long-term threat" of China is difficult because the country is not Caucasian.' She added: 'When we think about the Soviet Union in that competition (the Cold War), in a way it was a fight within the Western family.' She said: 'This is a fight with a really different civilization, and a different ideology and the US hasn't had that before . . .' It is clear that there are weighty actors in America who are convinced that anyone who competes with America or is not subject to its policy is, in their eyes, an enemy that must be surrounded and weakened.

However, it must be pointed that we respect the American civilization and its values, which are rooted in the 1776 American

Declaration of Independence. We welcome the principles proclaimed by President Wilson in 1918, the foremost of which is the right to self-determination of peoples, and we are impressed by America's democracy and its achievements, which have provided great services to all humanity. We consider all of these to be bright spots in human history.

Son: Let's review the position of China from this unprecedented American attitude: Chinese intellectuals remain calm and composed and show concern for the continuation of Sino-US relations. Hardliners are popular among netizens in China, the majority of them aiming to be 'Wang Hong' or a famous key opinion leader (KOL) whose statements are mostly what the netizens and some officials like to hear. If you examine carefully those voices, you will see that the economic factor is really important in driving their behaviour, numbers of followers became a major element crafting their opinions, but through my own personal experience, calm and more rational opinions are the main trend among China's respected thinkers that don't necessarily appear in the news. For example, Wang Jisi, Dean of the School of International Studies at Peking University, wrote an article on the current crisis in Sino-US relations: 'As we celebrate the fortieth anniversary of normalization, our relationship is fraught and sometimes frustrating for both sides, but it is not fragile and certainly not doomed to confrontation or conflict. We have problems and interests that sometimes conflict, but we also have a wide range of experience working together to resolve, manage and remove obstacles to cooperation.'

The Chinese researcher explains the following three reasons why these relations are not fragile:

First, after four decades of establishing diplomatic relations and launching what Americans describe as Chinese participation and engagement in reform and opening up, our relationship has become broader, deeper and stronger, though still constrained and frustrating. These relations are not seriously bad enough to be on the verge of a transition to armed conflict.

The second reason to challenge assertions of fragility is that they ignore or diminish the importance of interdependence, common interests and communication between leaders in both countries who have a great interest in maintaining at least minimal cooperation.

The third reason for challenging assertions of fragility is the desire of both sides to have a better relationship than they currently enjoy, and both are committed to addressing the problems that cause friction.

Yuan Peng, President of the China Institutes of Contemporary International Relations (CICIR), also addressed the tension in US-China relations and analyzed the expected US behaviour in dealing with the crisis with China:

'The Americans believe that if the traditional US communication strategy for integrating and changing China does not work, they will resort to one of the following two ways to do so. The first is to contain China, but the entanglement of deep interests between China and the United States makes it very difficult to achieve this. The second is to accept China as it is, but this is not desirable for the United States. Therefore, I expect that American behaviour shall range between containment and acceptance. In my view, the United States has not yet formed a whole new strategy for China, and in the current arsenal of tools to deal with strategic competitors, no useful tools have been found. Because China is a completely new adversary, but it is also an all-encompassing adversary, and at the same time, it is an adversary closely linked to US interests, or an adversary that insists on the path of peaceful development and peaceful advancement. Such an adversary is unprecedented in American history. Therefore, for a new historical phenomenon such as the rise of China, all strategic circles in the United States have engaged in collective debate and thinking, but so far, no firm answer has been found. Therefore, the current treatment of Sino-US relations is primarily geared toward individual cases and issues, and each case has a different approach to other issues.'

The Chinese researcher adds: 'There is now a problem in the United States, which is the conflict of decision between the Republican government and the Democratic opposition, in addition, the US Strategic Council lacks the presence of great thinkers such as Brzezinski and Kissinger, and this has reduced the influence of this complex and its staff, the current American research complex does not accept the positive views of other countries, such as building new relationships between the major powers, and it often handles things from a narrow point of view, any strategic step is seen as a tactical deception. Of course, there are many wise people in the United States, yet we must expect the worst, and I think our position should be shortened in three words: Prevention, Framework, and Readiness. Prevention to reduce the spreading of the impact of the crisis on the overall relations between the two countries, and the framework means that we have to take the initiative to form the desired direction towards the development of relations between China and the United States, and to find the new and final framework for these relations, because the existing frameworks are old and no longer fit to accommodate Sino-US relations, and prepare to face failure, and this means taking the risks of limited military confrontation.'

My friends in Beijing really enjoyed what Kishore Mahbubani stated in his newest book *Has China Won?* that Henry Kissinger told him, 'The USA has no comprehensive strategy to address China's threat to its global hegemony.' But China should not underestimate America's ability to develop a strategy and resort to ways to curb China's rise and even inflict severe harm on it. The prevailing atmosphere in America is not one of reconciliation and cooperation with Beijing.

What American political leader will be bold enough to recognize the reality of China's progress and the possibility of its superiority over America in many aspects, including becoming the biggest economy in the world in the foreseeable future? For many decades, Americans have been convinced that they are superior, and America means number one. For the average American, this idea of superiority has been linked to the question of America's affluence. It remains a conviction and culture that any harm to America's superiority means impinging on the fundamental beliefs of many Americans. The recognition of this fact by any American politician would be tantamount to political suicide.

3: China's Neighbourhood

The disagreements ranging from stable to explosive between China and its continental and maritime neighbours have raised the stakes of anti-China sentiment.

Father: China's geographical location represents a constant problem for China. It is located in a region teeming with historical problems and disputes and has a land and sea border with twenty countries, four of them nuclear states: India, Russia, Pakistan and North Korea. Despite China's constant assurances of good neighbourliness and its peaceful development, its sheer size raises concerns among its neighbours, particularly the smaller ones, such as the Philippines and Vietnam. China's size antagonizes its larger neighbours, like India, Japan and Russia.

Another issue is that several nationalities making up Chinese society have ethnic extensions in neighbouring countries, sometimes complicating China's relations with its neighbours. Taiwan remains a problem, as China regards it as part of its territory and demands its return, while Hong Kong and Macao have returned to Chinese sovereignty, but still enjoy special status.

Thus, China is in the heart of a frighteningly bustling and crowded region, encompassing about 50 per cent of the world's population.

The population of this region is composed of different races and religions, which cannot be compared with the neighbours of the single-race European countries. As we indicated earlier, the region is also teeming with historical differences and conflicts between nations, and mutual negative feelings exist among the populations towards each other.

Though it's dangerous to generalize, we believe that the people of India, Vietnam, the Philippines and Japan are not friendly towards China. The Chinese people view Japan, India, Mongolia and Vietnam negatively. There is mutual fear on the part of the peoples of China and Russia towards each other. All these complexities and historical problems have a negative impact on the creation of harmony between China and its neighbours.

The United States is fully aware of this fact and counts on this situation to put pressure on China. China is also surrounded by a circle of global crises and regional hotspots, including North Korea's nuclear issue, the Indo-Pak conflict, the tense situation in Afghanistan, and the existence of what China calls the 'three evil forces' of Terrorism, Separatism and Extremism in Central Asia. China has been the focus of external ambitions and invasions, which have amputated parts of the country, fragmented the unity of its people and its land, and created border problems, some of which are still blazing today. Border disputes have been resolved with the Russian Federation, but dormant problems occasionally erupt like a volcano, such as disagreements with India, that led to the deadly clashes between the two Asian giants.

One manifestation of this conflict is the sharp division of the two countries' positions on Pakistan. While Beijing supports the Pakistani regime and provides all kinds of military and economic support, India sees Pakistan as a threat and accuses the regime there of supporting the forces of terrorism and extremism. Things have reached the point of clashes between the armies of Pakistan and India. Beijing's position in support of the Pakistani government provokes anger in India, prompting it to take further action against the expansion of Chinese influence on the Asian continent. The military conflict in May 2020 between the two

Asian giants has changed the narrative of the relationship, especially from the Indian side, but despite the complexity of Sino–Indian relations, they are generally stable.

The same cannot be said of China's relations with its maritime neighbours. Incendiary problems with them can be summarized as the dispute over ownership of small islands scattered in the waters of the South and East China Seas. These problems threaten security and stability in the Southeast Asian region.

Son: It must be noted that the conflict over the islands in the South and East China Sea is no longer confined to local parties, but has acquired international status, and has become the heart of the struggle for influence and leadership between China and the United States of America.

Although America is thousands of kilometres away, Washington has become the main party to the islands problem, and the Chinese even hold the United States responsible for inciting some of the problems in the South China Sea, which at 3.6 million square kilometres is larger than the Mediterranean Sea. The sea is bordered by countries such as Vietnam, Malaysia and Singapore to the west; the Philippines and Brunei to the east.

The question arises as to why the islands' crisis erupted in the South and East China seas now? Several factors led to this:

The first factor was the Obama administration's enthusiasm since 2010 for 'equilibrium restoration' in the Southeast Asian balance of power. Chinese dominance there is something Washington has seen as a threat to US strategic interests. Washington has therefore decided to shift its priority back to Southeast Asia by sending more US troops to the South China Sea, and by reviving its alliances with some countries in the region, with the aim of restoring the balance that had been disrupted by China's growing military presence there.

In March 2013, US National Security Advisor Tom Donilon announced that: '60 per cent of the US Navy's fleet will be concentrated in the Pacific by 2020, and air force attention will also shift to the region over the next five years, and the Pentagon will work to prioritizing Pacific command for most modern US military capabilities, including fifth-generation submarines and fighters, as well as F-22s and F-35s, as well as working with allies to make rapid progress in deploying missile defence and radar systems.' Clearly, this US military build-up is intended for China.

The second factor is the growing strategic importance of the South China Sea, which carries more than 35 per cent of the world's maritime cargo trade, as well 60 to 80 per cent of the energy supply transiting to South Korea, Taiwan and Japan. It contains one-tenth of the world's fish resources. Moreover, the South China Sea contains proven oil reserves of ten billion barrels, as well as an enormous wealth of natural gas estimated at 1,000 trillion cubic meters (*Al Jazeera*, 22 January 2019). These large mineral and fish resources are important sources of income for the seven countries surrounding the South Sea. Furthermore, there are important countries such as China (64 per cent), Japan (42 per cent), Taiwan and South Korea whose maritime trade passes through the Malacca and Taiwan Straits in the South China Sea, while 15 per cent of America's maritime trade is also carried by the South China Sea.

The third factor is China's sense of danger, wary now that its interests in the region are threatened. The Chinese remember bitterly how America flexed its naval muscles when it sent its aircraft carriers to the Taiwan Strait in 1996, and they now look with concern at Washington's attempts to increase its military presence in the Malacca Straits. Beijing does not want China's main trade artery to remain threatened by the United States.

Father: A fourth factor relates to the internal situation in China, manifested in the conflict of interests between the various Chinese leaders, especially during the Hu Jintao era. The South China Sea problem has been an issue on the shelf for Beijing, but some forces in China have decided to highlight it in order to fan nationalist sentiments, to gain extra points. So the Chinese propaganda machine began to explain the importance of these islands, Chinese television hosted experts who began to inflame public opinion, and cameras were sent there until we reached the current situation. Another thing that has an impact on the continuity of this issue is the growing influence of the Chinese security establishment.

This influence increased with preparations for the 2008 Olympic Games when China's security establishment began to take control of the country under the pretext of ensuring the security of the Olympics. I noticed this during my meetings with Chinese officials at the time, where security concerns were foremost, above all other considerations. Chinese security officials even decided to use Israeli security expertise, which raised the ire of the Arab delegations participating in the Olympics. Visas had been restricted for foreign fans from Arab and Muslim countries, under the pretext of the fear of terrorist attacks. These measures also affected Western countries, whose ambassadors told me that Chinese security authorities scrutinized most requests for entry of fans of Western teams. These requests had also been subject to number reduction, under the pretext of preventing the infiltration of human rights advocates and defenders of Tibet and Xinjiang to China. The number of tourists and foreign investors had been reduced for the same reason.

Once the Olympic Games were over, the Chinese security establishment continued its tightened control and footprint on Chinese governmental decision-making. Some of the old files were reactivated and Chinese media started reporting about the strategic importance of the South China Sea, while academic circles started explaining the historical background of China's rights in the South China Sea, highlighting that this issue represented the bottom line for China's national security! Usually in China, it is difficult to return a file to the shelf once it has been deliberated.

Anyone who deals with China must understand that there are internal powers and networks which are trying to use some files with external extensions, to serve their domestic interests and settle the score with their competitors. The South China Sea issue is one of those files.

Moreover, Beijing realized that the US military presence encouraged the Philippines, Vietnam, Japan and others to take practical steps to control China's South and East Sea islands, areas that China considers part of its territory.

My conviction is that these accelerated developments have prompted Beijing to partly abandon the traditional policy of caution and strategic patience in that region and to launch the so-called pre-emptive policy toward the islands. In order to assert Chinese control of the disputed islands, it has resorted to dispatching Chinese naval forces, conducted some backfilling operations and developed infrastructure in the South China Sea.

Son: Two other phenomena in US–Sino relations are keeping the South China Sea crisis ablaze.

First, the lack of a common strategic denominator between the two countries. President Obama and former Chinese President Hu Jintao agreed to establish a council for joint strategic dialogue whose mission was to seek to crystallize their common strategic assets. As Evan Medeiros, Obama's Asia adviser, said in a speech on 5 April 2019: 'Presidents Obama and Xi have decided to establish a mechanism for strategic dialogue between the two countries in the Asia-Pacific region led by the two most important strategists: Cui Tiankai, China's Ambassador to Washington, and Kurt Campbell, Assistant Secretary of State for Asia and Pacific Affairs, and I have participated in this dialogue. After dozens of meetings between us, the two sides did not find a single common denominator, except for joint US–Chinese agricultural financing for a project in Eastern Timor.'

The second phenomenon that US–China relations are afflicted with, is embodied in the deep suspicion among various levels of the Chinese leadership of the intentions of the United States. This suspicion is likely justified, but the distrust causes the Chinese to question every decision or step taken by the Americans.

This largely determines China's actions regarding the South China Sea crisis. Before 2019, America basically stressed its neutrality, declaring that it was ready to mediate between the warring parties to resolve the crisis, calling for a peaceful solution, and claiming that its heavy military presence in that region was not directed against China, but aimed at securing international navigation routes. Nobody wants to resort to unilateral actions to change the status of the islands. Still, the Chinese believe that America's actions contradict its words, since it supports and incites Vietnam, Japan and the Philippines to take provocative steps against China regarding the disputed islands.

The Chinese Policy advisors cite a valid example of the US protection of the Filipinos' actions regarding some of the disputed islands. In 2012, the Philippines unilaterally changed the status quo on Huangyan Island when their President Aquino issued a decree declaring that the South China Sea is called the Western Philippine Sea. In 2013, the Philippines appealed to the International Court of Justice over the maritime dispute with China. In response, Beijing has already taken an anti-arbitration stance based on four Nos: No acceptance, No participation, No recognition, and No execution.

Beijing sent its own naval forces, took control of the island and ensured the security of China's maritime shipping routes there. However, Beijing breathed a sigh of relief when the Philippine President lost the 2017 presidential elections, and a new president Rodrigo Duterte was elected, who sought to improve the relationship with Beijing.

On 13 May 2014, demonstrations broke out in Vietnam when China sent an oil rig (excavator) to one of the islands disputed between the two countries. Vietnamese demonstrators stormed and burned Chinese enterprises and companies in Vietnam, and thousands of Vietnamese boats staged a naval demonstration against Chinese ships. Sino–Vietnamese relations were greatly strained by this. Beijing once again accused the United States of being behind the anti-China events in Vietnam by encouraging the Vietnamese government and sending some US naval forces to the disputed areas. It should be noted here that Vietnam claims sovereignty over all the islands of the South China Sea. The confrontation evolved between China and the US especially after the change of policy in 2019 when the Pentagon adopted pursuing a more aggressive straightforward action to push the Chinese back.

Father: It is not possible to conclude the discussion of China's differences with its neighbours without identifying the strained relations between Japan and China. The tension between the two countries is old with lots of history. The Chinese will not forget the atrocities of the Japanese army when it occupied part of China in the last century. The remnants of this occupation are still evident in three areas, firstly within the 'Chinese Comfort Women' during that occupation, the second, honouring the leading officers of the Japanese occupation of China, visiting their graves, and considering them heroes in Japan, and finally the disagreement over the content of history books in Japanese schools.

These three points are ticking time-bombs at the heart of the relationship between Beijing and Tokyo. The issues of the disputed islands as well as the demarcation of the maritime border have now emerged as a current, hot and dangerous point between the two countries.

The eight disputed islands between China and Japan are in the South China Sea. The Chinese call them Diaoyu, while Japan calls them Senkaku. The importance of these uninhabited rocky islands has grown following the discovery of significant natural resources, and the increase in the volume of international trade in the East China Sea. According to the US government's Energy Department, there are about 100 million barrels of oil and about 2 trillion feet of gas on the islands. In addition, the East China Sea contains important mineral resources such as precious coral stones, zircon, gold, titanium and platinum.

Moreover, the control of these islands means sovereignty over 40,000 square kilometres of surrounding waters, considered an exclusive economic zone, and the islands can be exploited militarily. China fears that Japan will establish air and sea reconnaissance systems that place maritime and air routes in the region and nearby areas of China under direct surveillance of the Japanese. The islands are already under Japanese administration, but China claims them as an integral part of its territory.

The relationship between Japan and China worsened considerably after the Japanese government's decision to buy and nationalize three of the five islands in September 2012. The disputes between China and Japan are not limited to the Diaoyu/Senkaku Islands. There are two maritime issues: the first one is the demarcation of each country's maritime boundaries within the East China Sea, and the second is around a coral reef known as Okinotorishima, which is located 1,100 miles east of Tokyo. While China does not claim sovereignty over the reef—which it considers to be a rock, not an island—it refuses to allow its use by Japan to claim an exclusive economic zone in the western Pacific.

Son: Disputes between Tokyo and Beijing over these islands and historical issues have contributed to changing the nature of the situations and alliances in that region. The Japanese–American military alliance was strengthened, and Tokyo took advantage of the opportunity to make amendments to its constitution so that it could send troops out of Japan.

Japan has also increased its military expenditure and acquired advanced weapons from the United States. Japan has developed its military cooperation with Southeast Asian countries and established an alliance with India and Australia. In cooperation with New Delhi, the two countries plan to establish the so-called Asia-Africa Growth Corridor (AAGC) in the Pacific Ocean area as an alternative to the Chinese Belt and Road Initiative. Japan has also moved to compete with China for AI, quantum computing, robotics and data-driven industries; China has an advantage in this area, as Chinese tech giants such as Baidu, Alibaba and Tencent harvest huge amounts of data from the country's 1.4 billion people. China only allows internal access to this data, so on 24 January 2019 at the World Economic Forum in Davos, Japanese ex-Prime Minister Shinzo Abe called for a global system to regulate data flow across borders.

President Biden announced on 28 January 2021 that the USA will guarantee Japan sovereignty over the Diaoyu/Sinkaku Islands! Defence Secretary Austen informed the Japanese Defence Minister that the USA considers the disputed islands as part of the defence agreement between USA and Japan.

I want to add some observations relating to the Chinese people's view of Japan. Through my experience of Chinese society, with my Chinese family and living among the Chinese people for the last twenty years, I have observed the complexity surrounding Sino–Japanese relations, where feelings are mixed with problems, admiration is accompanied by hate and opportunities always collide with realities on the ground. Most Chinese nationals are convinced that Chinese civilization is the basis of Japan's culture, i.e., the Japanese are disciples of the Chinese civilization, and the tragic history between the two neighbours keep bloody relics and scars in the memory of the Chinese people.

To give an example, my mother-in-law who was born in 1951 is, like all other Chinese mothers-in-law, keen to teach her grandchildren about the Japanese atrocities against China. These tragedies are also a rich leitmotif of the fast-growing television and film dramas in China, through which the Chinese passion for building their homeland is being sharpened. The moral of these stories is: 'When China weakens, other powers begin to smash its body, Chinese must work hard to prevent this from happening again.' With this message that China must focus on becoming a powerful nation that no country in the world can confront. However, the Chinese cherish driving Japan's most luxurious cars, Chinese officials meet frequently with their Japanese counterparts, economic relations are constantly evolving, and Chinese officials recognize Japan's contribution to China's renaissance through its heavy investment in, and fulfilling of, China's high-tech needs. The Chinese are eager to visit Japan, enjoy its pure air and fresh, uncontaminated food, and express their amazement at how the Japanese people are so well-organized, and the high standard of ethics of their community. These images reflect China's complex and contradictory feelings towards Japan.

I sense the same complex view among the Japanese when mixing with my Japanese friends, be they study colleagues or businessmen. They recognize the common origin of the civilization of the two countries but believe that they have the superior genes and features of this civilization, and that they are the sons of the miraculous nation of Japan, which— despite its limited national resources—has been able to achieve great accomplishments and defeat the greatest powers of the world when it wanted to. The Japanese attributed their surrender after World War II to mistakes in decisions by some leaders of allied countries.

It seems that many Japanese have an inferior view of the Chinese. Most Japanese refuse to refrain from visiting the shrines of their leaders. Instead, they justify and regret the behaviour of some of these heroes in committing crimes against China. But the Japanese glorify these leaders because—despite their mistakes—they have given their lives for the elevation of the Japanese nation, and therefore deserve recognition for their loyalty to Japan and their beloved emperor.

China's recent rise has trapped the Japanese in a difficult position. Their neighbour, who had been weaker in economics and industry, has taken the silver medal of the economy that Japan had prized for forty years. What scares many Japanese the most is that this Chinese renaissance was built with what they view as 'less capable Chinese hands'. The Japanese know that the Chinese people have not forgotten Japan's crimes against them, which could eventually turn into feelings of revenge.

On the other hand, the Japanese see China's rise as a great opportunity for Japanese companies and their economy to become the biggest beneficiary out of this. It is not in Japan's interest to antagonize their big neighbour nor to succumb to US pressure to side against China, so Tokyo is seeking a stable relationship between China and America that is in the interests of both countries and the stability of the region in general.

Father: Tensions over the problem of the disputed islands in the South and East China Sea reveal a sharp contrast in the positions of both China and the United States.

The essence of the conflict is that, as a quarter of US foreign trade and a large proportion of international trade pass through it, America considers the region vital to their interests, and therefore needs to ensure a positive outcome.

I am convinced that, having achieved what it wants by constructing five islands in the far reaches of the South China Sea, China will work to calm the situation there. I realize that China's objectives now regarding the South China Sea are: first, to seek to fortify its achievements there and maintain the status quo, and secondly, to prevent the establishment of a blockade or a pressure zone. If this were to happen, the South China Sea for China would represent what the Caribbean Sea represents for America—which is the fulcrum of the US naval force and its strategic range area that cannot be tampered with.

Continuing disagreement between China and other countries over the South China Sea islands results in constant tension in that region, stirring up ChinaPhobia and giving America justification to strengthen its military presence there.

4: Chinese Soft Power—The Hard Road to Effectiveness

Coined by Professor Joseph Nye in the late 1980s, the term 'soft power' means the ability of a country to persuade others to do what it wants without force or coercion.

Soft power is a supplemental and attractive approach to building great nations and spreading their influence throughout the world. In this chapter, we will ask whether China's soft power will be effective in boosting China's global presence.

Father: In contemporary history, there are three patterns of soft power that helped in the building of global empires or the emergence of regional states.

First, the American pattern. The United States has used soft power extensively in building the contemporary American empire. America's soft power was based on the great values put forward by US policy, such as the spread of democracy, the defence of human rights and freedom. Washington presented the American Dream, based on the launching of individual initiatives and achieving wealth, as a model for the peoples of the world. America has allocated a lot of money to consolidate its soft power and has extensively recruited the media to spread the American influence. Although the American pattern has made great achievements, it has also faced great resistance and failures.

The second pattern is the Soviet one, which was based mainly on the Soviet Communist ideology, specifically Leninism, that proposed a global program to eliminate capitalism and create a global Socialist system based on the attractive values of social justice, equality, abolition of exploitation and building world peace. Global communist parties and associated organizations contributed to the spread of the Soviet soft power. The fate of this Soviet pattern is already known.

Iran is a third example of soft power used by an emerging region. The Iranian pattern was based on infusing specific religious values among the people of the Middle East, reinforced by projecting hostility towards Israel and America. Iran has allocated large sums of money to spread its pattern and backed it by paramilitary organizations close to Iran in several Middle Eastern countries. This Iranian model is met with fierce resistance and hostility from many major countries in the world.

China, on the other hand, has chosen its own pattern of soft power based mainly on its growing economic power, as we will discuss in detail.

Son: China's interest in soft power awakened at the beginning of the third millennium during preparations for the Beijing Olympics when there was a need to highlight China's new face. In 2007, Chinese President Hu Jintao said that the Chinese government should start focusing on building soft power, for which significant financial resources were allocated—an annual budget of $12 billion according to some sources. This amount was budgeted about a decade and a half ago. Today, China spends much more on its soft power endeavours, but officials keep the figures classified, perhaps because Chinese officials know that they will be embarrassed, given the very modest outcome they have achieved.

China's soft power push promotes China's great economic achievements over the past forty years, providing an example of the ability of developing peoples to break out of poverty and underdevelopment. The political side has focused on China's peaceful rise and its benefits to the world, putting forward ideas to resist intellectual and political hegemony, building a new world order based on equality, and on the understanding that development and peace should be at the forefront of global concerns.

Beijing has built multiple foundations to globally exercise its soft power, initially setting up Confucius institutes around the world to teach Chinese and spread Chinese culture. Since the establishment of the first institute in 2004 in Uzbekistan, this network has continued to grow and expand, with currently more than 500 institutes in 154 countries, as well as about 1,000 separate classes. It is noticeable however that most of these Confucius institutes are located in foreign universities and do not have independent buildings of their own.

Objective assessment of this experiment suggests that it has achieved specific successes in some geographical areas, but the main problem is that Confucius institutes are Chinese government centres, despite all the face-lifting and change on the surface, they are still operated and run by government officials. As a result, the centres have not attained their goal of conveying China's great urban experience, explaining the rise of China or portraying the energy and enthusiasm one feels when visiting China's streets and cities. The fact that many of these are located in foreign universities has put a lot of pressure on their university administrations to prevent them from hosting personalities who disagree with the Chinese government's views. This has led to a great deal of sensitivity, particularly in the Western world, where universities are free think tanks. Any prejudice to intellectual freedom or the question of freedom of expression of opinion goes against the culture in Australia, America, Germany and other Western countries where these problems have occurred.

In Africa and some Asian and Latin American countries, where China contributes to the construction of their infrastructure, and keeps their economies moving through its energy purchases, it is important to note that Confucius centres are doing well. In India, the Philippines, Japan, Vietnam and other countries close to China, especially those with border problems with it, the limited number of Confucius centres have failed to improve China's image.

Father: I remember an incident I experienced in Hanoi, the Vietnamese capital, when I was ambassador there in 2004. As I wandered through the city centre, I spotted a historic Chinese-style building on which 'The Confucius Centre' was written in Chinese letters. I asked my Vietnamese companion if this was a centre of Chinese culture. He shot me an angry look, and answered seriously: 'China has nothing to do with this Centre, it is a Vietnamese heritage centre, and Confucius is part of our national heritage.' I did not argue, but I realized the extent of the disagreements between the two countries go as far as disputing the heritage of the philosopher Confucius!

In line with the suggestions of China's advisors to strengthen China's global footprint, the Chinese government established research centres in all fields, supporting China's decisions regarding its policy, worldwide. Although this is a new experience, initial evaluation of these centres are positive in principle, as the results of their research help decision-makers in Beijing in particular, to formulate foreign policy and improve China's international image. This has been reflected in the effectiveness of China's foreign policy, which has greatly improved its diplomatic environment.

A former senior official told me that when Xi Jinping came to power, China had few friends, and its direct neighbourhoods were full of problems. The Hu Jintao and Wen Jiabao administrations—despite providing massive financial assistance to some of their neighbours—failed to befriend them. In Vietnam, the Philippines, Mongolia, Thailand and North Korea, they used to say to the Chinese: 'Your money is welcome, but your people are not'.

After careful study of how other great powers project soft power, the Chinese government has allocated large amounts of funds to build a vast network of foreign-language official media around the world, using foreign aid funds and forums set up by the Chinese government to promote China. For example, the agreements for the establishment of the China–Africa Cooperation Forum in 2000 and the 2004 Arab–Chinese Cooperation Forum included lengthy paragraphs on cultural and media cooperation between China and those countries.

It should be noted that China's soft power has been widely accepted in developing countries, especially after the turn of the third millennium. This has helped China present itself as a developing country with no colonial past or aspirations, and it does not link its economic, cultural and health assistance to political conditions. China's focus on infrastructure projects, such as roads, railways, ports, health services, rural and other service projects benefit the lives of tens of millions of underdeveloped regions. In Africa alone, China has built infrastructure in 10,000 remote villages to receive satellite television via solar energy. China-backed companies are leading the new economy sector in Africa, this new economic sector of apps and products pushes China's image positively among the young generation in Africa.

Beijing has also declared it does not interfere in the internal affairs of these countries and does not seek to change the ruling regimes. China has presented its own concept of human rights, which is to eradicate poverty, illiteracy, epidemics and underdevelopment. These positions have been well-received by the ruling regimes there, who are fed up with criticism from the West about democracy and human rights.

Son: Even in America and some Western countries, China's use of soft power has had some success, going by USA Vice President Pence's remarks during his speech in 2018 at the Hudson Institute about China's activities within the United States. With particular reference to Chinese radio programs aimed at America, he made assertions about exploiting cultural centres, harnessing Chinese students and investing the presence of the Chinese students in US universities in favour of China, a practice that has been repeated in some European countries. But the problem with China's soft power today is reflected in the means it uses to reach the foreign public.

China started to understand its shortage in the soft power projection, it sees that the world is not understanding what's happening in China. In the end of May 2021, Chinese President Xi personally hosted a study session for the top Chinese leaders, lectured by prominent Chinese thinker Zhang Wei Wei, on how to address the problem of international communication. Xi emphasized that all

Chinese officials in charge at each level should allocate funds and be personally responsible for the mandate of international communication, an attempt to address the puzzle of the Chinese that the 'world still does not understand us'.

China's soft power has several gaps, the most important of which is the difficulty of the Chinese language. While America has relied on the widespread dissemination of English in the world, as did the Soviet Union—albeit to a lesser extent—when it encouraged the dissemination of Russian for decades, Chinese has not yet become a language of communication among the peoples of the world. The establishment of Confucius institutes has not helped much with the widespread dissemination of Chinese language and culture, particularly since several Western countries, led by the United States, have accused them of deviating from their cultural line and becoming political instruments in the hands of the Chinese government. Regardless of the veracity or error of these accusations, these allegations have reduced the proliferation and impact of Confucius institutes.

A key measure of the success of Chinese soft power will be when the world's media are able to correctly pronounce the names of Chinese officials and cities in the news, and when foreigners can look at Chinese characters with the same familiarity as their Latin counterparts that most of the earth's population recognize. The Chinese language has not yet entered the category of globally common languages, which limits China's ability to culturally communicate and influence the world's population. Therefore, it is true to say that China has a long way to go in this area. According to the latest polls, most of the world's population perceive China via the Great Wall, Chinese food, Kung Fu, hard work, good organization, authority's iron fist, the new iron wall, as well as other associations that are less appealing. The language barrier is a problem, as non-Chinese find it difficult to memorize and even pronounce the name of President Xi Jinping or China's most important university, Qing Hua.

Father: While domestic media is primarily geared towards the home audience, Chinese foreign media suffers from chronic problems, especially as it makes no allowance for differing opinions. The prevailing propaganda has greatly discredited it with the foreign public. Moreover, the lack of access to well-known, experienced and highly professional foreign correspondents results in the focus resting mainly on Chinese editors and broadcasters who read and write in foreign languages that do not appeal to the audience in other countries (at least this is what is happening in the Arab region).

Despite all the enormous investments and continued efforts, China does not have foreign-language media networks that can compete not only with the internationally recognized media establishments such as CNN and BBC, but it also failed to reproduce the platforms that reached a recognized success such as DW News, Russia Today, Al Jazeera and others. The media and social media have become the main platforms for any country wanting to strengthen its presence in the world.

Son: I want to elaborate on this issue. Although China has been re-modernizing its media platforms to keep pace with the new era, such as the official Xinhua news agency, Chinese television and other media outlets, all that has happened is that the studios have been updated and supplied with the latest equipment, and no further development has taken place. These platforms failed to attract new friends to China because they do not use a language comprehended by foreigners, and the content remains a literal translation of Chinese texts.

Chinese media may speak a foreign language but its message fails to enter to the minds and hearts of its international audience. Those who enter China's overseas-oriented media centres feel that they are in an official, gloomy, state-owned enterprise, unlike some of the offices of local Chinese media directed at the Chinese people. For example, those who listen to the Xinhua News Agency in Arabic or watch The Chinese Television Channel in Arabic immediately realize that those who are in-charge of these platforms are not Arabs, have not mastered the mysteries of the Arabic language and do not understand the Arabian intellectual level or taste.

Therefore, most of the media's audience is limited to diplomats in Beijing and those interested in Chinese affairs. And I always advise Chinese friends that they should have native speakers working on these platforms, providing and editing media materials, and that the role of the Chinese should be limited to monitoring the content. I know that this would be very difficult, given the way Chinese media officials think, and with its zero-mistake policy, no Chinese employee would want to take any responsibility for mistakes that foreigners may make in the Chinese media.

We understand that the working conditions of the media in China are very difficult; freedom of speech and independence do not exist. The Chinese journalist is strictly constrained by the party's instructions, which simultaneously lavishes funds on Chinese media institutions. Those in-charge of Chinese international media are government officials, selected on the basis of their mainly partisan affiliation.

China's international media are unable to speak an understandable universal language to bring the world closer to China. I felt this during my visit to Africa, where there is no Chinese media influence. Instead, one sees the effects of Western media activities seems to be aimed at undermining China's reputation and sabotaging its relations with Africa.

Therefore, I think that China will remain very far removed from the competitive American media networks, and far from their Russian counterparts, who it is fair to say have been able to achieve great success broadcasting to the homes of foreigners. Russia Today channel is popular among the Arab public and offers programs explaining various international issues from a Russian point of view.

Father: In August 2006, on the 50th anniversary of the establishment of relations between Syria and China, I met a number of Chinese television and press journalists. Over the course of two hours, I answered questions about the situation in the Middle East, relations between the two countries and Sino–Arab relations. I was surprised the next day that Xinhua published a brief story about the press conference in Arabic only. What's more, the Chinese agency deleted from my press interview everything related to the analysis of the situation in the Middle East, retaining only the part that valued bilateral and Sino–Arab relations, before adding paragraphs praising China and its policy. I inquired about the cause of this sudden manipulation of my conversation and demanded that it be published in full in the

Chinese-speaking media. The answer I received was: 'This was the result of an individual act by a journalist, and he will be punished.' I don't know whether the journalist was punished or not, but nothing was published in Chinese.

Traditionally the activities of the twenty-one Arab embassies in Beijing have been covered only in Arabic or English-speaking media, and the same applies to other foreign embassies whose activities are covered by Chinese media in foreign languages, but never in Chinese. I have tried to ask why China insists on this, given that China's ambassadors speak freely to all the national media in the countries where they are accredited. I have not received an answer, but I believe that some influential Chinese desire to build a Chinese media wall between Chinese society and the world. Such actions have created resentment among foreign embassies, and some countries have even reciprocated against the Chinese embassies accredited to them. This has had a negative impact on the spread of China's soft power in the world.

But what about Chinese literature, which is supposed to be one of the important sources of Chinese soft power? Unfortunately, this is not happening, and the reason is the language barrier. From my personal experience of more than sixty years of good cultural and political relations between China and Arab countries, I am aware that the number of Arab translators from Chinese to Arabic does not exceed the number of fingers on two hands. All their work is funded by the Chinese government. Chinese literature translated into Arabic was either translated from foreign languages other than Chinese, or translated by Chinese orientalists, despite the hundreds of thousands of Arab students who graduated from Chinese universities.

This is not solely due to the difficulty of the Chinese language, for there are other difficult languages, but also because the absolute majority of Arab graduates of Chinese institutes do not use Chinese in their home country. And they often work in areas which are not language-related. Moreover, Chinese companies operating in Arab countries bring their own national Chinese translators and usually do not use postgraduate Chinese-speaking Arabs who studied in

China. I think the same picture is being repeated in Africa, Latin America and other parts of the world. In other words, foreign graduates of Chinese universities do not receive proper support from Chinese cultural institutions, or interest from Chinese companies operating in their countries!

Son: China has increased its scholarships to foreign students, with the Chinese government now offering about 60,000 scholarships a year. In the coming years the number of foreign students studying at China's universities will exceed one million. These graduates can become ambassadors of China's soft power if they receive a good foundation. China sends close to one million students abroad annually, most of whom give a good impression of their home. These are all strengths that China is not yet leveraging nor maximizing.

China is far from having the soft power of the United States, which is characterized by the two H's: Harvard University and Hollywood. China's universities are still far from competing with America's leading universities. I tell my Chinese friends that China will be counted as a superpower when the world's rich and elite start sending their sons and daughters to Chinese universities, and when they begin to brag about it as they do in America and Britain, and when buying a residence in Shanghai, Beijing or Shenzhen will become a trend which necessitates entering the world-class elite, just like in New York or London or Paris. Despite the great progress in Chinese cinema, China still falls short of catching up with Hollywood, and can't even compete with Indian Bollywood. The film that represents China in the minds of the world's children is *Kung Fu Panda*—an American makeover of a Chinese story about the adventures of Kung Fu and a panda.

Father: Another issue that weakens China's soft power is its lack of ideological cover. The Communist Party of China abandoned the Leninist part of Marxism because Lenin was calling for the export of the revolution; the party stuck with Marx because he focused on the economic aspect of communism.

In November 2005, I met with Wang Jiarui, Minister of the International department of the Chinese Communist Party—the so-called foreign ministry of the CCP. During our conversation about the Party's role in China, the Chinese minister repeated the phrase 'Chinese characteristics' many times.

China is building socialism with Chinese characteristics; the party's revolutionary ideology has Chinese characteristics; culture should have Chinese characteristics, and development is on a path of Chinese characteristics. These ideas are repeated daily by China's leaders. I suspect that the insistence on the Chinese element of China's political thought, development and culture is what caused China to lose momentum in transiting to globalization. This may have been justified in the last century, when the Chinese Revolution was besieged, grappling and in conflict with the other rival socialist force at the time, the Soviet Union and its allies. It is puzzling to me why the focus on Chinese characteristics continues today, given China's great drive towards globalization, and becoming a great economic power in competition with America for the leadership of the world.

To take the leading role in the world by means of soft power, it will be necessary to emerge from a tightly knit domestic scene and adapt to a vast world horizon. Continuing to emphasize 'Chinese qualities' will complicate the path to becoming a world power and could make the Chinese experience in developing countries lose its attractive glow.

Look at the why American soft power has been effective. By championing liberalism around the world and increasing the number of liberal states, the United States of America has used soft power significantly and successfully over many years. American culture and the American way of life were greatly accepted by nations and peoples, especially after their victory in the Cold War, and the term 'Americanization' was widely disseminated in the political, economic, cultural and even in the daily lifestyles of the peoples of the world. While the soft power of the United States has begun to encounter problems as a result of President Trump's 'America first' policy, nevertheless, the soft power of the United States has not lost its global glow; its global positive image reserve and resilience are still effective because of the strong values and institutions on which it depends.

Some of the actions of official institutions towards foreign citizens also lower the credibility of China's soft power. Let me illustrate with a few examples of what is happening with Russia. Relations between the two leaders are known to be more than excellent, but at a time when the Russian and Chinese Presidents were participating in large-scale military exercises between the two armies and making statements about their friendship, the Bank of China was taking measures to limit the remittances of Russian citizens residing in China. At some Chinese airports, immigration and passport authorities were asking Russian citizens to hand over their mobile phones in order to check them out and make sure there were no anti-Chinese materials. This happened to the extent that the Russian foreign ministry had to formally ask the Chinese authorities to investigate the matter. At the same time, Chinese consulates in Russia doubled the cost of visas and increased the number of documents required from Chinese visa applicants. These measures sparked outrage among Russian citizens, as they complicated the procedures for Russians who want to obtain Chinese visas!

On the other hand, the oversights of some Chinese government agencies and companies in addressing such issues as debt in Sri Lanka, pollution of the environment in some parts of Africa, monopolizing of markets and competing with local industries, were all used by the West to fuel its anti-China campaigns, so they could accuse China of plundering the wealth of developing countries via the debt trap! The problem is compounded by the existence of the one-party system in China with its strong central decision-making. This gives the impression abroad that all Chinese companies—even if they are private—are governmental, and therefore represent China. In fact, most of the wrongdoing and dishonourable behaviour by the Chinese abroad are individual acts, but due to its centralized regime, China pays a heavy price.

The soft power of any country is manifest in its keenness to present the attractive and positive aspects of its political, economic and cultural practices. Any contradiction between words and actions causes great damage to the credibility of the soft power. This accounts for the negativity of some countries towards cooperation with China.

Son: Mistakes like these are to be expected in a major country such as China, which has complex relationships all over the world. The problem here is that there are international actors who are trolling these mistakes and amplifying them dozens of times in order to undermine China's standing and global influence. Despite all this, I believe that China, with its peaceful economic advancement, has provided great benefits to the whole world. It has a positive story it can export. It has largely eliminated poverty among its own people, created the largest consumer market in the world with its biggest middle-class population that is consuming goods from all countries around the world, fundamentally enhanced the quality of life for billions of people around the world by producing low-cost high-quality goods, formerly intended for wealthy classes, for hundreds of low-income consumers to enjoy. China's gigantic appetite for natural resources has driven prices up, helping the, mostly third world, exporting countries to develop their economies, positively affecting the lives of hundreds of millions of people. China's scientists might produce technologies that make life better for most people around the world 5G, e-payment, TikTok are best examples. China, with all its might and relative military regional superiority, had zero military conflicts and used zero bullets in last forty years, despite difficult border disputes with its twenty-one neighbours! These facts are not well-known and often ignored because China failed to tell this story in a universal language.

China's emerging soft power is not as secure as America's, as it suffers from both a lack of creativity and finance and its image is tarnished by its use of direct propaganda. These aspects have reduced the influence of China's soft power, compared with the United States who have long experience in dealing with the public through widespread use of media and a long list of public relations tools.

However, notwithstanding all the negatives we have pointed out, and even though China's endeavours toward this success invited attack and criticism from adversaries, an appealing and attractive side of China has now appeared.

5: Belt and Road Initiative

The Belt and Road initiative, launched by Chinese President Xi Jinping in 2013, has become the main driver of China's foreign policy. It has also accelerated 'ChinaPhobia'.

Father: At first, the West did not take this initiative seriously. Many Americans viewed it as another of the propaganda statements usually made by Chinese leaders when they come to power. President Jiang Zemin was known for his three representations theory, which was at the time, seen as a renewal of the Communist Party's theoretical arsenal. But this statement disappeared at once when the President left office. President Hu Jintao's utopian statement about a harmonious scientific society met with the same fate. Throughout his rule, Chinese officials and the media echoed his saying, seeing it to promote Chinese society. However, the statement evaporated at the end of President Hu's term.

What distinguishes the Belt and Road initiative from its predecessors is that—unlike Jiang Ze Min and Hu Jing Tao's theories—President Xi has taken this initiative as one of his main political endeavours, allocating funds, developing plans and building institutions to implement it. The Communist Party of China has also cemented the initiative into its constitution, and this constitution does not change, so this initiative will remain even when President Xi is no longer in power. It has thus been permanently partisan legitimized. Since its launch, this initiative has become the key driver of China's global influence and the main geopolitical tool in the hands of the Communist Party.

The initiative was launched in two speeches given by the Chinese President during visits to Kazakhstan and Indonesia in 2013. These two countries were not arbitrarily selected. Kazakhstan later became the focal point of the new Land Silk Road to the West, and Indonesia became a major station in the Maritime Silk Road to East Asia.

Son: I have been working on the Belt and Road Initiative for several years, through our involvement in different projects along the BRI countries. I participate in at least ten international and domestic conferences on this subject annually. So, let me offer some background on this initiative.

The idea of Belt and Road was born at the end of the 2000s when China became an important player in the world economy. It was not welcomed widely, especially in the West and the developed world. For example, Chinese companies have made great efforts to invest in Australia, but the general feeling in China was that they were unwelcome and have been treated inappropriately. I myself have witnessed the way the European institutions regarded Chinese investment. This prompted Chinese leaders to start moving their investment toward developing countries instead of developed countries, and Xi Jinping greatly encouraged this when he was Vice President. The initiative was therefore geared towards developing countries.

Much of the expansion of Chinese companies throughout the world has been chaotic and uncoordinated. As these companies were run in accordance with the interests of China's different domestic lobbies, the Chinese leadership was frequently unaware of many of the activities of their overseas enterprises. One of my Chinese friends told me that many senior Chinese officials were surprised to learn of the large scale of their investments in Sudan, which was under great pressure from the United Nations. Beijing vetoed the Security Council to preserve its interests there.

Large Chinese companies that have invested in minerals and energy in Africa and Latin America have also adopted aggressive tactics and policies. And they have made mistakes, such as allowing their staff to behave in a way that discredited China and provoked local communities against them. These companies continued illegal and devious practices they were carrying out within the Chinese market at the time, from corruption and lawlessness to money laundering. Those practices led to major problems within local communities. The Belt and Road Initiative seeks to end the chaos created by Chinese companies abroad, by creating mechanisms for coordination and central guidance.

China still suffers from a severe lack of human competence in undertaking international projects, particularly on the management side. Indeed, the famous Chinese 'win-win' cooperation slogan has become a popular sarcastic phrase among foreigners who believe, from their experience, that the real meaning of the Chinese slogan is that China wins twice! Although the BRI initiative is described as a global platform, the Chinese interest and flavour is by far the predominant one.

Nine years into the BRI, following twenty years of aggressive foreign operation by Chinese companies, currently in 2022, I am still one of very few foreigners engaged in this field. It is almost impossible for any foreigner to hold an active leadership position in Chinese companies, even Chinese multinationals, such as Alibaba, Huawei, Geely, Haier, Xiaomi and Tencent, where most of the faces remain local Chinese. Even if the heads of these companies deny it, it is really difficult for them to bring foreigners into their core inner circles. One reason they are unable to match their global competitors, such as Mercedes, Google and Facebook, is due to the closed nature of the Chinese mentality, where trust is primarily built on race, nationality and culture.

Another factor behind the Belt and Road nitiative was that China had reached the end of its internal construction infrastructure boom of cities, roads, ports, airports and factories which formed the basis of the Chinese renaissance. Over the last forty years, China has built a team of powerful companies and valuable know-how which it needs to preserve and protect. China has twenty-seven firms among the top 100 global contractors, up from nine in the 2000 Europe the traditional dominator went down from forty-one to thirty-seven and USA down from nineteen to seven.[2]

China's transformation into a world factory has produced a huge industrial power and a large surplus of factories and commodities, covering, indeed saturating, the needs of the Chinese market.

To become global leaders, China realized that its companies, especially those on the infrastructure team, needed to start making money from international markets instead of earning only in their own very closed circle. It was natural for the Chinese government to find new business markets for these companies.

BRI was key to achieving this. A large fiscal surplus in China encouraged President Xi to take up the BRI initiative. Estimated at several trillion dollars, this surplus was previously primarily invested in US bonds, a policy that many Chinese scholars warned against as too concentrated. They advocated for the government to hedge the risk by diversifying the portfolio of Chinese overseas investment.

Beijing started feeling a shift in the relationship with Washington from partnership to competition, containment and confrontation in the Obama administration. This forced Chinese leaders to consider a proactive and preventive step to avoid US pressure and thwart the containment policy. The move came in the form of the Belt and Road Initiative.

Another factor behind this initiative was the recent US administration's retreat from globalization, from which China had benefitted greatly. The US move prompted Beijing to take initiative to preserve international trade and protect globalization from the effects of US decisions. The surprising and overwhelming welcome given to BRI has shown that countries around the world are eager for global developing focus initiatives, hence the Belt and Road Initiative was described by many as 'Globalization V2'.

Father: The Chinese government has mobilized great potential to implement the initiative. A government committee comprising

---

[2] Deborah Brautigam and Meg Rithmire, 'The Chinese "debt trap" Is a Myth', The Atlantic, 6 February 2021.

representatives of all Chinese ministries led by standing committee members of the CCP has been set up to plan, supervise and provide financial support to the initiative projects. A large fund was established to finance the initiative, and banks were directed to grant loans to projects under which they are being implemented, and these projects have been given priority funding. BRI became a trending slogan in China for two years and between 2015–2018 most of the government-sponsored conferences for relative and unrelated subjects were linked to BRI!

Some companies resorted to trickery, trying to include some of their projects under the title of the BRI—although these projects had nothing to do with the initiative—in order to obtain financial facilities from banks. Government economic agencies have also set up special committees for negotiation and approval of projects with other countries. Media-wise, each television channel has created special programs to cover news on the initiative, and the media have been directed to give priority to activities under the initiative. Moreover, dedicated research centres such as Digital BRI Think Tank, Health Care BRI Think Tank, Maritime BRI, Artic BRI Space BRI etc. have been established, and thousands of international seminars have been held in China and other countries to explain the objectives of the Belt and Road Initiative.

On the political front, the Chinese President organized several summits for Heads of State from around the world to promote the initiative, most recently in Beijing in May 2019, which was attended by representatives of 150 countries and during which multi-billion-dollar contracts were signed. The United States of America did not attend this summit, instead painting a stinging criticism of the 'BRI Initiative', considering it a modern form of Chinese economic colonialism, and a means of pushing developing countries into the debt trap.

Son: It's not difficult to understand the background of the US position. The United States is eager to protect its global footprint and dominance. The USA cannot come up with a similar competing proposition; it has neither the financial mechanism nor the capacity to do so. Most importantly, America does not have the political will domestically to focus significant resources on the infrastructure that is urgently needed in developing countries, and to bring the continents of the world closer together by linking railways, sea and land routes which will promote cooperation among its peoples.

The United States under President Trump moved in an opposite direction, focusing instead on the dissolution of existing US-built international blocs and organizations, and the establishment of political and concrete walls to isolate itself from the rest of the globe. Its hostility towards the BRI has obstructed and distorted its implementation and pressurized participating countries.

China has been keen to give the initiative an international status by saying that while BRI was initiated by China, it belongs to the whole world, and by calling on all countries to participate and contribute. China has put pressure on Western countries by focusing on infrastructure projects in developing nations, an area that the West is reluctant to venture into because of the large investments required and the political risks in the developing world, as well the lack of competitive construction companies capable of executing such projects. China initially identified about twenty developing countries, then expanded to sixty countries and by the end of 2021, in excess of 145 countries and thirty-two international organizations had joined the BRI.

The BRI map was subsequently extended to most regions of the world except for most of the developed countries, in particular Japan, America and India, who openly declared their opposition. It is worth mentioning that these three countries are respectively the former, current and future competitors of China, so we can understand why they are opposing the Belt and Road Initiative.

On the other hand, developing countries, especially the poorer ones, welcomed the initiative and saw it as a good source of funds from a rich and benevolent China. It would appear that Chinese media's exaggeration of national actions and corporate achievements have fuelled this view of China. Leaders of developing countries seem to be under the impression that China is an inexhaustible source of funding, where the revenues of large companies often exceed the GDP of some of the developing countries.

As we have pointed out, the Western world saw this initiative as a challenge to its interests and economic leadership inherited from the colonial era. Western countries found that 'the Chinese dragon' could win on price, specification and speed of implementation. The new Chinese player did not engage with the laws and rules that govern the Western world, did not respect their norms and did not want to share with them.

Moreover, major Western countries find it hard to swallow the idea that China can offer global initiatives and plans that were once the preserve of the West (including Russia). The BRI Initiative also embarrassed the West, as many of the countries who broadly support China have also rejected Western criticism. One European politician told me that leaders from several developing countries suggested to him that if the West does not like what China is doing, they need to offer a suitable alternative. This is highly unlikely, because many pro Belt and Road countries are poor and cannot meet the conditions of international financial institutions. Additionally, the majority of Western companies have become less capable than their Chinese counterparts in recent decades, who are able to efficiently implement infrastructure projects at high speed.

Father: I'd like to add that a new decision by the Chinese government makes the proportion of international operations an important part of management assessment and KPI. This factor has sparked fierce competition among Chinese companies to win contracts in developing countries, under the Belt and Road Initiative. This increased competition has led to Chinese companies having to cut their profits, with two consequences. The developing countries managed to get the lowest prices and Western companies became unable to operate in developing countries due to China's low pricing of contracts.

We can see evidence of this in Kuwait or even in the UAE and other countries in Africa where infrastructure project profits used to run at about 30 per cent. Now, due to the involvement of Chinese companies, profits have fallen to less than 10 per cent. These eroded margins have effectively taken Western companies out of the global competition; these same companies' home markets have limited demand for infrastructure projects. This has led to loss of their skilled workers, so they are no longer able to invest in the latest technology required for a large volume of work.

We see this result reflected on the ground. Having lost one of its most important businesses in developing countries, the West withdrew from most foreign building and construction projects and moved instead to the trade, technology and service sectors.

China did not intentionally aim for this outcome, because fierce competition among Chinese companies also led to large losses, with their profit rate falling to low single digits. It has become very difficult for Chinese companies to maintain these prices, because their cost of their labour has risen sharply, and many young Chinese (children of the single-child policy generation) are no longer willing to work in Africa and difficult Arab countries. Having taken Western competitors out of the market, these companies began to raise their prices to try to make up for their losses. Ironically today, Chinese companies are locked in a bitter struggle with their Indian and Turkish counterparts, two of the most important and fierce opponents of Chinese construction in Asia and Africa.

It is helpful to understand the organizational structure of the BRI, which includes two main branches: The Land Road and the Maritime Road.

The Land Road includes five corridors:

- The Eurasian Corridor, extending from Western China to the Western regions of Russia.
- The China–Mongolia–Russia Corridor, which runs from Northern China to the Russian East.
- The China–Central Asia–West Asia Corridor, which runs from Western China to Turkey.
- The China–Pakistan Corridor, which runs from South-Western China to Pakistan.
- The Bangladesh–China–India–Myanmar Corridor, which runs from Southern China to India.

The Silk Road and the Maritime Belt extends from the Chinese coast through Singapore and India towards the Mediterranean and Africa, and another sea route extends to East Asian countries. The most important project carried out on land hubs is the railway linking China to Europe via Russia, which already operates. By the end of 2021, it will have transported over 14,000 trains of Chinese goods from sixty-two Chinese cities to over 170 European cities in twenty-three countries. In 2021, the total value of goods exchanged in both directions exceeded 40 billion euros.

The other giant project is the road and railway network linking the Western Chinese city of Kashgar with the port of Gwadar in Pakistan. The project cost more than $40 billion and has been in operation for several years. The Belt and Road Initiative has also been launched in Africa, where hundreds of kilometres of railways and highways have been constructed in Kenya, Uganda and Tanzania, in addition to other multi-billion-dollar infrastructure projects in most African countries.

China's land and sea routes under the BRI increased the value of China's foreign trade in 2021 to about 23 per cent. One of the objectives of BRI is to expand the scope of dealing with the Chinese currency, the Yuan, and to ease the pressure of the US dollar. Bilateral agreements have been signed with many countries to trade in RMB. With China's efforts to promote its electronic currency ECNY, which is already in use in some areas within the country, China is slowly but surely moving away from the US dollar. The ECNY will be promoted as the first option to the forty million foreigners visiting China annually, pushing international banks to buy large amounts of ECNY to serve their clients visiting China. A tourist from Portugal will be able to go to his local bank in Lisbon and exchange euro to ECNY to be directly transferred to his electronic wallet on his mobile phone, which will be used when he spends money in China. The businessman in Iran will exchange his Tuman directly into ECNY, and will be paying electronically to the merchants in Yiwu near Shanghai—the destination of hundreds of thousands of merchants from all over the world every year. This will be an important move to increase the RMB's role in international trade which is about 2 per cent against the 40+ per cent of the US dollar.

BRI is also developing in Europe. Following a successful start in Greece in 2018, more than twenty-two countries have joined the BRI including Hungary, Portugal, Italy, Luxembourg, with more to join in the coming years. Chinese efforts to promote the BRI have raised concerns within European capitals and in Washington. The fast-growing relationship between China and Eastern Europe through the 16+1 mechanism is being seen in important capitals of the western hemisphere as a dangerous effort by China to break the unity of Europe. Countries that oppose BRI have decided to jointly counter the BRI and coordinate their capacities to come up with alternative competing development programs such as 'Build Back Better World' as introduced by the Biden Administration and backed by G7 countries. In September 2021, the EU formally unveiled their new 'Global Gateway' Initiative as Europe's response to China's initiative.

India, Japan and Australia also oppose this project. The three countries have decided to jointly counter the BRI in Asia, and coordinate their capacities to come up with alternative development programs to compete with BRI.

Son: China has also been accused of using this initiative to strengthen its strategic influence throughout the world. When I participate in Belt and Road seminars, some Chinese speakers deny this. They are armed with universal goodwill slogans saying that the Belt and Road Initiative does not belong to China, but is an initiative launched by China to promote economic cooperation between countries, promote human relations and civilized communication, without political conditions. Of course, China has geopolitical ambitions behind this initiative, and rightly so; of course there are political conditions that go hand-in-hand with the Belt and Road Initiative.

Would a country that tries to recognize Taiwan's independence and support the rights of the Uighur and Tibetan people be allowed to join this initiative?!

It is also natural for China to seek to protect its interests in the world by resorting to security. We will certainly see more than one Chinese military base around the world to secure its global interests, just as with all the other great powers.

This Chinese denial is in line with the culture among Chinese officials of making sure that their true intentions are not shown. These practices are not limited to Chinese officials, but also common in the business sector, where you can sit in a meeting with Chinese businessmen for many hours while they circle around the issues, before finally announcing their intentions.

When I first arrived in China, I listened to many Chinese experts say that China would never build aircraft carriers because China has historically been a continental land force. Since then I have frequently heard that China will not build military bases because it does not need them and because they are expensive, and because there are other more effective ways to protect China's interests around the world. Of course today's reality is different from what the Chinese used to say, but that doesn't mean that those officials and experts were lying. They simply weren't aware of the nature of China's rapid rise. Your worldview is different when you're at the middle of the mountain than when you get to the top.

Chinese leadership customarily scrutinizes everything before taking any step. This is generally true, but does not apply to the Belt and Road Initiative. Let me explain this thoroughly.

The initiative developed and grew into a strategy from an idea put forward by President Xi Jinping, and then moved on to become one of the most important global initiatives of this era. However, this Initiative is still young, in need of care and with a long time yet to grow. China has not set firm and definitive targets for this initiative; its success depends not just on China, but on the world's acceptance of it. Finally, it is still called an initiative, not a plan. When China announces a plan, it details precisely its objectives and sets timetables with numbers and dates for implementation and appoints officials in-charge of the plan. For example, the 'Made in China 2025' plan and the 'End Poverty in China' by 2021 plan and others, were only approved after in-depth studies involving thousands of specialists and institutions, so China can control the progress of these plans in terms of adjustment or addition in order to ensure their implementation.

There is no place for the word 'failure' in the Chinese Communist Party dictionary. The Party's influence among the Chinese people is based on the credibility of its plans and its ability to achieve. As an example, China is one of the few countries in the world that predetermines the growth rate of the Chinese economy and therefore ensures that this growth is achieved. Other countries' plans are based on expectations for future growth; at the end of the fiscal year they announce actual growth rates, which may be higher or lower than predicted.

So it's unusual to have the Belt and Road Initiative constantly evolving, with its final features not yet configured. China has not developed a timescale for its implementation, and it did not appear as a result of in-depth studies and prior organization, but as an idea from above as a way to open up more to developing countries. Chinese executives then elaborated upon it; it is an evolving idea. While officially China doesn't like to talk about the obstacles, they are aware of them. That this idea has been welcomed by a large proportion of the world proves that China is able to deliver global leadership and global goods.

From my experience sitting on advisory boards of Chinese think tanks, Chinese officials don't pay much attention to the criticism and advice that comes from outsiders; they do listen seriously to the views of countries with whom that have agreed to cooperate and are interested in trying to resolve issues. That is what we saw during the second session of the Belt and Road Initiative held in the summer of 2019 in Beijing, where China announced a package of actions to address the problems posed by the participating countries. Execution remains to be seen. But a package put forward by China's most powerful leader is particularly significant and will inevitably lead to positive changes to address the shortcomings that have emerged during the development of this initiative, as is clearly indicated by China's decision to drop all coal-fuelled power projects globally.

6: China Abandons its Job as the 'Factory of the World'

For several decades, China has been seen as the factory that supplies cheap goods benefitting people around the world. That role is no longer viable due to a changing labour market, environmental costs of pollution and a shortage of natural materials.

Father: America was satisfied with China being the world's factory. The presence of cheap Chinese goods contributed to the welfare of American society, thereby minimizing the causes of social unrest. The trade equation between Washington and Beijing was generally based on the following rule: US companies design and create products, then send their orders to Chinese factories, where the goods are produced.

Over time, however, China developed real problems from the massive overproduction of cheap goods, including environmental pollution, overconsumption of natural resources, and an ageing workforce that led to a shortage of labour in China. Beijing realized that being the 'Factory of the World' was not sustainable.

Son: China has become one of the most polluted regions in the world with health and quality of life consequences. The atmosphere in Beijing, where I live, is dominated by a toxic fog coming from smoke emitted by tens of thousands of factories scattered in and around Beijing. The majority of these plants are coal-fired. Sometimes the air quality is so bad that my family doesn't venture out on the street for many days at a time, unless absolutely necessary. Beijing nights have no visible stars. A blue sky is a cause for family celebration. Severe pollution, tens of times the levels widely permitted globally, has led to the spread of respiratory diseases and an increase in the incidence of cancer among the population. The pollution has also prompted the city's residents to buy household air purifiers—a significant additional financial burden. Things have begun to improve in recent years, as China shifts to a pattern of less polluting production.

Father: I visited steel and iron factories in areas near Beijing, and it was really horrible. The clouds of black and coloured smoke emitted by the chimneys of the iron smelting furnaces were so dense that they reduced visibility even during the day. Moreover, these and other factories dumped their industrial waste into rivers and seas, so water, soil and agricultural crops were contaminated. Things had come to the point where many foreign embassies and companies had to import food and water from their home countries for fear of contamination.

In Beijing, the blue sky was glimpsed only on big occasions, such as the China–Africa Summit, the Arab–Chinese Summit or the 2008 Olympic Games. During these events, factories near Beijing stopped working, and the atmosphere became clear. Beijing residents were hoping to increase these events so they could continue to breathe clean air. The problem is compounded by the large expanses of desert surrounding Beijing, where strong winds carried dust across hundreds of kilometres, and the lack of forests exacerbates pollution. China ranks 100th in the world forest rankings.

Chinese leaders were aware of the frightening consequences of pollution. When I met with Chinese President Jiang Zemin to present my credentials as Ambassador, I told him of the frightening scale of the pollution in Beijing. He replied then: 'We know this, and we know the danger of pollution to the environment and the health of citizens, but we don't have the funds to fight pollution. It is a big tax that we pay to build China and we have to be patient and pay the price.'

The price was enormous, as pollution eradicated nature, water sources, and the health of people in China. When I came to Beijing to work in the winter of 2000, the snow was black, and I couldn't wear a white shirt and walk the streets of Beijing. Diplomats from Western countries regarded China as one of the more difficult and dangerous countries, and requested that embassy workers travel periodically with their families to environmentally clean areas inside and outside China.

In addition, as all Chinese funds and efforts were earmarked for economic construction, Chinese citizens had to bear the cost of medicine and private health services. Even education was mostly private in a country ruled by the Communist Party, whose objective was to provide basic services to citizens free of charge. The Chinese leadership had a difficult choice: either to use the money to develop the country's industrial base, or to spend it on pollution control. During the first twenty years of reform and opening up, Chinese leaders preferred to turn a blind eye to pollution and focus instead on industrial development.

Son: Natural resources were also depleted as traditional industrialization and overall development in China increased. China began importing oil in the early 1990's, as domestic production was no longer sufficient. In 2019, China imported more than 10 million barrels of oil per day. China is now the world's number one oil importer.

At the same time, China, which has one of the largest coal reserves, increased its dependence on coal, consuming about 10 million tons daily, of which about 1 million tons are imported. China annually produces 1.2 billion tons of steel—the largest quantity in the world. A relatively natural resource-poor China has become the world's leading importer of timber, cotton and asphalt. The Chinese economy is consuming tens of millions of tons of raw materials per day and has become the world's largest importer of these. The whole world's resources will not be enough for the Chinese industrial dragon's growing appetite.

Father: One of the reasons why China backtracked on the 'World Factory' tag is the lack of labour in the Chinese market, due to the widespread phenomenon of ageing in Chinese society. Wujiang District, part of east China's Jiangsu Province, is a microcosm of what the ageing population situation in China will be like in the coming years.

Qatar's Al Jazeera reported a bleak picture of the city in a report aired in October 2019: 'Its streets are almost deserted, lacking young faces, while there are plenty of older people who can be seen in the fields, in shops or even driving taxis. With nearly a million people, more than a third of whom are over sixty, Wujiang District is truly a city for the elderly only. A number of secondary schools have been closed due to a shortage of young students. Local companies are struggling to get young employees, and social services are struggling because of the increasing number of older people who are putting enormous pressure on them.'

'At the end of 2019, China had about 180 million people aged sixty-five and over, or 17.8 per cent of the total population,' the Chinese Ministry of Civil Affairs acknowledged in its August 2017 report. That is 10 per cent more than 2018 figures and much higher than the global standards set by the United Nations. According to these criteria, a country is considered an 'ageing society' when the number of adults over sixty is about 10 per cent of the population.

It was not only the one-child policy that reduced the number of births. The massive industrial revolution that took place in China led to radical urbanization. The demand for urban jobs increased and women's employment opportunities improved, thus delaying the age of marriage or postponing childbearing. Economic development and subsequent improvements in the standard of living also brought about an increase in the number of smokers, alcohol consumers and unhealthy diets, and high rates of pollution. All these factors have had a direct impact on fertility, both for men and women. China experienced a rapid and historically unprecedented decline in fertility from 5.8 children per woman in 1970 to 2.8 in 1979, to only 1.5 in 2010, meaning that every two women had only three children throughout their lives. In 2020, newborn figures reached a new record low, 10,003,500 compared to 17,230,000 in 2017.[3]

Son: The result is that China's population is getting older than anywhere else in the world. According to the United Nations, China is ageing faster than almost any country in modern times, and its dependency ratio could rise to 44 per cent by 2050. This is the

---

[3] (China's internal ministry report 8 February 2021).

proportion of the population which does not work but lives off the earnings of the rest of the working population. The elderly will get the lion's share, followed by those who are too young to be employed. This will have significant economic consequences, including a shortage of productive labour, a significant decline in inventions and innovations, and severe pressure on the state's financial resources to finance unproductive pension and health insurance funds.

This will also be reflected in the nature of the Chinese economy, which formerly boasted of a huge surplus of export goods. Signs now point to a lack of production, a shortage of exports and increased imports. The Chinese government has begun importing food and some goods from abroad; soon China will also have to import foreign labour.

The annual China International Import Expo in Shanghai that was launched in 2018 is tasked with encouraging imports and has become a global platform where the world's companies race to sell their products to the Chinese market. There is a verbal directive from the Chinese leadership that any company participating in the exhibition cannot return empty-handed. The Chinese President participated in the opening of its four sessions. This demonstrates the Chinese government's determination to open its doors to the world's products.

In its fourth exposition in 2021 more than 127 countries and 3,000 regions signed over 70 billion USD of import contracts.

Father: I suspect declining fertility rates will continue to be a problem. I don't think that the Communist Party's retreat several years ago from the one-child policy will lead to an increase in births in China. The modern Chinese family often does not want to have children and take on the heavy responsibility of their upbringing. It's estimated that it costs $140,000 to raise a child in China, a number that is out of reach for many young families. There is a significant trend among the younger Chinese generation, especially in major cities such as Shanghai, towards 'Families without Children'! To address this, China has begun to consider financial incentives to increase births. However, the experiences of other countries, such as Japan, Germany and Russia, have not yielded positive results, despite the great financial inducements offered by their governments for newborns.

Experts are predicting that China will lose half of its population in less than one century, unless there is a magical solution. China's population is likely to decline by the end of this century to about 800 million, mostly adults. Such a decline will present a major obstacle to China's drive towards world leadership. The problem of labour scarcity is already a reality affecting economic life, and is no longer just an assumption or prediction.

One reason for moving foreign companies outside China, especially those requiring a large workforce, is the lack of available labour, which has led to higher production costs. A family housekeeper in Beijing in 2003 cost about $100/month. Today it costs $1000 for the same service! The Chinese believe that new technology such as robotics and artificial intelligence, which is now advanced in China, can solve this problem. But experiments in a number of countries around the world in substituting robots point to the emergence of new social problems. These problems will be even greater in China due to its high population density. Denying work to hundreds of millions of people in favour of robots is contrary to the fundamental principle of China's Socialist system, which is to guarantee the right to work for every human being.

Son: In a meeting with a Chinese official in the summer of 2014, I was complaining about the government's continued raising of minimum salaries in different cities around the country that was pushing many foreign companies to leave China, and raising the cost of living for expats. I explained to him that this would have a significant impact on China's economy, which is heavily dependent on exports. His answer opened my eyes when he said 'we are aware of this issue, and trying to manage this pattern but will not stop it. If our people, especially the lower-income level, can't earn more money, how we will move to a consumer-based economy just like the USA? We've done our job and contributed well to humanity. Let other countries like India and Vietnam and Indonesia start to play their role as well. We wish them all the best!'

These three problems have prompted China to gradually abandon the slogan of 'China is the Factory of the World', and to redirect the economy to focus on future industries, which do not pollute the environment and do not need large quantities of raw materials, energy or a large workforce.

Those industries were, until a few years ago, the best partners of American and Western companies. China's intrusion into world-class qualitative production has caused it to collide with the United States, which is now deeply concerned about Chinese competition in leading global inventions and innovations, creating an additional reason for hostility to China.

If China had remained within the limits of traditional industrial commodity production, as 'Factory of the World', Sino–US relations might still be within the bounds of partnership. China's move to promote itself as the 'Inventor and Innovator of the World' and its steady progress to becoming the biggest consumer and import market in the world, has challenged US hegemony over the global technology market and US influence on the world. This shifting economic landscape is a primary source of American ChinaPhobia and related hostility.

7: COVID-19

The coronavirus pandemic that disrupted the entire world has accelerated and been used to justify ChinaPhobia in the United States and other countries.

Father: COVID-19 has caused major losses to the world economy, and humanity in its entirety has been confined to the prison called quarantine. The pandemic has disrupted peoples' lives and claimed a large number of victims. This type of global disaster will deeply affect the whole world for some time to come. Because the virus was first spread in China, it will inevitably affect attitudes toward China in other countries.

The pandemic presented an important opportunity to enhance global solidarity and to build bridges of cooperation and mutual trust to fight this virus, based on the principle that misfortune and human disasters unite people. Instead, the coronavirus caused a serious new international crack, particularly in American–Chinese relations, leading to opposing attitudes about the origins of the virus, the demand for an international investigation, the relationship with the World Health Organization, and the demand for compensation from China for the massive losses.

Relations between Washington and Beijing have grown more complicated after the pandemic and attitudes towards each other have become more extreme. Gone is the flexibility that prevailed between them during the past forty years. Old problems like Hong Kong, the Uighurs, and Taiwan also continue to cause distress. These will be discussed in greater detail later.

Son: What are the most important effects that the coronavirus pandemic has had on American–Chinese relations, and on the broader international situation? From our perspective, these effects can be summarized in the following points:

First, the coronavirus has united large segments of public opinion against China. The Pew Report of October 2020 shows how negative COVID-19 was for China's image, especially in the developed world. The economic damage, fear and death toll from the pandemic have been devastating. The focus on Chinese responsibility for this devastation can be attributed to the charges that Washington made against China, and its critical call to conduct an international investigation into the spread of the virus which started in the city of Wuhan.

America insists that Beijing's approach to the pandemic was far from transparent, as it concealed the disease and punished the doctor who initially warned against it. America claims that the Chinese leaders did not take the necessary precautions to prevent the spread of the virus, especially in the early weeks. It did not suspend flights to and from China, and instead allowed millions of Chinese to travel to other countries, transmitting the virus. Moreover, Beijing withheld the truth at first when it announced that the virus could not be transmitted from human to human. The persisting human and financial haemorrhage in the USA caused by the pandemic massively negatively affects bilateral relations and inflames America's revengeful feelings towards China.

According to the Americans, China is responsible for the losses suffered by the American economy and its citizens. President Trump went as far as declaring the pandemic an attack against the United States more dangerous than the Japanese military aircraft attacks on Pearl Harbour on 7 December 1941 which drove America into World War II.

Moreover, the two major parties in America—the Republicans and the Democrats—are unanimous in their accusations that China is the reason behind the disasters inflicted upon America due to the coronavirus. President Trump is not the only one accusing Beijing. Biden, the then Democratic presidential candidate, also declared that holding China accountable would be a main article on his agenda if he wins the upcoming elections, which he did.

Father: These accusations against China are not mere words. Some American entities, with official support, have commenced legal proceedings, with District Attorneys of eighteen states filing class action lawsuits against China, claiming compensation for the losses inflicted upon America. These class action lawsuits are expected to expand. Some important circles in America want to deprive Chinese properties in the United States of the attribute of sovereignty, as a prelude to confiscating Chinese financial assets in America by way of damages. The Republican Party formed a nationwide committee, headed by Representative Liz Cheney, to coordinate all American actions and lawsuits against China. The American administration is still exerting considerable efforts to form an international alliance to condemn the Chinese government's handling of the coronavirus pandemic.

Beijing has denied all of America's accusations, and confirmed that relevant Chinese entities took all necessary precautions to prevent the spread of the disease. The Chinese view the overall campaign conducted against them by the Trump administration as a smokescreen, aimed at hiding America's failures in fighting the pandemic.

It is important to highlight a significant element that has come to the forefront in the relations between China and America, and that is the aggravation of anti-USA sentiment in Chinese public opinion. Many people in China believe that their leadership succeeded in containing the pandemic and preventing a catastrophic death toll by prioritizing the safety of the people and the economy. National media's focus on America's comparative weakness and confusion served to enhance Chinese national sentiment, and public opinion has pressured the leadership not to make any concessions to Washington, after they witnessed America's poor response to COVID-19.

Another issue that must be pointed out is that the coronavirus pandemic inflamed national and racial sentiments around the world, hindering communication among peoples. Initially, racist hostilities rose against the Chinese in America, Europe and even in Russia. At a later stage, hatred towards foreigners spread throughout China. Such hostilities have widened the gap between the Chinese and other nations including America, creating an atmosphere conducive to the spread of mutual phobias and diffidence.

Son: Another important consequence of the coronavirus pandemic is the retreat of the United States from its leading global role. This retreat started three years ago as a result of the protectionist and isolationist policy of President Trump, and his withdrawal from many international conventions and organizations. The American administration's confusion and failure to respond to the coronavirus led the world to reconsider its attitude towards the feasibility of America's global leadership, especially as Trump's procedures were focused on isolating the United States from the rest of the world and closing its borders. He was so occupied with his popularity inside America, and making deals that benefitted Americans, that he neglected to lead and coordinate international efforts to form an alliance to provide financial resources and produce vaccines. All of these actions damaged the reputation of the United States and its global leadership position.

The world was amazed at Trump's attempts to get exclusive access to a promising German vaccine and his administration's refusal to participate in global vaccine efforts led predominantly by US allies in Europe and other developed countries. Trump's 'medical' Tweets that defied science subjected America to the world's mockery; mass media ridiculed his suggestions for treating the virus, and his lack of a plan for immunizing Americans against COVID-19, even after having prioritized 'warp speed' development of a vaccine by multiple US firms.

The United States proved itself incapable or unwilling politically to effectively control the pandemic, thus greatly affecting its worldwide influence and global role. Its moral standing was further eroded by Trump's brutality concerning the American June 2020 protests, in response to the killing of an African American man, which shocked the world and undermined the credibility of the United States and damaged its soft image. It undermined American claims that US policy defends democracy, freedom and human rights in the world. When President Trump referred to peaceful protestors in America as 'thieves and terrorists', encouraged police to use violence and threatened military intervention to suppress them, he acted more like a third-world dictator. President Biden tried to reverse a lot of this policies, by rejoining global organization and reopening the borders to refugees and Muslims with the slogan 'America is Back'!

Beijing attempted to take advantage of America's confusion in dealing with COVID-19 by showing that it could control and conquering the deadly coronavirus. It also played a responsible role on the international stage by offering aid to many countries, and allocating billions of dollars in additional grants, relieving the debt burden owed to Beijing by over seventy-seven countries. China hoped thereby to strengthen its global leadership position.

Many factors blocked Beijing's opportunity to fill the space vacated by the US on the international stage at that time. In the early stage of the pandemic, Chinese officials made massive efforts to deny and condemn any claim that COVID-19 came from China. Chinese diplomacy was tense about any suggestion linking China to the Coronavirus, and this attitude surprised journalists around the world, particularly those in Western countries, who spared no expenses in making accusations against China.

When I wrote an article about the global attack against China, I indicated that it was inaccurate and far from the truth to describe the Coronavirus as being 'Chinese', and more correct to say that the Coronavirus first spread in China. However, several of my Chinese friends rejected this description and suggested instead that, due to the efforts of the Chinese authorities, COVID-19 was first discovered in China, and that the international community should be grateful to Beijing for all of its efforts in identifying the virus and the resulting swift measures that prevented a potential global catastrophe.

Father: Chinese authorities also celebrated their initial victory over Coronavirus, which they attributed to the privileges of China's authoritarian political regime, and its excellence compared to Western democracy. At the same time, Chinese mass media highlighted the confusion experienced by some Western democratic states, which showed the disappointment of Western peoples with their governments. Chinese media broadcast interviews with Western citizens demanding that their governments learn from the impressive Chinese experience and accept aid from China. Special focus was placed on a group of foreigners who raised the Chinese flag as if seeking to join China! This demagogic propaganda annoyed many foreign countries, including those close to China. High-ranking officials in Italy, the only country in the Group of Seven which joined the Belt and Road Initiative with Beijing, were forced to tell Beijing to stop such behaviour and refrain from its 'provocative media coverage'!

Moreover, the Chinese government's policy of offering aid to help countries respond to the Coronavirus, which was referred to as the 'Mask Diplomacy' was not a success story. On the one hand, many countries highlighted the bad quality of the personal protective equipment provided by China, describing shipments of PPE as aid even though importers had paid for the goods. The continuing changes to the export rules for COVID-19-related items made it extremely difficult for importers, which was seen as Beijing trying to leverage the supply chain for political gain. On the other hand, the Chinese Ministry of Foreign Affairs was confused because so many entities and ministries were in charge of the aid programme that the overall coordination suffered from serious issues and failed to achieve its goals.

As one example, I cite what happened regarding medical assistance offered by China to Syria in May 2020. Media in Syria announced that China was providing urgent medical aid to Damascus to help fight the corona pandemic. Syria's Deputy Foreign Minister and the Chinese Ambassador to Damascus, along with a number of senior officials, went to Damascus Airport to receive the Chinese aid consignment, accompanied by media representatives and many trucks. However, everyone was surprised to see that the aid consisted of two small cartons that were placed on the ground in front of the receivers—an awkward situation for everyone present, which was mocked on social media. Later, Chinese officials explained that a Chinese aeroplane was distributing simple medical aid to a number of countries, including Syria.

To add insult to injury, beneficiaries were frequently asked to express their gratitude to China for this aid and acknowledge its positive attributes. European diplomats told me that some Chinese embassies demanded the governments of their aid-receiving countries to arrange media coverage in praise of Beijing. One of my foreign acquaintances described the atmosphere surrounding this Chinese diplomatic behaviour as: *'Our general feeling is that China is offering this aid for advertising rather than humanitarian purposes. It is inappropriate for Beijing to offer a gift on the condition of receiving praise for the Chinese leadership in return. Moreover, Chinese diplomats indirectly give the impression that failure to express gratitude will reflect negatively on relations between the beneficiary country and China, and it will affect the leadership's evaluation of their own performance in their embassies.'*

Son: At the same time, Chinese mass media and diplomats were ordered to become more involved in administering international public opinion campaigns. Think tanks and researchers in China were instructed to organize a counterattack against America's accusations, and to set about confusing global public opinion as to which side was responsible for the Coronavirus, by exchanging accusations about its origin.

Obviously, China was the weaker party in this public relations battle due in part to unequal capabilities, experience, and administrative capacities. China might have won the battle if it had stuck with a calm, low-key strategy. One Chinese expert asked me to advise what Beijing was supposed to do in response to the unfair attack it was subjected to during the early period of Coronavirus. My answer was that if the spokespersons in the Chinese Ministry of Foreign Affairs and other propaganda hawks had remained silent, China's international situation would have been much better! Beijing would have gained the world's sympathy if it had kept quiet regarding what it considered hostile behaviour by other countries. Had China not indulged in provocative protests or claimed to be a victim of Washington's attacks, America's past record and Trump's methods and reputation alone were enough to defeat American strategy, without China's intervention.

Father: Assigning the management of the corona crisis to the Chinese Communist Party apparatus also contributed to China's inability to take maximum advantage of America's chaotic pandemic situation. Although this management responded successfully to the pandemic internally, the Propaganda Department of the CPC central committee failed to manage the external media battle which had a seriously negative impact on China's efforts to gain the sympathy of international public opinion. Officials in this department simply do not have the specialized entities, research centres or experts to conduct scientific evaluation of the methods and efficacy of Chinese tactics, which other government-related ministries and departments have access to. China's external propaganda was further affected by the inexperienced officials allocated to the job, who just sat in their offices and gave instructions to the relevant state bodies, without researching, evaluating and allowing corrective discussions on the implementation of this method and its outcomes.

Without underestimating the position and ability of the officials in the Propaganda Department of the CPC central committee, I note that their work experience is based on managing internal public opinion, and they do not have sufficient experience or knowledge, nor do they have the tools or budgets to navigate the minefield of international public opinion.

Additionally, inexperienced members of the youth groups involved in the state bodies ardently attempted to prove first their loyalty to the leadership, and secondly their ability and efficiency. The consequence of such a strategy was that officials from different ministries resorted to a confrontation to address any criticism against China, repeatedly stressing the ability of the Party and State to successfully manage the corona crisis. Chinese diplomats made several mistakes when ambassadors were instructed to adopt an aggressive attitude in responding to China-Phobia campaigns. In what is currently called 'wolf warrior diplomacy', each Chinese diplomat abroad was to become a 'wolf warrior' when addressing external campaigns against China. This term was coined from the 2015 Chinese movie of the same title about the heroic deeds of a Chinese soldier who fought against the mercenary, in a direct imitation of the American Rambo movies.

This strategy reached its peak when some officials classified as 'wolf warriors', such as the spokesperson of the Chinese Foreign Ministry

Zhao Li Jian, stated that the United States was responsible for spreading the pandemic in Wuhan. This statement led to formal American protests which the Chinese Ambassador in Washington failed to calm despite explaining that he is the one who represents China's official state policy towards the USA and that the spokesperson's opinion does not necessarily reflect the attitude of the Chinese government towards America.

A statement made by the Chinese Ambassador to France accused the French government of abandoning its citizens to die of Coronavirus in old people's care homes, which caused a crisis between Beijing and Paris. Beijing's Ambassador to Australia threatened that Australia would pay a high price if they continued their hostile policies towards China. A long list of assertive and aggressive statements was made by Chinese officials in a tone that the world was not used to hearing from China's foreign policy representatives, where it was impossible to distinguish between statements from the Foreign Ministry or from the Defence Ministry! I believe that these 'wolf warriors' exaggerated in expressing their attitudes, which reflected negatively on the relationship between China and a number of countries around the world. This new strong language and assertiveness has not helped China reach its goals of enhancing its global image.

It seems that America's criticism of China worked to negatively affect European attitudes towards Beijing. As can be seen from the British government's attitude on matters important to the bilateral relationship such as Huawei, nuclear power stations and other vital projects.

This tension was also reflected in the video summit that took place in June 2020 between the leaders of the European Union and Chinese President Xi Jingpin. The President of the European Commission, Ursula von der Leyen, stated that during the summit, leaders of the European Union expressed their great concern towards the national security law in Hong Kong to their Chinese counterparts President Xi Jinping and the Premier Li Keqiang. She added that she had stressed that such law will have 'very negative consequences,' and she reminded the leaders that Hong Kong owes its economic success to its relative autonomy.

In a press conference following the summit, she said: 'We were very clear that this law is not in line with the situation of Hong Kong nor with China's international commitments'. In his turn, Charles Michel, President of the European Council, stressed that the Europeans expressed their grave concern about the aforementioned law, adding: 'We demanded of China to fulfil its promises to the people of Hong Kong and the international community regarding the autonomy of the previous British colony, and guarantee freedoms there'.

Beijing severely criticized the EU following these statements, stressing that this is an internal issue, and that China does not accept any foreign interference in its internal affairs. This is the first serious EU–China confrontation, and it indicates that the general orientation in European policy has changed direction and is now drifting away from China and converging with America. This represents a serious failure of the Chinese policy that was successful in the past at coaxing Europe away from America.

Son: A review of these details indicates that there is much interaction and tension between the different directions and forces within Chinese policy, which often goes ignored or unnoticed by international public opinion and world decision-makers. China outwardly appears to be a solid dry country with one opinion, an inaccurate image which Beijing presents to the outside world. It is worth noting that it is the nature of Chinese culture to keep conflicts inside the household and hide or conceal them as much as possible.

Despite that, it is important to note that when the second and third wave of Coronavirus struck different Chinese cities in May 2020, the world saw the Chinese government apply a new methodology. The total lockdown was abandoned, as opposed to what had happened in Wuhan, three months prior. The specialized health systems hastened to announce the pandemic, define the infected areas, and follow the procedure of immediate isolation of any person who came close to the infected areas. Even so, this effective policy and impressive performance left other areas open. I did not feel any change in our lifestyle in Beijing as we live on the other side of the infected city. Mass media were allowed more freedom to write about the second wave, reflecting the desire of the Chinese policymakers to develop, reflect, and keep learning from their mistakes.

Now that we are discussing the factors that limited China's ability to fill the void left by America on a global level, it is important to highlight Beijing's delay in introducing global initiatives to fight the pandemic, such as intensifying international efforts to produce mutual vaccines, and failing to try to establish an international fund to aid the afflicted countries. Beijing's reaction was limited to offering bilateral efforts through sending some aid whilst maintaining a defensive stance. It did not initiate or lead international efforts to respond to the Coronavirus when America withdrew.

In addition, the accusations by the United States and other nations that China concealed information about COVID-19 and failed to disclose its ability to be transmitted from human to human, as well as not closing its borders to prevent large numbers of Chinese citizens from leaving, cast international doubts over the credibility of the Chinese government, decreasing its popularity in many countries. The ordinary people in particular—whose lives were dramatically affected for the worse—were easily influenced by their local media who echoed US sentiments, as they continued to hear Chinese officials and media reporting on the supremacy of the Communist Party and their great success in containing the pandemic.

Father: I believe that the fourth consequence of the corona pandemic, (which we have already partially referred to) which inflamed ChinaPhobia inside America, can be seen from the fierce competition between the ruling regime in China and American and Western democrats.

China's successful victory over the Coronavirus is the reason this problem emerged. Beijing was quickly able to defeat COVID-19, and it summarized its pioneering experience in controlling the pandemic in a white paper released by the Chinese government on 6 June 2020. This paper attributed China's success in dealing with the pandemic to its swift and decisive management in concentrating the nation's resources to contain the affected areas, combining China's advanced industrial and constructional capacities with the latest technologies, making use of traditional Chinese medicine, and providing free treatment for patients.

These achievements earned worldwide praise and positive media coverage for China's regime, compared to the liberal democratic system in many countries that resulted in disorder and confusion, and an increased number of coronavirus victims. This comparison has restarted the debate about which system of government is better. Obviously, the shift of international public opinion raised the fears of the American ruling class and initiated attacks against the Chinese regime which it accused of being totalitarian and cult-like, and of opposing democracy and human rights. On this topic, the famous American thinker Fukuyama wrote in 'American Interest' on 18 May 2020:

'The dangers of a regime that seeks totalitarian control were laid bare in the early days of the COVID-19 crisis, when speaking honestly about the unfolding epidemic, as Dr Li Wenliang did, was severely punished. For all we know, the flow of misinformation is continuing today. It is wrong to hold up the CCP's totalitarian approach in dealing with the virus as a model to be emulated by other countries. Nearby South Korea and Taiwan, both healthy liberal democracies, achieved even better results in the pandemic without the draconian methods used by China.'

Fukuyama added: 'One of the great dangers today is that the world looks to Xi's totalitarian model, rather than a broader East Asian model that combines strong state capacity with technocratic competence, as the winning formula in facing future crises.'

He continued: 'What Americans need to keep in mind is that their enemy and rival right now is not China, but a Chinese Communist Party that has shifted into high-totalitarian mode. The CCP's aspiration toward total control unfortunately now reaches into liberal democracies around the world. The hundreds of thousands of Chinese who study, work, and live abroad do so because they want to better their lives, and find that foreign countries offer better opportunities than their own. But the CCP wants to keep them loyal to China and use them where possible to advance the interests of Chinese foreign policy. This then unfairly casts suspicion on ethnic Chinese citizens and leads to prejudice and unfounded charges of dual loyalty.'

American leadership appeared to spare no effort in attacking China and blackening the reputation of the Chinese Communist Party, as was manifested in the speech of Michael R. Pompeo, the Secretary of State,[4] in front of a number of Chinese opposition figures.

---

[4] In the Richard Nixon Library & Museum, on 23 July 2020.

The Secretary's speech included a comprehensive strategy to face China, and he clarified the depth of the negative changes that had taken place in American policy towards Beijing, following corona, which inflamed ChinaPhobia in America. We will elaborate on the most significant parts of the speech as it shows the ChinaPhobia advocator's logic and narrative. The American Secretary stated:

'We imagined engagement with China would produce a future with bright promise of comity and cooperation. But today we're all still wearing masks and watching the pandemic's body count rise because the CCP failed in its promises to the world. We're seeing staggering statistics of Chinese trade abuses that cost American jobs, and struck enormous blows to the economies all across America. And we're watching a Chinese military that grows stronger and stronger, and indeed more menacing.'

The Secretary posed the following questions:

'What do the American people have to show now fifty years on from engagement with China? Did the theories of our leaders that proposed a Chinese evolution towards freedom and democracy prove to be true? Is America safer? Do we have a greater likelihood of peace for ourselves and peace for the generations which will follow us?'

Pompeo answered:

'We must admit a hard truth, that if we want to have a free 21st century, and not the Chinese century of which Xi Jinping dreams, the old paradigm of blind engagement with China simply won't get it done. We must not continue it and we must not return to it.'

The Secretary added:

'In 1967, in a very famous Foreign Affairs article, Nixon explained his future strategy towards China. He said, "We simply cannot afford to leave China forever outside of the family of nations ... The world cannot be safe until China changes. Thus, our aim—to the extent we can—we must influence events. Our goal should be to induce change."'

The American Secretary of State continued:

'As time went on, American policymakers increasingly presumed that as China became more prosperous, it would open up, it would become freer at home, and indeed present less of a threat abroad, it'd be friendlier. But the kind of engagement we have been pursuing has not brought the kind of change inside of China that President Nixon had hoped to induce.'

Pompeo added:

'Our policies resurrected China's failing economy, only to see Beijing bite the international hands that were feeding it. We opened our arms to Chinese citizens, only to see the Chinese Communist Party exploit our free and open society. We marginalized our friends in Taiwan, and did not listen to our friends in the Chinese opposition. We gave the Chinese regime itself special economic treatment, only to see the CCP insist on silence over its human rights abuses as the price of admission for Western companies entering China. Hollywood, the epicentre of American creative freedom, self-censors even the most mildly unfavourable reference to China.'

The American Secretary asked again:

'How was this flattery rewarded? We are convinced that the ultimate ambition of China's rulers isn't to trade with the United States. It is to raid the United States. China ripped off our prized intellectual property and trade secrets, costing millions of jobs across America. It sucked supply chains away from America and made the world's key waterways less safe for international commerce.'

Pompeo continued posing questions:

'Why did free nations allow these bad things to happen for all these years?' He answers, 'Perhaps we were naïve about China's virulent strain of communism, or triumphalist after our victory in the Cold War, or cravenly capitalist, or hoodwinked by Beijing's talk of a 'peaceful rise'.

He went on:

'Whatever the reason, today China is increasingly authoritarian at home, and more aggressive in its hostility to freedom everywhere else. So, as President Trump has said: enough.'

The American Secretary proceeded:

'The only way to truly change communist China is to act not on the basis of what Chinese leaders say, but how they behave. President Reagan said that he dealt with the Soviet Union on the basis of "trust but verify". When it comes to the CCP, I say we must distrust and verify.'

Pompeo added:

'We know that the Communist Party dominated all Chinese companies. A good example is Huawei. We stopped pretending Huawei is an innocent telecommunications company that's just showing up to make sure you can talk to your friends. We've called it what it is—a true national security threat—and we've acted accordingly. We know too that if our companies invest in China, they may wittingly or unwittingly support the Communist Party's gross human rights violations. We know too that not all Chinese students and employees are just normal students and workers that are coming here to make a little bit of money and to garner themselves some knowledge. Too many of them come here to steal our intellectual property and to take this back to their country.

We know that the People's Liberation Army is not a normal army, too. Its purpose is to uphold the absolute rule of the Chinese Communist Party elites and expand a Chinese empire.'

The American Secretary defined how America will respond to the Chinese behaviour, saying:

'Frankly, we've built out a new set of policies at the State Department dealing with China, pushing President Trump's goals for fairness and reciprocity, to rewrite the imbalances that have grown over decades. Just this week, we announced the closure of the Chinese consulate in Houston because it was a hub of spying and intellectual property theft. We reversed, two weeks ago, eight years of cheek-turning with respect to international law in the South China Sea. We've called on China to conform its nuclear capabilities to the strategic realities of our time. And the State Department—at every level, across the world— has engaged with our Chinese counterparts simply to demand fairness and reciprocity.'

He added:

'We can't ignore it any longer. They know as well as anyone that we can never go back to the status quo. But changing the CCP's behaviour cannot be the mission of the Chinese people alone. Free nations have to work to defend freedom. It's the furthest thing from easy.'

The American Secretary went on:

'I have faith because the CCP is repeating some of the same mistakes that the Soviet Union made—alienating potential allies, breaking trust at home and abroad, rejecting property rights and predictable rules of law.'

'But' he added 'there are differences. Unlike the Soviet Union, China is deeply integrated into the global economy. But Beijing is more dependent on us than we are on them.'

He continued:

'Our approach isn't destined to fail because America is in decline. As I said in Munich earlier this year, the free world is still winning. We just need to believe it and know it and be proud of it. People from all over the world still want to come to open societies. They come here to study, they come here to work, they come here to build a life for their families. They're not desperate to settle in China.'

The Secretary of State added:

'It's time for free nations to act. Every nation will have to come to its own understanding of how to protect its own sovereignty, how to protect its own economic prosperity, and how to protect its ideals from the tentacles of the Chinese Communist Party.

'Indeed, this is what the United States did recently when we rejected China's unlawful claims in the South China Sea once and for all, as we have urged countries to become Clean Countries so that their citizens' private information doesn't end up in the hand of the Chinese Communist Party. We did it by setting standards. And if we don't act now, ultimately the CCP will erode our freedoms and subvert the rules-based order that our societies have worked so hard to build. If we bend the knee now, our children's children may be at the mercy of the Chinese Communist Party, whose actions are the primary challenge today in the free world.'

Pompeo added:

'Now, this isn't about containment (like what happened with the Soviet Union). Don't buy that. It's about a complex new challenge that we've never faced before. The USSR was closed off from the free world. Communist China is already within our borders.

If the free world doesn't change, communist China will surely change us. There can't be a return to the past practices because they're comfortable or because they're convenient.

Securing our freedoms from the Chinese Communist Party is the mission of our time, and America is perfectly positioned to lead it.'

The American Secretary ended his speech saying:

'Today the danger is clear, and today the awakening is happening. Today the free world must respond. We can never go back to the past.'[5]

Son: We must mention the fifth consequence of COVID-19.

The corona pandemic drew attention to the risk of the West's reliance on Chinese manufacturing, particularly in the pharmaceutical sector, in times of difficulty. During the corona pandemic the Chinese government had to instruct its pharmaceutical factories to prioritize supplies for the increasing demands of the home market. Pharmaceutical sectors in the United States and Europe depended heavily on imports from China and they suffered a scarcity of medicines, at a time when COVID-19 was spreading rapidly. We believe that the emergence of deglobalization, moving the supply chain out of China to a more regional facility, is another consequence of the Coronavirus.

In this regard, it is worth mentioning that a number of global factories had moved their businesses out of China before corona, for other reasons (which we will discuss in more detail elsewhere in the book), and this represented a loss for China. Moreover, the growing trend of moving strategic industries out of China back to their countries of origin will cause a serious blow to the economic globalization that opened the world's markets to Chinese goods. This will aggravate the faltering global economic crisis initiated by the COVID-19 pandemic.

Finally, we have reviewed the most important outcomes of the corona pandemic on the relationship between Washington and Beijing, and on the international scene. As the Coronavirus is not over, and is still killing thousands every day, aggravating the economic and social

---

[5] We've included this speech by Pompeo because it embodies ChinaPhobia in America and outlines their new set of policies and programme for dealing with China. At the same time, it indicates that stress between the two countries has taken, following the spread of COVID-19, an irreversible approach considering Trump's administration. The rapid imposition of sanctions by the Congress against China that was kept by the Biden Administration emphasizes that bilateral cooperation between Beijing and Washington will never go back to its old times, a permanent shift has accrued.

crises, all its effects on international relations have not yet appeared. The world before coronavirus may have been different from the one which might appear after defeating the pandemic. Despite that, what is happening today makes us think that ChinaPhobia will not disappear. Instead, it will multiply and take new forms, and it will continue to spread throughout the world.

Chapter 2

Means of Hostility Towards China

In this chapter, we will talk about the means used to actually apply an anti-China approach.

Father: I will resort to a little bit of history to explain the future of the current relations between China and America. During World War II, America and the Soviet Union were partners against Nazi Germany, and America provided huge military and economic assistance to the Soviet Union. After the end of the Second World War, relations began to change between the two countries, because America felt that its war ally was threatening its leadership position in the world by competing economically and militarily, and that the Soviet Communist totalitarian regime aspired to replace the Western regime. Therefore, America laid down general principles of the Cold War, to which all subsequent Presidents of America committed themselves, in order to exhaust the Soviet Union, deplete it and thus destroy it. This goal was fully implemented in 1991 with the dissolution of the Soviet Union. These historical facts remind me of what is happening now with Sino–American relations.

America has provided tremendous assistance to China for over thirty years, and now after China's rise, it is in dispute with America over world leadership. Washington considers that it has failed to turn China into a Western liberal state, evidenced by the arrival of hard-liner communist Xi Jinping in 2013, his decisions to roll back the strict party control over everything in China.

Of course China is not a replica of the Soviet Union, but the American political and research faculty finds it difficult to realize this, and seeks to portray China not only as an existential threat to America but as a fundamental threat to its interests and role in the world. The problem is that the US vision is no longer just a conspiracy theory, there are those in America who strive to begin operational steps to contain and exhaust China.

Son: I don't think this comparison reflects the final picture of China. Chinese leadership focuses on peaceful advancement. Evidence shows that China is the only major power that had no war in the last forty years and fired no bullets since it adopted reforms and opening-up policies in the late 1970's. Beijing's leadership says that it does not compete with America and has no ambition to take its place as a world leader, and that it does not interfere in the affairs of others, while rejecting the policy of alliances, axes and global military confrontations.

Father: All of this may be true, but the important thing is that America is not looking at China as a partner, but as a competitor, and a threat. America has therefore begun to resort to the means it experimented with in its Cold War with the Soviet Union, the most important of which are the Trade War, the Arms Race and the promotion of Chinese separatist movements. And that is what we will talk about in detail.

1: Trade War

The trade war between the United States and China is one of Washington's means of containing China's economic development, reflecting its concerns about the growth in power of those Chinese companies which are in strong economic competition with the US. The continuing trade frictions between China and America have become one of the most important factors in feeding hostility towards China.

Father: The trade war began as a way of limiting China's growing influence in the world. The decisions and steps taken by the Chinese leadership have increased the concern of America and the West in general, especially the 'Made in China 2025' plan adopted in 2015, through which the Chinese wanted to make a quantum leap in development and in the implementation of President Xi Jinping's vision.

Son: I want to make it clear that the operational details of the China 2025 plan were dominated by overzealousness and some flattery of leadership that provoked America and Europe and sparked their concern. Western resentment is clear from the detailed response of the EU representatives in Beijing, who said the plan deprives foreign companies of fair play in China. Government subsidies to Chinese companies, whether through concessional loans or aid, or forcing foreign companies wishing to operate in China to transfer to high technology, violates the principle of a market economy that controls economic relations with the West. This accelerates the state's dominance of the market through its large companies and puts foreign companies in a vulnerable position in the Chinese market.

In turn, American circles believe the 'Made in China 2025' plan is ultimately aimed at extracting global pioneering technology from US and Western companies in general. At the same time, US concern has increased regarding China's pursuit of the Belt and Road Initiative put forward by President Xi. It can therefore be said that the Belt and Road Initiative and the 'China 2025' plan, in addition to China's huge trade surplus, provided the right ground for the trade war that followed.

We will now introduce the 'China 2025' plan in some detail. In 2015, the Chinese government adopted a comprehensive 'Made in China 2025' plan to develop ten key industries through 2025. These industries include advanced information technology; automated machine tools and robotics; aerospace and aeronautical equipment; ocean engineering equipment and high-tech shipping; modern rail transport equipment; energy-saving and new energy vehicles; power equipment; new materials; medicine and medical devices; and agricultural equipment.

In line with the plan, the Chinese government is providing funds to establish forty innovation centres by 2025 to develop IT integration mechanisms in manufacturing and promote local research and development, particularly in aircraft, alternative energy vehicles and medical equipment. They plan to build 1,000 green plants by 2020 to determine best emissions practices. The Chinese government has justified the adoption of this plan in seeking to move the Chinese economy from high-speed quantitative growth to high-quality development, improving innovation capacity, promoting scientific research, technological development and upgrading industry.

The Chinese government said its plan would provide the required opportunities and energies to boost China's economy and ensure its global pioneering status. The plan identified implementation in three phases as follows. The first phase is to enter into the ranks of the industrial powers by 2025. The second phase will end by 2035, when China's manufacturing industry will reach the middle level of the world's industrial power, and the third phase will end when the new China reaches 100 years of age, that is in 2049, at which time the country will enter the phase of global dominance and global industrial power.

Due to strong European and US opposition to the plan, the Chinese government has been forced to backtrack a little and obscure the plan, while continuing to implement it quietly and without fuss. China adheres to this plan because it seeks to catch up and control the Fourth Industrial Revolution. This is very sensitive in China. There is a deep moral wound in the memory of the Chinese, namely not catching up with the First Industrial Revolution because of the opium wars imposed by the West on China. China also failed to catch up with the Second Industrial Revolution because of foreign occupations and wars, and the country therefore remained lagging behind. It took more than a century for China to begin its industrial progress in the 1950's and early 1960's and catch up with the remnants of the Third Industrial Revolution, thanks to the help of the Soviet Union, which sent 11,000 Russian experts to China, built 852 heavy industry projects and trained 40,000 Chinese engineers. These efforts have resulted in the construction of an industrial base, a nuclear bomb and a satellite.

After Deng Xiaoping came to power, he worked on establishing national industry committees. Under his reign, advanced technology and industry became the prerogative of the second man in power, the Prime Minister, to demonstrate the importance of technology in China. China has also pursued a policy of localizing technology in China and then transferring this technology, or 'studying' as China calls it, rather than stealing, and then modifying it to suit China's requirements—a policy which continued until the end of the 2000's. This practice became a major problem for the world for which China has subsequently come under international pressure. It's fair to state that China's late catch-up was based on Soviet Union aid, and was completed by generous and genuine support from Western countries and its allies such as Japan and South Korea.

China decided to be one of the founders of the Fourth Industrial Revolution, and therefore adopted a new economic policy based on the principle of supporting local scientific research, focusing on science and high technology, through which China can make big advances without repeating the efforts of Western scientists in the past. Electric cars are such an example.

There are many people in China who compare the opium war waged by Europe and in particular Great Britain in the 18th century with today's American trade war, remarking that the goal of both is to prevent China from catching up with global industrial revolutions, and they say 'this will never happen again'.

Another matter of concern to the Chinese is their realization that after several decades, China's biggest obstacle towards realizing its dream of building a rich and prosperous country is its ageing population. China will be the first country in human history that will get old before it gets rich. Therefore, we see the Chinese leadership currently investing all its efforts and energies to speed up China's construction. In this sense, the 'Made in China 2025' plan is, in a way, a defensive plan to anticipate time. There is a firm conviction in China that those who lead in science and technology will lead the world. China has advantages in this area, the most important of which are—as we mentioned elsewhere in the book—its 8 million graduates annually, of which 65 per cent are in the scientific field and 50 per cent are engineers, in addition to its ability to set goals and implement them. This element in itself enables China to advance its technical competitors.

Moreover, another important advantage for China is its huge consumer market, which absorbs the transformation of inventions into low-cost products. This does not exist in many countries of the world, including America, so they are forced to sell their scientific inventions to China. China's determination to enter and control the Fourth Industrial Revolution globally is demonstrated by the new strategy adopted by the Chinese government to move directly to new generations of the revolution's industries, instead of standing still at the levels reached by global companies. An example is the automotive industry, where the Chinese government realized it would not benefit much from the production of conventional cars, so it immediately jumped to planning to produce electric cars, where China is now ahead of the world's major automobile companies.

Father: Europeans and Americans have realized that China has moved from a position of trade partnership to a state of strong competition that threatens the leading position of the US economy in the world. It is this sentiment that sparked the trade war between America and China.

Son: In the first two decades of that relationship, US companies and US business communities played a major role in lobbying the US government to stabilize and develop US–China relations. These companies were driven by two factors: first, there was a suitable and very profitable working environment in China, and the second was the unwillingness of US businessmen for the US government to intervene to solve their problems with China. Major US companies have therefore invested in China and made significant profits. For example, Apple's sales in the Chinese market reached $52 billion, General Motors was making 43 per cent of its cars in China, and Caterpillar's turnover reached $12 billion. Boeing's China subsidiary was the world's largest branch outside America. Nike was distributing clothing and sneakers to the Chinese market for $5 billion, and Starbucks for $15 billion. These companies formed what looked like a strong Chinese lobby in America, where they were countering any US government move against China.

But things turned upside down. In 2015, I noticed that the position of these companies began to change, as China began to exercise a protection policy in its domestic markets, business in China became more difficult and profits began to plunge. This was accompanied by Chinese President Xi's policy of relying on Chinese state-owned companies and strengthening their role in the Chinese economy. I have always told foreign friends who complain about these measures that their situation is much better than that of Chinese private companies in China, because foreign governments can at least defend their companies and criticize Chinese government practices, whereas Chinese businessmen have no one to complain to.

In addition, I have begun to feel that foreigners are definitely not that welcome in this country; the general feeling among foreigners living in China is that the country has become less hospitable. Compared with their parents, China's young generation generally regard foreigners living in China as having a lower status. The increase in the cost of living, accompanied by the bad pollution that limits and affects the lifestyle of expats in China have combined to decrease China's soft power and international image, declining profitability, empty promises by local governments and an increasingly difficult business environment. These are the reasons why America's business sector has refrained from defending China's position when the trade war storm hit the Chinese economy, simply business community had less interest and was fed up with their Chinese counterparts and authorities. It is therefore possible to say that China has lost an internal ally in US decision-making positions, and China's friends in Washington are heavily besieged. Thus, the situation for foreign companies in China is getting worse, with new problems and complications emerging. Author Thomas Finger summarizes these problems as follows:

First, Chinese measures are increasingly alienating international companies, including those located in the United States, with intellectual property theft, no distinctive national treatment, pressure for technology transfer, and unfulfilled promises to open additional sectors, industries and markets to US foreign companies.

The second factor is the curtailment of interest in the private sector, as the Chinese government provides all forms of support to state-owned enterprises, forcing foreign companies to compete with entities owned and financed by the Chinese government, which have access to capital and legal protection.

The third factor is the loss of China's advantage as a source of low-cost, abundant employment due to the demographic change in China and the growing ageing rate in Chinese society, and this has alienated companies from the Chinese market which have migrated to other countries with better advantages.

These shifts have led many American circles to question the feasibility of continuing to support China and open up US markets. Since Trump's entry into the White House, a new factor has been putting pressure on China–America trade relations, that of the President's populist economic policy, which has led to further tension in trade relations with China. Peter Navarro, the President's economic adviser and one of the administration's hawks, played an important role in these tensions, and can even be described as the commercial devil lurking in Trump's mind and the 'bad man' in China.

In fact, Navarro's thoughts played an important role in inspiring the idea of the current trade war between America and China. Navarro had expressed early on his negative vision of China in his 2006 book: *China's Next Wars*. He addressed the negative impact on America of China's rise, noting that the Chinese incursion into the US markets has led to thousands of Americans losing their jobs. For Navarro, this was the first warning bell that it could turn into a trade and possibly military war with China.

In 2011, Navarro released his second book: *Death by China* which in 2012 became a documentary directed by Navarro himself. In the book, Navarro accuses China of causing death not only to America but also to our entire planet by polluting it and rendering it unfit for life. These ideas were admired by then-businessman Trump. Trump announced his adoption of his advisor's ideas, and blamed China for the decline in US industry and the loss of hundreds of thousands of American jobs, due to the influx of cheap Chinese goods into the US markets, which, Trump says, led to the closure of some 70,000 US plants and the emergence of the so-called Rust Belt.

As of March 2017, the Trump administration began implementing the idea of tariffs on Chinese goods. Thus, Trump entered relations with China amid a trade war, which he later began to use for electoral purposes, especially as the presidential election is on the way. The President believed that trade pressure on China will enable him to maintain his base in the next election by exploiting the indignation of those American industrialists and workers who have been affected by Chinese competition.

President Trump began a series of decisions to dismantle trade relations with China. In November 2017, the United States backtracked on its earlier decision recognizing China's 'market economy status'. Since its adoption in 1980, that decision has contributed to raising the total trade volume between China and the United States from $4 billion in 1980 to $635 billion in 2017. China moved from 24th place in partnership with America, to first place. The US Department of Commerce justified this in a note: 'This decision was based on the increasing role of the Chinese State in the economy and its relationship with markets and the private sector, and this leads to fundamental distortions in the Chinese economy.'

In a 2017 report submitted to Congress on China's compliance with WTO requirements, the US Trade Representative said US policymakers had 'expressed hope that the terms of China's WTO accession protocol would dismantle China's current state-led policies and practices, but those hopes had evaporated. China continues to largely support today's state-led economy.' Washington has thus eliminated many of the advantages granted to Chinese companies and China as a sponsored country. Washington has promoted the argument that the Chinese government has intervened directly and significantly in domestic economic activities to support Chinese companies (especially state-owned enterprises) through unfair means that have caused severe suffering and defects in the United States.

On 22 March 2018, the United States officially announced the results of the 'Section 301 Investigation' which criticized China for: (1) forced technology transfer, (2) unfair licensing requirements, (3) theft of US secrets over the Internet and (4) China's efforts to acquire US technology and intellectual property through acquisitions to support its industrial plans. US economic circles say America's losses due to the illegal practices of technology theft and forced patent transfer on the part of Chinese companies, have reached $1.2 trillion. The mechanisms for scientific and technical cooperation established forty years ago between the two countries, including the Sino–American Joint Committee for Cooperation in Science and Technology, and the China–American Dialogue and Innovation Commission, have been frozen. These two mechanisms have contributed to the strengthening of Sino–American cooperation in science and technology over the past four decades. On 15 June 2017, the US Department of Commerce issued a new export policy to China, subjecting exports to China of aircraft parts, aviation electronics, navigation systems, lasers, underwater cameras, propulsion systems and individual communications equipment to prior approval from the ministry.

At the same time, the Trump administration introduced a series of resolutions to tax hundreds of billions of dollars on Chinese goods exported to the United States to ease the trade deficit, which the US President said was the basis of the problem between the two countries. The Biden administration kept most of Trump's measures against China, with the biggest change being a more targeted approach towards China, aiming for 'recoupling' rather than 'decoupling'. The basic line of this administration is that it will deal with China when it suits the USA's interest and will look upon China as an adversary for the rest of the mandates. Beijing did not experience much change in the hostile attitude from Washington.

Son: Thus, the trade war produced sub-wars between China and America. Among them was a tariff war that affected Chinese and US goods by hundreds of billions of dollars, followed by the 'investment' war, which led to a reduction in Chinese investment in the United States, US investment in China, and a war between staff and students.

The procedure has affected over 300,000 Chinese students studying annually at US universities and institutes, as well as thousands of Chinese researchers, in addition to disrupting the large exchange between research centres in both countries, whereby many US universities and research centres were closed to Chinese students and researchers, on the pretext that the open US economic system makes it difficult to reliably cut advanced technologies from China.

Washington claimed that Beijing has recruited its researchers and graduate students in America for espionage and theft of technical secrets. In the field of technical relations, Americans argue that the qualitative development in Chinese technology companies is the result of China's massive investment in biotechnology, and their public and secret forced acquisitions of US technologies through investments in leading US technology companies and start-ups, and cyber and industrial espionage. The Americans, therefore, ignited a technical war that led to the punishment of major Chinese technology companies. ZTE has been subjected to US fines of about $1.2 billion for allegedly violating US sanctions on Iran and North Korea. Now a major campaign is underway against Huawei after it was accused of having links with Chinese security agencies, and at the request of the US government, the daughter of the Huawei founder was arrested in Canada and held for over three years.

The US growing blacklist now includes 250 giant Chinese computer manufacturers, high-resolution technology and artificial intelligence. It is believed that these hostile American actions against advanced Chinese companies came after the Americans realized that Chinese companies, scientists and government experts are increasingly capable of unique scientific achievements that qualify them to set worldwide standards for global communications control and high technology systems, at the expense of US interests.

Moreover, America claims that China has used its advanced technological capacities such as facial recognition and supercomputing technology to implement surveillance and 'social management' of its local population, raising ethical questions for the United States and other governments about dealing with the Chinese companies that have been involved in the development of some of these technology platforms. In other words, the trade war between the United States and China, with all its ramifications, threatens the overall framework of economic, financial and technical cooperation that has taken place between the two countries over the past forty years, and is a major source of widespread hostility towards China in America.

With its newly announced dual circulation strategy, prioritizing local economy, China is moving towards accelerating the local consumption role instead of depending on its export economy. We can see that in wanting to ease import measures, China is on track to becoming the world's largest consumer market with a middle class of over 800 million people within the coming twenty years. This situation will impose a new way of dealing with Western companies. China, which has evolved technically—especially over the past ten years—no longer welcomes the entry of foreign medium-tech companies, for two reasons. First of all, these companies are unable to compete with many similar companies within China. As leaders in many fields of technology, China is primarily interested in foreign companies with the advanced technology that it needs. What I want to say is that the entry of advanced technology into the Chinese market is now regulated and imposed by market laws, not just by the Chinese government's decisions to forcibly transfer technology. An example of this are the champions of the German auto industry Volkswagen, Daimler and BMW compared with French Peugeot and Renault. Firms from both countries entered China in a similar situation and under similar conditions, however, the French venture failed to compete in China because they refrained from providing the best technology and products to the market. At that time, China and Iran were at the same level of development, hence the French management's mentality was to treat the Chinese market similar to the Iranian market, by refraining from introducing its latest and top products, insisting on doing business the French way, without sufficient adjustment to the local business culture and best practices, and that is why they are basically now out of China's market! Whoever wants a piece of the Chinese market cake must give their best. This will greatly change the nature of trade relations between China and all countries throughout the world. My friend Jim McGregor whom I regard as one of the most knowledgeable China experts put it as follows: there's two types of foreign companies in China, ones that need China, and ones that China needs, and if you want to have a good time in China, you better be the latter!

Being the biggest industrial power in the world, China really needs to look hard at the list of goods it needs to import. Just ask the foreign ambassadors in Beijing who, when they work hard to balance the trade deficit with China, mostly end up with a list of agricultural products. But even with agriculture products, it's very difficult to find products that China needs. I still remember the moment around ten years ago when we were discussing business opportunities wherein China wanted to help few Arab countries with their reconstruction projects and be paid by way of a barter deal in agricultural products to be imported to China. After looking at the list of crops that those countries could provide and noting that China didn't need most of them, I saw chickpeas and thought that this could be a good potential product. However, I was shocked to learn that China is one of the biggest exporters of chickpeas and that the majority of the delicious Middle Eastern hummus is actually made from imported Chinese chickpeas!

Many foreigners forget that China all through its history was an agriculture-based economy and society. Compared with other societies, food is of paramount importance in Chinese life. Eating well has produced the famous abundant Chinese cuisine. The country went through many dark times of starvation, the last of which is still remembered by people over sixty. When I arrived in Beijing and started learning Chinese, *'Chi fan le ma'* which means 'have you eaten well?' was the local way to greet people. Most of the important issues in Chinese life are discussed around circular dinner tables. This is why for any leader in this country, abundant food production within China is of importance above anything else.

We should also note the policy of food self-sufficiency for all Chinese regions. Since Mao Zedong, China has pursued a policy that every region in China must attain domestic self-sufficiency in the production of food and basic goods. Although this policy was imposed by the states of blockade and destitution experienced by China in its early founding years, this approach still exists. Commercially, this means that China is very much self-sufficient in many aspects, and it explains why Chinese authorities are making it difficult to import food products from abroad. China's economic growth and the complexity of its trade relations with the outside world force it to reconsider this policy of self-sufficiency, but administrative and party bureaucracy make the application of this trend very slow. This, in my view, is one of the reasons for the emergence of China's trade deficit with most countries in the world.

Father: The most important question now is where the trade war is going, will it continue to expand and are there any opportunities for trade relaxation between China and America? When Trump began his threats of a trade war with China, Chinese leaders thought they could absorb these threats based on their past experience when they have been able to tame any new US President and contain his threats.

This was effected through closed bilateral meetings, seeking to capture the keys of US negotiators, asking China's supporters within America to influence these officials, and urging major US companies with interests in China to convince the public of the need to pressure the US administration to talk with China and solve problems behind closed doors.

I am not saying here that China was offering direct bribes to US administrations and officials, but Beijing used a method of pushing the associated US parties to maximize the size of China's financial interests in America among the US decision-making circles.

Neither do I wish to say that Beijing was leading this influential process or overseeing the overall relationship with the Chinese lobby in America. This relationship was equal and based on the exchange of interests between the two parties. Chinese actors have been sponsoring the interests of the US circles representing the 'Chinese lobby' in America, and in turn these American actors helped large Chinese families bring their children to America's best universities and provide them with best possible conditions for a successful start in their professional lives. A look at the biographies of the children of the first, second and third tier of Chinese families confirms this. In addition, these children's investments in America and international markets (which are, of course, in US dollars) are also facilitated. In short, a deep and complex network of mutual interests between the influential circles of the two countries prevented bilateral relations from declining to the stage of war in its various forms.

Son: The question now is: what really happened to start the current trade war? I think it is America that changed, and not China. Trump came to power with the support of America's poor white class, not with communities of traditional ruling political power. Trump therefore was not obliged to abide by the compass of these forces. The general anti-China atmosphere in America has also become ripe for them to launch their attacks against Beijing. A vivid moment of change in the narrative of the relationship was realized when the drums of the fantastic opening of 2008 Olympic games were announcing the Chinese Dream, while the financial crisis was playing out what felt like the death march of the American Dream.

This was followed by Obama's 'return to Asia' policy, the South China Sea issue that changed the Pentagon's view on China, Xi's 'China Dream' ('Make China Great Again'), the Belt and Road Initiative, the 'Made in China 2025' plan and Trump's 'make USA great again' policy. Historians will need to look at these pivotal moments to explain the reason for the breakup of the marriage between the two giants.

China, who I thought could rearrange these cards and domesticate Trump, has failed to read this change. I am convinced of this point of view, especially after my conversation with James Green, who oversaw the China file for many years. When I asked him in November 2019 about his objective assessment of China's performance over the past two years 2018 and 2019, he replied in Chinese: '不好' (*bu hao* = not good). When I asked him why, he noted that China had made many mistakes in managing this confrontation and failed to take advantage of the golden opportunities provided by the mistakes and hasty decisions of the Trump administration.

'Beijing has not taken advantage of Trump's withdrawal from the Trans-Pacific Partnership (TPP) (Pacific Free Trade Area) Treaty, which was negotiated by previous US administrations to reduce China's role in Asia. This was a golden opportunity for China to present its competitive "Initiative" of the "TPP" and take the lead in Asia.' Although he acknowledged that China's performance in managing this confrontation had improved significantly over the past year, it 'failed to read the change in America', which is the job of the specialists responsible for the American file. These specialists did not reflect the true picture of the situation on the ground, and Beijing did not help its traditional friends in America, companies, former officials and businessmen.

'At that point, I was in direct contact with some of these friends, and I sensed then that the general feeling among them was their frustration with Beijing's actions, where there was a greater tightening of the business of foreign companies in China, and the atmosphere of public life in China, particularly in Beijing, became gloomier to foreigners, and the Chinese government and Party interference in all walks of life became apparent,' Green said. 'At the same time, representatives of foreign companies are fed up with China's unfulfilled promises, so many members of China's lobby are recommending a tough policy against China. But most of them opposed Trump's approach to, and methods of negotiating with, Beijing.'

Father: By observing the course of the trade war between the United States and China, I feel that the Chinese leadership has taken a weak defensive stance from the beginning, limited to its forced reactions to US steps. Beijing appears to have found itself in a difficult position since the beginning of the crisis. It did not believe there was a new situation in Washington. The Chinese have tried to find out the truth about what is going on, and their previous network of relationships has not helped them. Chinese leaders found Washington's doors locked in their faces and tried every means to figure out what was going on behind those doors. Beijing even had to knock on the doors of some people who never dreamed of becoming intermediaries between Beijing and Washington. China turned to all of Trump's friends and sons to get into the inner chambers to find out the truth about Trump's demands, failing to understand that what is needed is a change of Chinese regime.

Beijing was willing to adjust the trade surplus and even reverse it in favour of America by starting to buy American oil and gas together with the traditional Chinese shopping list, which it sources in any case from foreign markets. A look at the oil-supplying countries will make it clear that most of them are at risk of losing their contracts in favour of the USA. But the problem is that America's demands have reached out to the Chinese Party by insisting on monitoring state policy, interfering with economic and industrial policies that will eventually affect the grip of the Communist Party on the country as well as keeping the sanctions scissors on China's neck in the event of China breaching its previous commitments. The United States has also conditioned China's pledge not to respond to or surrender to US sanctions.

Son: One of the participants described to me the negotiations that followed the start of the Trade War as 'Cross-Purposes Dialogue'.

The two sides exchanged accusations and threats, followed by the start of Trump's sanctions against Beijing, which tried to absorb the first wave at the attack and suppress its anger. But Trump's provocative public approach has forced China to adopt a hard-liner policy by keeping pace with him at every step of the escalation, without abandoning the policy of calling for a return to negotiations, knowing that it will be the weakest party in the confrontation. When the effects of this war began to appear on both sides, the two adversaries returned to the negotiating table and the US side came up with a list of demands that surprised the Chinese with its audacity. The Americans demanded that the Chinese Communist Party's grip within China be weakened. The negotiations were overshadowed by a heavy atmosphere of mistrust between the two sides, particularly regarding China's commitments, and there was a lengthy discussion about what would happen if China breached its pledges (and the US has been confident that China will manipulate these pledges).

But the worsening of Trump's domestic crises has changed the course of the negotiations, so that the balance has begun to tilt in favour of China, especially regarding the US midterm and presidential elections. The West's electoral system has always been its weak feature, and it has been the focus of China's attention. Over recent decades, China has learned how to take advantage of the uninterrupted knowledge and experience between its different generations of its officials and, a great advantage for China compared to other countries, where officials pack their bags when their parties lose power. In China, the overlap between all age groups is maintained in state institutions. Knowledge (not necessarily wisdom and experience) is thus guaranteed to be passed between generations. This is evident in the images of US and Chinese negotiators. The Chinese delegates were at least a generation younger than their counterparts. However, I see the US trade war on China, despite its cruelty, as an excellent experience for the rising Chinese giant. China has not been accustomed to such cruel treatment during the past forty years in which most of the current leadership generation grew up. China is used to being welcomed and facilitated internationally.

In addition, the harsh conditions of the United States have put the Chinese leadership under pressure to be open with its own people, asking them to be patient with the significant negative effects of Trump's strikes. These conditions have also created problems within the Chinese decision-making kitchen, where a dispute over how to deal with this war has erupted. China's powerful ruler Xi Jinping has been forced to listen to the various views of Chinese leaders and to try to explain his style and plans for dealing with the new reality of Sino–US relations. China's future is the political cost of this dossier, and it exceeds the views of any Chinese leader, even one the size of Xi Jinping.

Moreover, the influence of former President Jiang Zemin, which will only end upon his death, cannot be overlooked. Zemin's influence on the Party and the government remains strong. Furthermore, Beijing's current decision-making circles are obliged to consider the influence of the families of the founding leaders of the new China. In China, there is a subtle balance, and any Chinese leader must work hard to be reconciled with all its parties, particularly in the fundamental decisions that will affect China's future, especially since the members of these families believe that they have a stake in the ruling regime because their ancestors and fathers contributed to its construction.

Father: My conviction is that the trade frictions between the two countries will not end because the causes of the dispute remain, foremost of which is China's technical and economic rise, which is now threatening the American leadership.

Then there is a psychological reason: the Americans are shocked by China's rapid and unexpected emergence. This has inflamed feelings ranging from resentment, remorse and anxiety among US leadership circles, who claim that China's boom and growth is thanks to 'our' care and help, for 'we' provided them with advanced technology and opened our markets to them. 'Millions of Chinese specialists graduated from our universities, and after all that the Chinese started breaking into our markets and competing for the leadership positions in the world!' is the general US feeling.

America cannot easily swallow and acknowledge these feelings. It is hard for America to realize that China has achieved an unprecedented miracle in history thanks primarily to the efforts and sacrifices of its people, and secondly to its leadership of international situations with skill and intelligence to serve Chinese interests.

An observer of China's performance in the management of the trade war can conclude that Beijing can bear the negative consequences of these wars far more than America, because, firstly, its economy is centrally managed, and the secondly as China controls the media and information within China, it can control public opinion according to the interests of the state. This is in contrast with the freedom of media that exists in America, which has become one of the most important points China plays upon in its war against the US administration.

This brings to mind the following incident. The claims of US soybean farmers had become a top concern for President Trump, following their continued complaints in US media about the Chinese market being shut down in their faces as a result of the American President's sanctions. China won the round of trade negotiations in October 2019, by making an offer to double the number of soybeans it imports from the US. Trump said he was pleased with the Chinese offer, which satisfies soy farmers in Ohio and elsewhere, and eases media pressure on him. In fact, China realized that the best way to counter the White House is with targeted therapy. Trump needed to appease American peasants in counties like Ohio and other soy-growing provinces who also knew very well how to use targeted therapy and leveraged their voting tools to be a vital voice in any presidential election.

Actually, increasing soy imports does not hurt China because eventually it needs the produce. But Beijing was able to play this card, supposedly to be secondary to the trade problems between the two countries, to become the most important achievement announced by the US President in his office in the presence of the Chinese Deputy Prime Minister Liu He. This is an example of China's greater maneuverability than America's, in the trade war.

Son: Another point I would like to refer to is that the tariffs imposed by President Trump on Chinese products led to a decline in the level of development of the Chinese economy. The Chinese leadership was able to bear and thus absorb these effects, turning this trade battle into a steadfast defiance of the Chinese nation in the face of American arrogance, which, as the Chinese say, targets the rise of China to the ranks of the leading nations of this world.

The phase-1 deal also reveals the Chinese leadership's willingness to give financial 'gifts' to Washington, regardless of the amounts, in order to buy time and avoid a clash with America. In this regard, it is useful to note that Beijing has proved that it does not accept any concession to America affecting the structure of the political system built by the Communist Party of China. To clarify, Chinese leadership is ready to buy US satisfaction with money, but not through a change in their political system.

2: Arms Race

Dragging China into an exhausting arms race is no longer an assumption but has now become an obvious American strategy.

Son: Up until a few years ago, China's military capability had not been of concern to the United States, because in the past the Chinese could build their military capacities in silence, with skill and effectiveness, without raising any American doubts. America surrendered to the illusion that its army's superiority surpassed China's military capacities. Thus, the Pentagon leaders were not worried about China because American military dogma—earlier programmed to fight the threat of communism—has been preoccupied since 2001 with fighting what they call 'Islamic terrorism'. That is why they did not pay attention to American military intelligence and reconnaissance reports about the speed of China's military construction. After reporting on the Chinese military threat in the East China Sea, one officer said that his superior asked him, 'Are you hallucinating, or did you spend your mission drinking?'

In my opinion, the Pentagon has failed in two areas: first in estimating the speed of the Chinese in building their military arsenal, and second in interpreting China's military intentions and ambition, which transcend the claim that it is merely their defence policy. This is true, but the question here is: What are they defending? Are they defending Chinese mainland territories, including Taiwan? Or are they defending Chinese interests in the world, which are experiencing significant growth? I believe that Chinese interests and red lines have moved beyond Taiwan and the Diaoyu Islands in the East China Sea and have gone as far as was announced by the Chinese President Xi Jinping in 2014 that the South China Sea is now a red line. In Chinese dogma and rules of engagement, red lines mean that they are ready to go to war to defend them. China's defence policy is expanding in line with its international growth, which is a cause of great concern for the US.

Another issue that worries America is that China's military industry is based on China's industrial power, which is the biggest and strongest in the world. China can manufacture large parts of its military apparatus itself and is capable of selling its products in the local market; unlike some militarily advanced countries like Israel, South Korea, Czechia, and Ukraine, where the defence industry is developed but lacking the support of a large local market.

China's military industry has a key advantage because worldwide marketing of its products is not subjected to many of the controls that competing military countries have to adhere to. A lot of European countries refrain from providing arms to countries that violate human rights. For example, Berlin refrained from selling arms to Saudi Arabia after the assassination of Jamal Khashoggi. American drone manufacturers cannot sell their planes to many Third World countries because of controls set by the Congress, and out of fear that these sales can affect the safety of America's allies (like Israel).

Moreover, China adopts a policy of limiting exporting arms with established governments which ensures that China has strong G2G (Government to Government) relationships and more freedom when dealing with sovereign-elected governments. Having military cooperation agreements between the government of China and foreign governments enables any Chinese defence contractor to have military dealings with these countries, without having to obtain further approvals.

They only have to inform the higher authorities about these contracts. In other words, while closing an arms deal with a foreign party in America requires the approval of the administration, the Congress, and other entities, it is not like this in China. This enhances the abilities of Chinese companies to export their reliable quality arms in less time, and usually their prices are much more competitive than their Western counterparts, an advantage of latecomers!

Exporting Chinese arms is not related to political conditions that complicate sale and purchase, and most importantly Chinese companies sell arms to their clients with the ability to provide finance and loans from China. As if this was not enough, China decided to adopt the US method by combining the arms market between civil and military players and fields. Opening the arms manufacturing industry to allow the private sector to enter helps the state-owned sector to speed up the development of the defence industry.

This move will unleash the potential and address the weak points by engaging vibrant hard-working tech-driven Chinese entrepreneurs! Similar to the USA, the R&D, technology and industry of the defence sector will be shared with the civil sector so the cost of innovation and development will be distributed and well-sustained. Because of this, China will strengthen its place in the global arms market, and will be a fierce competitor for Russia, America and other countries. Within a few years, experts estimate that China will surpass Russia and become the world's second biggest arms exporter after the USA.

The new generation of Chinese military leaders understands the Chinese army needs to prove itself in front of their people. It has been a long time since the Chinese military apparatus has had practical experience in the battlefield (their last military confrontation was with Vietnam at the end of the 1970s). This has caused the army's role and public image to decline in China, especially after it was allowed to become involved in commercial life in the 1990s; this decision was an attempt to ease financial pressure and burden on the army. The army became a competitor and a monopolizer of the most important pillars of commerce, and many military officers indulged in different commercial activities and even smuggling, without any control. This created frustration among the general public. In a few years Chinese leadership realized the side-effects of this policy and decided to get the army back to its military bases with tighter control on its economic activities. Xi's arrival heralded the start of a brutal anti-corruption campaign which ended the era of military interference in economic life.

The new generation in China is no longer satisfied with memories of the past sacrifices of the Red Army, especially now that the only military operations over the past decades were drills and maneuvers, or military video games in luxurious air-conditioned halls. This public pressure, alongside Xi Jinping's approach of projecting China's confidence and the authority of the Communist Party, has raised the assertiveness of the Chinese Army, and toughened up its officers to tackle China's problems, especially boundary issues (like the militarization of the South China Sea). Behind closed doors in China, one can feel the eagerness of these officers to show their strength, despite the official denial of the Chinese leadership.

These developments put China under the observation of American military leadership, which concluded that China represents the most serious threat to America's global dominance. To an objective observer, it is difficult to doubt such an analysis because the expansion of China's power will definitely come at the expense of America's influence, which is the strongest in the world.

I believe that America will spare no effort in dragging China into an arms race. Although China realizes the gravity of this matter, it hastens to build its military capacities only out of necessity. The West tells only half the truth when it describes China's military-building capacity, especially its navy, as a dangerous expansion of a domination-seeking Chinese Army, while ignoring the fact that for more than two decades China made no attempt to build these forces.

This means that many Chinese naval ships will be decommissioned. A military commentator declared that for every two ships that are placed into active service, one of the old ships is decommissioned. If we compare the two armies, in particular their navy and air forces, which would be the main units involved in any potential confrontation between the two opponents, we will notice the vast difference between them. Thus, I strongly believe that China will keep investing heavily in building its armed forces to bridge the gap between the two countries, and to achieve its strategic goal of preventing America from taking a huge military victory over the Chinese army, particularly in East Asia. China will not hesitate in involving itself in an arms race if necessary.

Father: In 2012, American military presence in the South China Sea began to increase when President Obama declared a new military strategy of transferring American military fleets to the Pacific Ocean and increasing the number of American troops stationed there. The purpose of this strategy was obviously to confront China. In response, after the ascent of President Xi to authority, Beijing decided to increase its military presence in the disputed islands in the South China Sea. America saw these Chinese military procedures as a threat to American interests and to the freedom of international navigation in the region. The two sides became trapped in a classic security dilemma, where each defensive move was seen as a threat and aggression from the other side.

In early 2018, President Donald Trump's administration announced a new national defence strategy that included moving the focus of the American army from fighting terrorism, as had been the case since September attacks in 2001, to confronting threats resulting from the military rise of China and Russia. President Trump decided to set up the United States Space Force with the aim of producing new types of space weapons. Both China and Russia considered this a threat to militarize aerospace. America has also withdrawn from the Anti-Ballistic Missile Treaty signed with the Soviet Union, mainly due to the imbalance with China concerning missiles, which was not a part of that Treaty, and fears were raised in America against the Chinese military threat.

In October 2019, the *Washington Post* published a study from The Centre for a New American Security (CNAS), written by former Deputy Defence Secretary Robert O. Work and his former special assistant, Greg Grant. The authors expressed their deep concern about the growth of Chinese military capacities. The study says that China is planning to surpass America military superiority in the long term, and it seeks to commence in the Pacific Ocean.

The study says that the People's Liberation Army has been observing the American Army patiently for two decades. The Chinese have studied America's favourite war tactics and put in place a strategy to take advantage of its weaknesses and undermine its strength, especially its technological military force. Work emphasized that the Chinese are proceeding with their plans.

Navarro, Trump's economic adviser, wrote that 'each dollar paid in buying Chinese goods in America is used in China for supporting the Chinese army, which directly threatens American national security.'

In the speech given by Mark Esper, US ex-Secretary of Defense, at the 10th Munich Security Conference (February 2020), the main message was a warning to the USA against the threats of China. Esper summarized these three Chinese threats: 5G technology produced by the Chinese company Huawei, the applications used by the Chinese government in the domain of artificial intelligence, and the policy of the Communist Party of China. Esper said, 'Huawei has become an example of China's heinous industrial strategy that is based on theft, coercion, and exploitation of free market economies, private companies, and colleges and universities. The Chinese Communist Party is heading even faster and further in the wrong direction—more internal repression, more predatory economic practices, more heavy-handedness, and a more aggressive military posture. It is necessary then for the international community to awaken to the Chinese challenge it is facing.' For his part, Central Intelligence Agency (CIA) Director William J. Burns announced on 7 October 2021 adjustments to CIA's organizational structure and approach to best position it to address current and future national security challenges.

Director Burns announced the formation of a China Mission Centre (CMC) to address the global challenge posed by the People's Republic of China that cuts across all of the Agency's mission areas. Emphasizing that the threat is from the Chinese government, not its people, Director Burns explained that the new mission centre will bring a whole-of-Agency response and unify the exceptional work CIA is already doing against this key rival. 'CMC will further strengthen our collective work on the most important geopolitical threat we face in the twenty-first century, an increasingly adversarial Chinese government,' Director Burns said.[6]

A large number of American politicians think that the problem with China is significant because, as we mentioned earlier, China's strengths combine all of America's previous competitors at the same time. It possesses Soviet military power, the economic growth of the Japanese, and Germany's historical aspirations. Two further elements are added: the large population, coupled with the fact that China is perceived by America as hiding its real ambitions and goals behind the slogan of a 'peaceful rise'. America has never faced an enemy with these characteristics.

Son: China has clearly become a great power, but America is exaggerating China's military capabilities to justify the large increase in its own military spending, to make other countries fear China, and to convince the Americans of a serious external danger to distract them from the country's large internal problems.

Now that we are discussing the American point of view, we might as well present Chinese attitudes from their primary sources. In 2019, the Chinese government issued a white paper about the Chinese army, which I read carefully. The paper lists figures which indicate a reduction in the members of the Chinese army by about 300,000, decreasing to 2 million in 2017, and a reduction in defence expenses from around 5 per cent of the national GDP in 1979, to 1.5 per cent in 2017, at a time when military spending was at 3.5 per cent in America and 4.4 per cent in Russia.

The Chinese white paper holds America responsible for the unrest in East Asia, saying that the US is strengthening its Asia-Pacific military alliances and reinforcing military deployment and intervention, adding complexity to regional security. The deployment of the Terminal High Altitude Area Defence (THAAD) system in South Korea by the US has severely undermined the regional strategic balance and the strategic

---

[6] https://www.cia.gov/stories/story/cia-makes-changes-to-adapt-to-future-challenges/

security interests of regional countries, to circumvent the post-war mechanism. The paper adds: 'The US has adjusted its national security and defence strategies and adopted unilateral policies. Washington significantly increased its defence expenditure, and pushed for additional capacity in nuclear, outer space, cyber and missile defense, and undermined global strategic stability.'

Japan has adjusted its military and security policies and increased input accordingly, thus becoming more outward-looking in its military endeavours. Australia continues to strengthen its military alliance with the US and its military engagement in Asia-Pacific, seeking a bigger role in security affairs. The established AUKUS (Australia, UK, USA) alignment and the nuclear submarine deal has changed profoundly Australia's position in the ongoing arms race.

Father: In my opinion, the biggest problem is the insistence of both parties in accusing each other of aggressive behaviour and of threatening security and stability. America says that China threatens free international navigation, and its increased military troops mean that it has become dangerous for America. Beijing, on the other hand, holds Washington liable for the tension and militarization of the seas, skies, and oceans, and for forming military alliances against China.

We will not go through the complexities of refuting either opinion, although facts reveal that China did not send ships and planes to threaten American waters, nor does it attempt to constitute alliances against America. Despite that, the sad truth is that aggravating the dispute between China and America, and the lack of any bridges of understanding on either side, creates the conditions for an arms race, and for augmenting all types of enmity between them.

Some Chinese researchers talk about another issue which pushes China towards an arms race, which is China's ability to deviate from the main branches of the American army. American satellites are no longer safe now that Beijing has developed anti-satellite missiles. American fleets and aircraft carriers no longer dare to go near Chinese coasts, fearing Chinese anti-ship missiles. Beijing has launched a satellite that can discover and locate American nuclear submarines. It is also difficult for American bombers to fly in Chinese airspace because of China's advanced air defence systems.

Regardless of the truth of these claims, just talking about them causes Americans to feel the gravity of the danger from China, increases American enmity toward China, and encourages America to look for all possible means of fighting or weakening its opponent.

The Chinese claim that they will not be dragged into an arms race with America, but the evolving situation might force them to. When America deployed its THAAD missiles in South Korea under the pretext of countering the North Korean threat, China discovered that these missiles and radars cover a large area of its territories. Apart from that, some reports hint that the United States is seriously thinking of deploying a large number of surface-to-surface missiles to stop China in the Pacific Ocean. On 19 October 2018, the *New York Times* reported the intention of the American army to install Tomahawk launching pads, alongside expanding its plans to develop and establish land-based systems, with a rage exceeding 1,000 km. Weapons of this sort will be seen as a direct threat to China, particularly if spread widely in sensitive areas like Okinawa Island in the western Pacific Ocean.

This was confirmed by the US Secretary of Defence and the Secretary of State when they announced that their country will spread medium-range surface-to-surface missiles in the countries surrounding China. China denounced these declarations and considered them a threat to its security and interests. If America proceeds in that endeavour, Beijing will have to have a defence against these missiles. Such an action can only be called an arms race. The arms race will encompass nuclear weapons as well.

In a visit to Moscow in 1957, Mao Zedong stated that he was not afraid of the nuclear war, saying that even if half of China's population were to perish in a radioactive inferno, 300 million would remain. Despite that, the fear of a nuclear war led Mao himself to possess such weapons and to set off the first Chinese nuclear bomb in 1964. Nowadays, China rarely speaks about its nuclear weapons, but it emphasizes, according to the 2019 Chinese white paper about the army, that 'China is always committed to a nuclear policy of no first use, and these weapons are for the purpose of self-defence.

Nuclear capability is the cornerstone to safeguarding national sovereignty and security, and the goal of the Chinese nuclear weapons is to deter enemies from using nuclear weapons against China.'

In January 2019, the *Economist* magazine mentioned that China's nuclear stockpile represents 2 per cent of the world's total, and that Beijing follows a different approach than that of Russia and America, who keep nuclear warheads attached to missiles. These are the things that would make China slower to engage this weapon first, and more liable to being pre-empted. Fiona Cunningham, from George Washington University, says that China's attitudes towards nuclear weapons have remained relatively constant since Mao Zedong.

The Economist thinks that China is working on developing its arsenal by making it smarter. An example is the DF-41 missile which was first seen in a military parade in celebration of China's 70th anniversary in October 2019. This missile can hit any part of America. The magazine adds: 'Because new weapons require new nuclear warheads, this is also driving nuclear expansion toward manufacturing new nuclear weapons.' Admiral Michael Brooke, the Director of Intelligence for America's Strategic Command, stated in August 2019 that China's armed forces 'doubled their nuclear arsenal in the last decade, and they are on track to double it again in the next decade.'

I think that China's modernization of its nuclear arsenal is natural, considering increased American military threats, particularly after Washington revived its programme of space weapons and introduced new types of tactical nuclear weapons, together with the fierce intelligence assertiveness against China, where it was clear that Beijing needed to make more investment in the nuclear arsenal field to ensure the capacity of nuclear deterrence. China's nuclear weapon arsenal remains much smaller than America's, (according to the latest reports, China has over 200 nuclear heads compared with around 6,000 to the USA) and its purpose is to prevent any attack and deter any assault against China by being able to counterattack.

Son: The arms race between China and America will not be traditional and will not be measured only by the number of tanks, planes, ships, and the like. Rather, it will take a modern technical form, at a very high cost. With the lack of official information from either

America or China concerning the main tendencies in the new arms race, we will resort to articles written by American military officials, and to what some Chinese media says in this regard.

According to a study published by the *Washington Post* in October 2019, for the Centre for a New American Security, written by former Deputy Defence Secretary Robert O. Work and his former special assistant, Greg Grant, the Chinese resorted to developing these concepts and capabilities in order to take advantage of the weaknesses in the American defence network. They also developed 'black capabilities' that are held in reserve until unveiled in the event of war to surprise with attacks from unexpected vectors. Furthermore, they have worked on becoming the world leader in AI and then deploying that technology for military use. Thus, AI represents the primary way the new arms race will be fought between America and China.

The Chinese newspaper the *Global Times* mentioned earlier in 2019 that the Chinese State Council (government) has put forward an ambitious plan for China to become a world leader in artificial intelligence. According to the plan, the country's investments in AI will amount to $150 billion by 2030. The newspaper talked about three reasons for China's support of AI.

- First, AI is the most important factor for the success of the 'Made in China 2025' plan that represents the major industrial strategy in China.
- Second, AI can be the solution for expensive labour costs and the ageing population.
- The third reason, according to the newspaper, is that AI is a critical element in preserving national security, and this was emphasized in the 19th National Congress for the Communist Party of China.
- *The Global* ended its article by saying: 'Thus, AI technology is playing a major role in national defence.'

China is certainly developing AI technology remarkably quickly. In June 2019, *Fortune* magazine hinted as much, referring to the reasons behind China's progress in the AI race which lies in the structural advantage and availability of massive data flow on the large population, computational power, and substance of qualified engineers. China refuses to share with others the data it possesses as a basis for AI.

The other domain of the fierce arms race between China and America is quantum technology. In September 2019, the Centre for a New American Security published a study by a retired Colonel in the US marine corps, who served in the Pentagon in the Obama era and at the beginning of Trump's administration. He emphasized that China's army is constructing quantum factories and laboratories in many Chinese universities. China has launched a satellite for quantum communication that sends quantum coded messages. Beijing spares no effort in establishing its own space quantum mechanics, in addition to quantum sea navigation system. The study also states that China has a quantum radar that locates American Stealth aircraft, and that every communication system used by the American army is faced with a Chinese electronic warfare system, designed to disable it in case of dispute. China's plan is to achieve victory against American troops through paralyzing the digital networks and communications that enable the USA to navigate and coordinate its units.

This does not mean that China is not developing other weapons like intercontinental ballistic missiles; a model of the most modern supersonic missile was presented in the military parade in Beijing, marking China's 70th anniversary. China is building its third carrier and will not stop there. In short, there is a serious arms race between China and the United States, but it is taking place silently.

As expected, the arms race is no longer an academic assumption, but unfortunately a reality that is negatively affecting both countries. This arms race has resulted in a large increase in the defence expenditures of both America and China. Observing the Chinese situation, one can notice a steady increase in military expenditure, particularly since the ascent of President Xi Jinping in 2013. Figures reveal that America maintains its global leading position in military expenditure, and that Washington during the time of Trump has raised the Pentagon budget to numbers unprecedented in American history. In 2018, this budget amounted to $649 billion, equalling 4.6 per cent of the American national income. With that, America's spending on its army in 2018 equals the military spending of the world's largest eight countries, including China, in the same year.

At the same time, the Chinese leadership is steadily increasing its military expenditure. In March 2019, the Chinese Ministry of Finance announced the allocation of $167.5 billion as an annual budget for the Ministry of National Defence, an increase of 7.5 per cent from the 2018 budget. The Stockholm International Peace Research Institute declares that the actual figure is $250 billion. The Pentagon, on the other hand, claims that China's military expenditure far exceeds that. In this case, China has surpassed Russia and become the world's second largest military spender, behind the United States. Since 2013, China has been allocating around 2 per cent of its domestic product for defence purposes, on which it is currently spending more than Japan, South Korea, the Philippines, and Vietnam combined.

The question to be asked is whether this military mobilization will lead to a new cold war that divides the world into conflicting campaigns, and to proxy regional wars, as was the case between the Soviet Union and America. The answer is unclear. The current fierce conflicts, manifested in commercial and media wars and the arms race, will remain mostly between America and China. America's allies, i.e. the European Union, Japan, and even Australia and South Korea, will need to think seriously before joining American efforts against China.

Moreover, China knows its own limits and does not seek to dominate the world; China is one of the major beneficiaries of the existing international order. The Chinese do not have military allies around the world, and in principle, are not in favour of forming alliances. Hence, the current cold war between China and America most probably will not transform into a global cold war.

3: Fostering Ethnic Separatist Movements

Sympathizers of some religious and ethnic minorities with separatist tendencies, together with supporters of intervention in Hong Kong, are exerting growing pressure on China.

Father: There are two old ethnic problems in China. The first is the situation with the Muslim Uighur minority living in the Xinjiang region in China, and the other is the Buddhist Tibetan minority that inhabits the Tibet region. Recently, events in Hong Kong have also come to light. The United States is persistently providing support for activists, on the pretext of defending human rights and protecting religious minorities and democracy in China.

    Son: I want to highlight a significant point in relation to America's intervention in these issues, which in my opinion, can be attributed to many reasons.

    Americans think that their beliefs and principles and their values of individual liberty, human rights, and freedom of expression are inalienable rights for all the peoples of the world, as per the Declaration of Independence of their Founding Fathers. It is also part of American mentality that they have to defend this belief and help support and distribute it throughout the world. This thinking has been internalized by all previous American generations, and it will persist in the future. So, ordinary Americans do not consider it a violation of the privacy of others when they share their beliefs of individual liberty, free society and human rights worldwide, because they truly believe them to be universal beliefs that all humans share. Consequently, American officials cannot overlook any violations of these beliefs anywhere in the world, because ignoring them, especially when highlighted in the local American press, will cause them to lose their voters. These issues are used by American foreign policy officials to achieve their objectives in maintaining America's unilateral hegemony over the world.

Father: President Trump's administration ignored the problems of the Uighurs and Tibet in its relationship with China for the first 2 years in office. However, in 2019, as the presidential election approached, the US administration noticeably increased its adoption of the attitudes of the Chinese separatist movements. Trump also approved a decision for protecting democracy in Hong Kong. We will not dwell on the origins of these problems, but we will just comment on the American attitude, particularly in relation to the Uighurs, which has become one of the sensitive issues between Washington and Beijing.

The United States is using what is happening in Xinjiang to put pressure on China and defame its image externally, on the pretext of protecting human rights and fighting religious persecution. Remarkably, Trump's administration has included this issue in its efforts aimed at containing and weakening China, and keeping it occupied with internal issues. Washington could justify its current campaign against China by the decision of the Chinese government to establish centres for large numbers of Uighurs that Beijing calls 'vocational education and training centres' but America calls 'mass detention camps'.

The Chinese government claims that the purpose of establishing these centres is to fight religious extremism, active terrorist organizations and separatist forces in that area. Moreover, it says that enrollment to and exit from these centres is optional, and lessons there focus on patriotism, teaching languages, culture and history. Their goal is to enhance national unity of the Chinese nation. Washington, however, is depicting a totally different image of these centres.

The support of Trump's administration towards Muslims in China is surprising because not such a long time ago, it launched a worldwide campaign against Muslims. The United States government fostered Islamophobia, in addition to linking Islam with terrorism and prohibiting the citizens of several Muslim countries from entering its territories. However, now we see Washington claiming to protect the Muslims of China, and organizing large campaigns in their favour. As we said, the reason for this American attitude is more to undermine China than to protect the Muslims.

The American administration did not stop at verbal statements and condemnation but went as far as taking punitive measures against Chinese institutions and officials.

Son: In this regard, it is important to mention that China and America had come to terms in relation to this issue when America acknowledged that some Uighur organizations are terrorist, and confessed that China's efforts in Xinjiang are to combat terrorism. However, the Chinese government has failed to contain extremist organizations with the policies it used in the last decades, which varied over the past ten years from 'carrot and stick' and development policies, to extreme measures where hundreds of billions were spent to improve development in Xinjiang.

Remarkably, seventy years since its establishment, the government is still working on convincing the Uighurs that they are Chinese and that Xinjiang is an inseparable part of China. History will record the policy of Chinese officials towards Xinjiang, and we are not here to judge it, but we can say that these measures have triggered the West to suddenly rise up in support of a victory for the Muslims in Xinjiang. I can safely say that the West's claimed interest and support for Islam in China will end when China pays the right price to the West.

Since we are talking about at the US sanctions and measures, it is important to go into detail here.

On 27 March 2019, the US Secretary of State, Pompeo, called for 'prompt' release of the Uighur Muslims from what he called 'detention camps' in China. He said this in Washington, during a meeting he had with a family of the 'survivors' who spoke to the American press about extensive torture of the Muslim minority in Chinese prisons. Pompeo celebrated the 'courage' of these 'survivors' who dared to 'reject China's violations'. He tweeted that 'China must release all those arbitrarily detained and end its repression.'

The following day, Beijing strongly protested this statement by the American Secretary of State. The spokesman for China's Foreign Ministry said that Pompeo's statements are 'extremely silly and they constitute a brazen intervention in the Chinese internal affairs.' He added: 'We demand the US to respect facts and stop distorting them maliciously.'

The US continued escalating their attitude towards China.

In September 2019, the United States Senate approved a draft law putting more pressure on China in the so-called Uighur detention issue, demanding that the American administration examine the massive detention operations of this minority. US Intelligence was assigned to prepare a report, within 6 months, about the campaign in the Xinjiang region in the northwest of China. The US Department of State was required to assign a coordinator for the Xinjiang file, and mandated the FBI to go through reports about China's harassment of American nationals of this minority. Secretary of State, Mike Pompeo, was encouraged to consider the possibility of imposing sanctions on Chinese officials who were responsible for these practices.

In October 2019, Washington announced sanctions against Chinese persons and entities. It put twenty-eight Chinese companies and government and security offices on the United States' 'blacklist' due to claims of their involvement in human rights violations in Xinjiang. It also prohibited several Chinese officials from entering the United States.

The US Department of Commerce explained these sanctions, saying that these entities 'were involved in human rights violation and abuse during the implementation of China's campaign of repression and mass arbitrary detention, in addition to high-tech operations against the Uighurs, Kazakhs and other Muslims minorities in Xinjiang.'

Secretary of Commerce Wilbur Ross said: 'The US Government and Department of Commerce cannot and will not tolerate the brutal suppression of ethnic minorities within China.' He emphasized that this action will ensure that American technologies: 'fostered in an environment of individual liberty and free enterprise,' are not used to repress defenseless minorities.

The United States demanded that the UN Forum tasked with protecting indigenous people worldwide cancel China's membership. Prior to the elections of the organization's members, American diplomat Courtney Nemroff said that China's treatment of Uighurs should be a factor in deciding if Beijing could remain a member of this organization. She added 'The United States is alarmed that more than a million Uighurs, Kazakhs, Kyrgyz, and other Muslims have suffered arbitrary detention, forced labour, torture, and death in camps in China's Xinjiang region. These atrocities must be stopped. We call on member states to bear this in mind in this important forum,' she continued.

Washington invited the head of the World Uighur Congress, Dolkun Isa, to address the UN Permanent Forum on Indigenous Issues (UNPFII), which infuriated China.

Biden's administration kept the same tone, Secretary Blinken acknowledged the description of genocides happening in Xinjiang, sanctions on Xinjiang products severely harmed Xinjiang's economy which represents one-sixth of China's GDP.

After presenting these American attitudes, it is obvious that Washington considers the Uighur issue a good opportunity for undermining China's policy and defaming Beijing's attitudes on the world stage.

Father: I have visited Xinjiang several times, and I was impressed with how the Uighurs preserve their national heritage, their language, derived from Turkish, and their religious nature. Last time I visited this region was in 2007, and a local driver took me from Urumqi Diwopu International Airport to the hotel. On the way, he talked about the history of the region and the difficulties it faced. Every now and then, he would point to street name signs in Urumqi city, saying: 'Notice how

Chinese language is given priority in these signs, while place names are written in the Uighur language in small font. A few years ago, it was vice versa.' He continued, 'In these streets, signs are written in Chinese only. The Uighurs used to represent the majority of population in the past, but now they number less than half.'

On the same day, I met Taimur Dawamati, head of the Chinese–Arab Friendship Association at that time. He is a veteran politician who occupied several posts in Xinjiang and in Beijing. Before leaving the hotel, management warned us against roaming the streets due to terrorists. In the house of Mr Dawamati, there were lots of officials, including the Secretary of the party organization, who belongs to the Han people, the Governor of the area who is Uighur, and head of the office of external affairs in the local government who is a Kazakh, in addition to a number of other officials from different ethnicities. Upon introducing the guests, our host said, 'these people represent most of the ethnicities of the Chinese community, and we live in cooperation and fraternity, and work together for the development of the region and prosperity of China.'

After the invitation, I wandered this beautiful city freely, and visited its fascinating eastern markets. I did not see any signs of stress or 'terrorists,' rather, stability and development pervaded. The question is: What happened so the situation has changed there? What has pushed the Chinese authorities to take assertive action to start the re-education campaign? How could extremists control the minds of such a big population despite the important economic projects that were implemented there in the past ten years, the extensive presence of the Party's entities, the educational infrastructure and official local media? I do not have a specific answer, but I think that negligence of local authorities in Xinjiang, and condescending attitudes towards the local people have provided the right circumstances for extremists to take to the streets. Mistakes were made there, and it is essential to study them and learn from them. This is even more important and much more effective than putting people into education camps that have cost China a lot of money and impacted its worldwide reputation, leading America and other countries to interfere in China's internal affairs.

Son: All in all, China will not stay silent concerning American interventions in what it considers its internal affairs, and it has responded to these American attempts.

In July 2019, the State Council Information Office issued a white paper about historical issues in the Xinjiang region, in the northwest of China. This paper strongly refuted everything that America and Uighur supporters say concerning the existence of a Muslim Uighur race independent from the Chinese nation, and about the existence of the state of Turkistan in history.

The paper says: 'Xinjiang has never been called East Turkistan, and there has never been a state of that name. The advocacy of this so-called state has become a political tool and program for separatists and anti-China forces attempting to split China.

'Xinjiang has long been an inseparable part of Chinese territory. The Uighur ethnic group did not come into being from Turkic origins, but it is a part of the Chinese nation. The Uighur conversion to Islam was not a voluntary choice made by the common people, but a result of religious wars and imposition by the ruling class, though this fact does not undermine our respect for the Muslims' right to their beliefs. Moreover, Islam is not the sole religion of this area; there are other religions in Xinjiang including Buddhism, Taoism, Protestantism, Catholicism, and the Eastern Orthodox Church. It has 24,800 venues for religious activities, including mosques, churches, Buddhist and Taoist temples, with 29,300 religious staff.'

From this uncompromising position Beijing indicates that it will not tolerate separatist movements, and that all claims of religious or ethnic persecution in Xinjiang are lies with no historical basis. American attitudes in this regard are driven by anti-China political desires, and not based on facts.

As we mentioned earlier, the Chinese government denies America's claims of the existence of detention camps for Muslim Uighurs. What America calls camps are in fact vocational education and training centres to fight terrorism and extremism. China went as far as sending a memorandum to the UN, signed by about fifty countries, including thirty Muslim nations, denying the American charges, and approving of the efforts of the Chinese government in Xinjiang.

Chinese media organized a campaign accusing the American administration of violating human rights and rights of religious minorities, particularly Muslims. The Chinese Press stated the fact that the United States, as a permanent member of the UN, did not sign the International Covenant on Economic, Social, and Cultural Rights, and it withdrew from the United Nations Human Rights Council. China has focused on reports published by the Council on American–Islamic Relations, saying that the status of human rights in the United States is not at its best. According to these reports, anti-Muslim incidents increased by 17 per cent on an annual basis in 2017, and hate crimes increased by 15 per cent. More than a third of anti-Islamic incidents were motivated by agencies of the Federal Government of the United States, including 464 incidents related to the unconstitutional 'travel ban' preventing Muslims from entering the United States.

Washington and Beijing represent two extremes regarding the Uighurs issue that has become the heart of the ChinaPhobia campaign, led by the United States.

Father: The same thing is repeated in the Tibet issue, where the US is accusing China of organizing persecution campaigns against these indigenous people, and of practices that violate human rights and religious and public freedom. China, on the other hand, is denying that, and accusing the United States and other countries of supporting the separatists in Tibet, under the leadership of the Dalai Lama.

I would like to point out that the Dalai Lama is highly respected in the West, and he is considered an icon by Western elite. The Chinese leadership is aware of that, therefore it cannot belittle him. All its attempts to marginalize this spiritual leader ended in failure due to his charisma. Beijing awaits his death because it realizes that his successor will not be able to fill that void. China also seeks to replace him with a figure who is Beijing-friendly. All this comes after China's success in reducing the Dalai Lama's official international role, after threatening to punish any government that receives him officially. China rightly considers any official reception of the Dalai Lama as a rude intervention in its internal affairs, because the Dalai Lama is calling in real terms for Tibet's independence from China, and this goes against the decisions of the United Nations.

The Tibet issue has been considerably weakened during the past thirty years, with the growth of China's international position and footprint. It is hardly mentioned now except on rare occasions.

As with Xinjiang, the Chinese government issued several white papers, emphasizing that Tibet is part of China, and that opposition movements are no more than terrorist groups seeking to separate this region from China, but Beijing will not allow this. The Chinese government criticizes American Presidents for receiving the Dalai Lama and other Tibetan opposition figures, which it considers a flagrant intervention in Chinese internal affairs.

Son: In relation to the Hong Kong issue, Beijing is facing the most recent problem of sovereignty, and it reveals the weakness of the Chinese system in dealing with such issues. Beijing blames foreign forces and accuses them of augmenting this problem, which is true. However, decision-making centres in Beijing realize that the underlying problem is their unsuccessful policy for attracting the youth of Hong Kong to the mother country. Additionally, Hong Kong leaders over two decades have failed to find new methods of development, and their politicians are dependent on big families in Hong Kong. These families are closely connected to the leaders of Beijing. The educational system, despite being described as the most advanced in aspects of organization and management, failed to plant the seeds of national identity in the youth of Hong Kong. They do not see themselves as brothers of China's youth, and the West does not treat them as if they are!

The new generation has inherited the condescending attitude towards inhabitants of mainland China that was way beyond Hong Kong when sovereignty was transferred. In the 1990's, Hong Kong was a centre of modernity and civilization, and an intellectual destination for the Chinese. However, this situation has changed radically, and the Hong Kong that used to represent more than 30 per cent of China's GDP in 1997, is now producing less than 2 per cent. This transformation occurred within less than thirty years, and many Hong Kong people could not digest this change. Most of Hong Kong's youth still live in the illusion of the past, and many of them do not even speak Mandarin, the official language of China. A significant proportion of them could not—for financial reasons—visit the mainland, but at the same time

Beijing is considered a magical world and a fairytale land for the wealthy elite of Hong Kong who spend fantastic times in the Chinese capital.

From my acquaintance with a lot of my friends from Hong Kong, I can safely say that the majority of young people are not aware of what is going on in mainland China, particularly in relation to political and administrative issues, despite their knowledge of China's official language. A number of my friends in China whose businesses are in new economy fields such as TMT, find it difficult to hire young people from Hong Kong due to their weakness in the required fields such as engineering, software, and other future sciences. Most graduates of local universities in Hong Kong are from the financial sciences and law—majors which will not be required by companies in the future.

Another complicated problem in Hong Kong is that big families can limit the authority of the Hong Kong government and prevent it from executing real long-term reforms that are not in their interest. Housing is a good example. Influential families prevented the government from giving residential licenses, causing house prices in Hong Kong to multiply tens of times during the past thirty years. Owning a house has become an unattainable dream for young people because they would have to save money for sixty years in order to afford even modest accommodation. Moreover, the Hong Kong government has refrained from issuing building licenses for twenty years, creating a housing crisis. Despite the external and good-looking prosperity, the result is that most of Hong Kong's inhabitants live in very small apartments, many of which could be described as inhuman conditions. The floor area per person there is the smallest in the world.

These are the real reasons behind the outrage in Hong Kong, but its leaders are trying to use the extradition bill to Beijing and later the national security law as a pretext. It is worth mentioning that factors for the crisis were already there, and that global anti-China forces were preparing this scenario with or without that law. I believe that exaggerated enthusiasm and the tolerance of the leadership which dominates China now is what encouraged Hong Kong officials to create this problem.

The assertive and high-pitched attitude of the policy maker in China has gone some way to encourage the local officials in Hong Kong and mainland China to take some provocative measures which poured oil on the fire. Proposing the extradition bill was the spark that ignited the fire, but the situation was already ripe for the explosion. The best description of the crisis between Beijing and Hong Kong was made by one of the important former Chinese leaders, when he confirmed that people in-charge of this Hong Kong file lacked innovation and imagination, and failed to form creative policies to manage it. The bureaucrats of Beijing adopted the traditional policy that they use on the mainland in managing this crisis, which proved to be the wrong approach, given the fact that Beijing was aware that US administration and other hostile circles would use this issue against it.

America has seized the opportunity of this crisis to increase pressure on Beijing. We can understand the American attitude towards Hong Kong if we view the city as the main platform for Beijing's plans of globalization of the Chinese Yuan, and its point of departure to international markets. That is the bottom line as there is a public awareness that the Yuan is the only currency that can break the hegemony of the dollar in international transactions. Hong Kong has been one of Beijing's most important sources of hard currency, representing an advanced base for China in the body of global capitalism, just as it highlights a point of venerability in the Chinese Communist body.

Here lies the strength of Hong Kong which no one can contest, including Singapore, despite working hard to inherit Hong Kong's international potential. Due to its independence, Singapore will never win the acceptance of Beijing, or of any of the proposed local areas such as Shenzhen, Hainan, or even Shanghai, as these cities are not independent practitioners of the rule of law.

To sum up, America's support for the independent ambitions of China's ethnic and religious minorities, and its taking advantage of the worsening situation in Hong Kong against the Chinese government, are now at the heart of the ChinaPhobia campaign, led by the United States and its allies.

Chapter 3

1: China's Ambition for Global Leadership

China seeks to play a leading role in world affairs, especially now that it has built up economic, technical, and, in part, military might, not to mention an ambitious and determined leadership. However, the road to global dominance for China is not going to be a smooth one.

Father: China anticipates two major events which will significantly help accelerate its efforts to seize a significant and influential global leading role. The first is the centenary celebration of the founding of the Communist Party of China which took place on 30 July 2021. According to the Chinese, during this period, the Communist Party managed to pull China out of the quagmires of poverty, underdevelopment, and dependency, ultimately ending the 'Century of Humiliation' by foreign powers, unifying Chinese lands, and paving the way for China's progress and prosperity. Chinese achievements prove the validity and the soundness of the Communist Party's doctrine and approach. Therefore, President Xi Jinping has begun re-consolidating the Communist Party's authority in the country; he is adhering to the Communist path that upholds Chinese characteristics while letting go of some of the liberal capitalist reforms initiated by Deng Xiaoping in 1978.

The second anticipated celebration is the centenary of the founding of the People's Republic of China on 1 October 1949. Over the past seven decades, successive Chinese leaders have built a vast industrial base and integrated infrastructure in anticipation of the rise of China. President Xi has developed his ambitious industrial upgrading and economic plan, which includes three phases ending in 2025, 2035 and the third in 2049. The plan aims to transform China into the world's epicentre of inventions and advanced technology while realizing the aspirations of the Chinese people by ensuring a prosperous life and restoring the historical glory of the Chinese nation. Some Chinese researchers predict that after 2049, China will likely overtake America in all areas.

In 2013, President Xi adopted the Belt and Road Initiative to secure stable and robust means to enhance China's global economic influence. He approved various military initiatives and measures including:

- building a modern and flexible army possessing knowledge and technology,
- changing the Chinese military strategy from defending China to protecting Chinese interests and institutions in the world, and
- transforming China from a land-based military power to one with a powerful navy and large fleets, capable of protecting Chinese interests and its power transmission lines.

However, there are two obstacles in the path of China's achieving global leadership, namely, the strong US opposition to China's progress and rise, which we have discussed in detail in the chapters of this book, as well as internal difficulties. We will review both at length.

Son: The main domestic difficulties can be summarized as follows. Many Chinese experts promote the premise that China has no historical colonial experience that would help it become the number one country in the world. When they possessed the largest naval power in the fourteenth century, 200 years before Marco Polo, with ships ten times bigger than the Italian explorer's fleet, the Chinese emperors did not use their ships to expand and occupy other countries. Instead, they harnessed this power to enhance commercial and cultural exchanges between China and the ancient world. As an example, the Chinese like to cite the voyages that took place under the leadership of the Chinese Muslim General Zheng He (Islamic name: Hajji Mahmoud Shams), who in 1371 led the largest naval fleet the world had known at that time. With 30,000 sailors on board, he undertook several peace voyages to East Asia, Africa and the Arab region.

Today, there is a divergence of views among experts on whether China lacks the historical experience and the resources that would enable it to lead the world. Some maintain that China adopts a principle of discretion and prudence by not announcing its global plans and ambitions to the world. Supporters of this argument believe that China's claim of having no colonial history is a delusion. Historically, the size of China had been continuously expanding. Even ancient China, which was unified by its mighty Emperor Qin Shi Huang, extended geographically across present-day Central China only. This empire then expanded to include new regions, such as Xinjiang, Tibet, and Yunnan, which were inhabited by the non-Han tribes. Even today, the Ministry of Foreign Affairs of the People's Republic of China rejects the idea that the Mongols were part of China's history, that Chinese soldiers participated in the invasions led by the Mongols, or that they were more vicious than their Mongol leaders. This group of experts claim that, if given the opportunity to expand globally, the Chinese would be more unjust and more aggressively powerful than the United States.

Other experts contend that China and Chinese history and culture (based on Confucianism, Taoism and Buddhism) rely mainly on the ideas of focusing the attention on the self, refining it, and seeking to attain what it wants using thought and resourcefulness. According to Chinese beliefs, the best way to win a war is to do so without firing a single shot.

My personal conviction on the matter stems from observing China's actions and plans, and not through what the Chinese people and leaders say. I do not believe that China is a lurking monster, nor is it a peaceful kitten. Speaking from my knowledge of the Chinese people and of their way of thinking (which I acquired from interacting with them daily for the last twenty years), I don't believe the Chinese have any ambition to dominate other lands, especially those of their neighbours. Moreover, Chinese leadership has neither the creative thinking nor the need to lead and unite the people of the world behind them, or even behind their principles. Any specialized researcher in Chinese affairs, including foreigners like myself, in the absolute majority, who have lived with the Chinese, will agree that the objective of Chinese leadership is for the world, especially the West, to recognize the legitimacy of the Communist Party and their right to rule, and ensure the security of China.

You will not hear any serious talk inside China—even behind closed doors—about a plan to pursue China's international aspirations through force or war, including those related to rich African mining resources, Burma's dense forests, and Siberian water resources. All that China has in mind now is to use conventional commercial and financial means—including loans and other political and economic tools to exert its influence in the world. It is worth noting that this method has not been the first choice for the world's great powers over the past centuries who mainly resorted to bullying and oppression, in addition to using a wide range of instruments of financial, cultural and economic pressures in pursuit of their colonial agendas.

There is also a fundamental argument that dispels the claim that China is seeking colonial expansion in the world, namely, the social contract in China between its various social components, especially between the government and the people. This contract does not include having the families of China send their children to battlefields unless to protect Chinese territory. This is contrary to what we see in the United States where many American families are proud to send their children to military service to invade Iraq, Afghanistan, or Syria, under the pretext of defending human rights and freedom. These are values that are worth protecting for them, values that are somehow universal in nature.

In China, neither the values of Chinese culture nor the doctrine of the Communist Party calls for this type of sacrifice. The Chinese social contract obligates the youth to care for their parents, focus on their lives, and carry out their obligations towards their children and wives. The people of China will not let their young die in the forests of Africa or the Arabian deserts, under the pretext of protecting the interests of the Chinese nation. Moreover, because of its ageing society, China will not have a sufficient human reservoir for global expansion and domination. On average, China adds 15 million babies against almost 20 million people retiring each year. An expansionist rising state with hegemonical aspirations requires a young nation.

Father: Despite the enormity of the Chinese economy, which is competing with the American economy today, China suffers from a shortage of internal capital accumulation, where most of the profit is generated domestically. Unlike the USA, China's income and profit pool lack fresh outsources. China's top corporates generate 80 per cent of profits from internal markets, whereas US competitors rely on the international market for over 70 per cent of their profits. China's domestic debt is massive, and unlike the USA, China suffers from a lack of natural resources. China is also energy-poor and has become the world's largest importer of oil and gas. It is losing, in this regard, compared to the United States, which possesses enormous natural resources, and which has been able to invest in the world's wealth through its huge financial institutions. Moreover, China still primarily relies on the US dollar in foreign trade. The role of the Chinese yuan remains limited in global transactions, barely occupying 1.5 to 2 per cent of the global financial trading volume. SWIFT's June 2020 RMB tracker statistics list the RMB as the 6th most active currency for global payment by value behind US Dollar, Euro, Pound, Yen and Swiss Franc. For the RMB to become an international currency, it needs a transparent banking system, and this is not currently available in China. The Chinese financial system still widely depends on financial institutions set up by the United States.

Now we will elaborate on other areas which we alluded to briefly. Unlike China, former colonial powers such as Portugal, Spain, France, Germany and England managed to compile great wealth by expanding and plundering the goods of their colonies. This enabled them to secure great financial resources, which funded the hegemony of their empires.

As for America, it made its wealth through proper speculation in the First and Second World Wars, and then it ensured the continuity of its financial dominance by stabilizing the dollar as the world's currency. China's monies are hard-earned and generated by conventional trade and economic activities that cannot fund a hegemony.

On the other hand, there are hotheads in China, who seriously believe that America's days are numbered, and that America will end at the hands of China. For these hotheads, we present the following two examples:

- A pack of ten shirts, which China sells to America for $100, actually costs the Chinese economy about $92 to produce, wasting 4,500 liters of water that China desperately needs. On the other hand, the cost of printing the US 100-dollar bill, with which America buys the pack of shirts, costs only two cents! Therefore, no power in the world today—including China—can stand up to America's financial might, as long as the US dollar remains the backbone of the global economy.

- The second example: On 1 February 2020, Al-Jazeera's website published an article by the former Defence Intelligence Agency officer, Patrick Collins, about the level of US military spending, stating the following:

  ○ Washington's spending on defence in 2018 amounted to $649 billion, which is higher than that spent on defence by China, Saudi Arabia, India, France, Russia, Britain, and Germany combined ($609 billion) in the same year. Collins clarified that America has treaties obliging it to defend fifty-one countries in the world, twenty-eight of these belong to NATO, eighteen to the Treaty of Rio, and two to Anzos, namely Australia and New Zealand. There are also bilateral treaties with Japan, South Korea, and the Philippines, as well as close ties and evident security interests with other countries. And occasionally, Washington is compelled to deploy its forces in countries that do not have formal treaties with it, such as Taiwan, Israel, Saudi

Arabia, Iraq, Afghanistan, Jordan, the Emirates and Qatar. This protection costs the US Treasury about $320 billion annually, which means that US military spending is $962 billion every year.

   °   Astronomical military spending is one of the essential pillars on which the global leadership of America is based. I believe that China is incapable of allocating a trillion dollars annually for military spending just to be on the same footing as US military power!

   °   On the other hand, it took China about forty years to create a foreign currency reserve estimated at $3 trillion, which is the largest in the world, and it is a huge figure, but—at the same time—it is a very fragile reserve for a country the size of China. In 2018 alone, the Chinese government had to spend about $600 billion in less than four months to protect its currency from the speculation that it was subjected to!

Son: Anyone following Chinese economic affairs can easily see the substantial internal pressures facing China's financial budget. At the same time, the financial resources of this budget are at risk of losing growth prospects, and the possibility of their decline is on the rise. On the other hand, there is an increasingly rapid and continuous growth of expenditure. China's education budget is still a problem and a massive burden on the Chinese government because many schools in many regions of China lack the minimum requirements. The service sector is also a sinkhole, draining enormous resources. For example, China admits that there are more than 200 million Chinese people without sanitary latrines. Thus, China still needs massive financing for the sanitation sector.

In the health sector, things are far worse. Although China was able to secure basic health insurance for about 90 per cent of its population, the quality of services in this sector is still ranked in 50th place among the worst in the world! And although the average life expectancy of people has risen to 72 years, the level of individual health is around 62 years, which is the lowest in the developed world.

The rapid ageing of Chinese society has placed tremendous burdens on finance. According to some estimates, serving the unproductive elderly will cost the Chinese economy more than 20 per cent of the country's GDP, which is far more than the budgets required by defence and military. Moreover, governmental obligations towards these older adults are considered a political and non-negotiable responsibility. The legitimacy of the Chinese Communist Party is based on these obligations, because the party presents itself as the official caretaker and servant of all Chinese people, of their well-being and fundamental rights, and it is on that basis that the Communist Party leads Chinese society. Therefore, any violation of these obligations will result in the destabilization of the public political authorization of this leadership.

COVID-19 is an example, where peoples' lives were priority number one at any cost! As a result, China paid an enormous economical price for its low death rate, a path that most governments around the world would avoid! Those who live in China today readily realize that when any Chinese law collides with the fundamental rights of the Chinese individual, the Chinese administration seeks to find a quick way out that satisfies the people. A Chinese farmer, for instance, does not care about what his government pledges to local or foreign investors if his basic rights are compromised. And even if this Chinese farmer is at fault, the official authorities are obligated to take his rights into account.

Moreover, the Chinese government cannot turn a blind eye when many of its citizens lose their money in failed crowd-financed commercial investment ventures, even when there are no legal irregularities involved. The Chinese authorities compensate these citizens by pressuring the owners of the enterprises and then obligating the local governments to compensate families who have lost out. The logic behind this is that people lost money to a venture that was registered and marketed in China under the eyes of different government departments, and therefore they believe the government is at fault for allowing such businessmen to conduct a business, just as a father should be held responsible for his children's behaviour.

Furthermore, the government cannot compel certain groups of society, especially Chinese minorities, to abide by many of its plans and regulations. It often turns a blind eye to this to maintain civil peace, even if these plans are valid and well-studied. Inner Mongolia is an excellent example of this. Mughal herders in Inner Mongolia are a major headache for government officials because members of this social group refrain from adhering to government plans—even when they are valid. In other words, the limited financial resources, and the heavy and compulsory commitment to the welfare of the Chinese people, make it imperative for China to focus on the domestic needs of the Chinese people instead of fulfilling the financial obligations of its international aspirations.

Father: Moving on to another point, China has recently made significant technological breakthroughs in the field of artificial intelligence, communications systems and more. However, Chinese educational institutions are still traditional and politicized; moreover, they lack an atmosphere of creativity, hence it is rare to find a Chinese university listed among the best universities in the world.

On the other hand, China's unbalanced development created serious choke points slowing its way to national rejuvenation, while the world can live without China's products, China still depends on the import of high-tech products such as chips and semiconductors, most aspects of current Chinese technological advancement are made possible by the purchase, transfers/copy of foreign inventions. China is still lacking way behind in the basic science field, which is called 'zero to one' inventions (concepts become reality), where most of the funds invested might lead nowhere, but that is exactly what builds super tech powers; this is how computers and the internet were invented.

The ingenuity of the Chinese lies not only in imitating what others invent but in the speed of turning these inventions into reality and in improving some of their features. For example, the high-speed trains that China now produces came from Siemens in Germany. The WeChat App, China's competitor of the global WhatsApp, comes from Israel, and the comprehensive online payment system in China is based on an American program.

There are indeed hundreds of thousands of Chinese scientists and hundreds of specialized technical institutes and universities. Yet it is also true that China cannot establish its own 'Silicon Valley' like America, because most workers in the scientific sector are state employees who value the privileges that come with their jobs over other things. Also, scientific creativity requires an atmosphere of freedom of action, and tolerance for failure, and the public sector does not provide such an atmosphere.

Son: I disagree that technical innovation will stand in the way of the rise of China. On the contrary, what scares China's competitors is the excellent progress that is taking place in China, especially now during the Fourth Industrial Revolution. China, the US, and to some extent Germany, stand in the front row of the fourth industrial revolution as they are the majority leaders for future technology, whereas countries like Russia, France, Israel, Korea, and Japan, come second because they possess advantages in some sectors. Other countries will realize very soon that they are just followers.

To overtake America, China still lacks an education system that shifts away from the currently followed methods of blind memorization and student rivalry. These approaches to education certainly have many advantages, but they contradict creative thinking and the qualities required to develop this skill. Besides, Chinese universities have not yet been able to find a critical thinking teaching method which would give students space for free intellectual and philosophical thinking and lead to technical and technological inventions. We notice, for example, the failure of Chinese universities to graduate any nominees for the Nobel Prize or other prizes in different scientific fields. And this prevents China from having its own Silicon Valley, despite the efforts of the Chinese government to make Shenzhen a close rival to California. The reason is that inventions do not come as a result of administrative decisions from above, but rather through governmental support for a system of innovation that grants people intellectual space and unrestricted freedom to think and express opinions. Such a system accepts everyone's views in various aspects of life.

Many observers believe that China is capable of innovation in the technical sciences where there is no room for politics, but not in fields of human sciences as the political party is the one that leads and creates the digital science environment. I disagree with this statement. Creativity happens only when there is freedom of choice. China's progress is undeniable, but we are talking here about the obstacles that hinder its autonomous scientific superiority.

Another point about the educational system is the fact that China will not become a dominant global power unless its universities start attracting top science students or upper-class students from all over the world. I always say that the true indication of reaching the top is when a businessman from Nigeria or Poland starts donating to the endowment funds of top Chinese universities such as Tsinghua University, Peking University, Renmin University, or Fudan University in Shanghai, to increase the chances of his children securing admission to these universities. When the Brazilian President, for example, sends his children to one of the boarding schools in Su Zhou, then the elite families of Brazil will start following by sending their children to these schools, they will surely purchase luxury homes nearby to keep mothers close to their children, as happens in England and Switzerland. Only then can it be said that China is at the centre of global leadership. I asked a lot of university professors and some foreign officials of the joint universities established in China whether this can be achieved in China. All of them answered that they do not envisage this scenario during the next fifty years.

Father: Many other things hinder China's endeavours to becoming number one in the world. First and foremost, global leadership is not a privileged position. It carries with it significant financial responsibilities, such as the aid given to developing countries, charitable work, and other humanitarian duties. The size of China's foreign aid now amounts to several billion dollars, and this is limited to government aid only. The private sector cannot establish charitable funds to provide assistance to foreign organizations as it is prohibited to do so by Chinese law.

In contrast, the aid provided by the US government and private sector funds is at least ten times more than the Chinese donation.

Moreover, Chinese law prohibits the reception of refugees, regardless of their nationality; China now has 'zero tolerance' for refugees. This is inconsistent with international laws and norms, by which a country aspiring to global leadership should abide.

Son: Foreign aid is one of the means of achieving global power and of wielding influence over the world, but Chinese foreign aid remains one of the country's secrets. Therefore, whatever aid China provides remains small relative to its global ambitions, especially when compared to what other major countries give, such as Japan, Germany, and even Kuwait. The prevailing social opinion is that the Chinese are more deserving of their money than others, therefore any increase in Chinese foreign aid is met with opposition.

In addition, the culture of charity and giving is not as widespread in China as it is in America, and that is due to cultural differences. This does not mean that the Chinese are stingy people; they are actually hospitable. They honour their guests and offer them the best of what they have, which is one of their best qualities. You witness this when you are a guest of a Chinese family.

First of all, most wealthy people in China prefer to take care of their own families and relatives and meet their basic needs. After that, their charitable interests extend to their own town, county, city and province, and end at the borders of China.

It should not be forgotten, however, that such practices will continue even after China becomes the premier economic power in the world. Many Chinese businessmen who perform minor global philanthropic deeds are criticized and even attacked. Therefore, many of them are afraid to declare their international donations, even if they serve essential Chinese interests and help improve China's reputation. This reality undermines China's ability to compete with America as a benefactor.

Some people may wonder about the importance of the Chinese people's opinion in a country governed by an overly holistic central system. I want to point out here that the Chinese leadership is attentive to people's views and the general mood, which form the basis of all government decisions. The decisions of the Communist Party of China are not made without listening to the opinions of the Chinese people. For example, in 2018, the Chinese leadership was forced to reduce the sums given to African countries and instruct the media to stay low-key and avoid publicizing the funds announced during the China–Africa Cooperation Forum. Public pressure rejected government generosity at a time when the Chinese economy was going through a difficult stage. It is worth noting that most of these sums were not donations, but debts guaranteed by high interest when compared to the global average. Also, most of this money stays in China, provides many opportunities for Chinese companies, and serves Chinese interests. But the Chinese government cannot explain these details to the Chinese people for fear that the foreign media will use this story to attack China's worldwide expansion attempts. This is a factor that explains the ambiguity of Chinese foreign investments.

Father: Several other obstacles are standing in the way of China's ambition to become the global leader. The first of these obstacles is economic: even though China today stands in second place, with an economy at around $15 trillion compared to America's $21 trillion economy. In China however, the per capita income is low, and lower than countries like Turkey, for example, at a modest $10,000 per person compared to $70,000 in America. Additionally, there are tens of millions of poor people in China and about 100 million poor migrants coming from the countryside into the cities. Many foreign observers and even Chinese people were surprised when Chinese premier Li Ke Qiang announced at the end of the 2019 that more than 900 million people in China live on less than $160 per month!

The second obstacle is social, mainly due to the Confucian values prevalent in Chinese society. Confucian and Taoism philosophy is based on family ties and the internal solidarity of the Chinese family. Therefore, Confucian traditions dictate that it will not be socially acceptable—as indicated above—for any Chinese party to give foreign aid, at a time when family 'members' are suffering from poverty and destitution.

Here, I must point out as well that Confucian and Taoism values are the primary values and customs of the Han Chinese. It is not easy for these values to become universal; Chinese popular feasts, the food, and ways to eat it, folk myths, and Chinese customs and traditions all carry the local Chinese character. Social values usually assist a country aspiring to lead the world. While we see all children everywhere cherish Santa Claus and celebrate Halloween, it's difficult to imagine Arab children celebrating the Chinese moon festival in the next fifty years.

Finally, the difficulty of the Chinese language and its limited outreach presents a cultural obstacle. The challenge of learning the Chinese language limits the spread of Chinese culture and literature in the world, at a time when English has become the primary language of communication between people and is the language of literature and science. Even in parts of Africa where French is spoken, and in Latin America, where people speak Spanish, people found themselves having to give up these two languages and switch to English—the language which unites Africa, India and other countries.

In short, despite its richness and 5,000-year history, China's culture has become an obstacle to reaching the position of the number one country in the world.

Son: Another hurdle in China's path to global supremacy is its lack of allies and supporters around the world. The United States has managed to establish a wide network of partners and affiliated organizations, which enabled it to be at the top of the world order. The developed and prosperous Western countries—in addition to Japan and South Korea—still consider themselves America's allies. Moreover, America has bolstered its world influence through a vast network of international military, economic and financial organizations. NATO, which is the strongest military power in the world, is under US leadership. The International Monetary Fund and the World Bank also guarantee the hegemony of the US dollar.

On the other hand, the Soviet Union became second in world rankings not only because of its powerful military but also because its international affiliations enabled it to reach the hearts and minds of people through its deep-rooted relations with countries of the

Socialist camp, the Warsaw Pact, international communist parties, and the liberation movement in developing countries, which Moscow was able to draw to its side through slogans denouncing colonialism and imperialism and calling for progressive regimes.

China currently does not have these privileges. Beijing still formally declares its opposition to the idea of forming alliances in the world, although it maintains working relations with worldwide political parties, regardless of their political identity, whether they are reactionary, liberal, conservative, communist or religious. As a result, there are no global allies for China. China is not aiming to produce an internationally accepted doctrine or a global value system, essential elements for any superpower seeking dominance, like the USSR and the USA.

America presented itself as a champion of freedom, democracy, and human rights, which won the minds of hundreds of millions of people, regardless of how committed the US was to these values. Furthermore, Hollywood and American media networks, which have huge international influence, helped spread American values and the American lifestyle. As for the Soviet Union, it put forward slogans for establishing a just socialist system in the world by ending the exploitative capitalist system and limiting the imperialist domination based on aggression and the subjugation of peoples.

China does not have allies in the world, nor does it put forward a coherent global ideology. It does not have capable global military, or financial organizations or a 'Hollywood'. Most of the slogans put forward by China to this day are domestic and focus on China itself, such as building an advanced economy, eradicating poverty, and giving the Chinese people a good life. On the international level, Beijing is content with offering the principle of peace and development, enhancing cooperation with all, and building mutually beneficial business partnerships. These are all economic and temporary systems, with no ideology behind them, even though the Communist Party is the ruler in China.

Father: A current phenomenon interferes with China's ambition to lead the world, and that is their unwelcoming attitude towards foreigners and the growing feelings of hostility against them. History explains the origin of these feelings. Chinese emperors used to believe that their country was the centre of the world and that the rest of the countries of that time were on its outskirts. These emperors practiced closed-door and self-sufficiency policies—a culture of not needing foreigners. For example, when one of the British kings wanted to establish relations with China in the eighteenth century, he sent a letter to the Chinese Emperor, to which he received the following reply: 'We agree, provided the ambassador becomes a Chinese citizen. He is to wear, eat, and live like the Chinese and subject himself to Chinese laws.'

Later, after China opened up a little, foreign ambassadors wishing to meet the Emperor were obliged to kneel before him because he was the 'Son of Heaven'! When the West conquered China by force of arms and drowned it in opium, the Chinese gained nothing but humiliation, oppression and violence from contact with the outside world. These violent Western colonial practices have left a deep wound in the minds of today's Chinese which is seen in their cautious behaviour when dealing with foreigners.

And although Deng's reform and opening-up policy have alleviated these sentiments, they do not seem to have been completely cancelled. The rapid rise of China to one of the superpowers has revived nationalist enthusiasm and pride, reflected in slogans like 'restoring the glories of China' and 'the Chinese dream'. As a result, suspicion and mistrust began to rise among foreigners now residing in China, feelings which are reflected in actions on the ground.

The *Financial Post* stated that China has become less welcoming to foreign businesses after it imposed constraints on foreign companies. The lives of foreigners have also become more difficult following the introduction of complicated procedures for their residency documents, imposing taxes on them, and establishing pension systems that they will never receive. The number of foreigners expelled from China every year has also increased, as has harassment against them and the number of random arrests. Even foreigners married to Chinese women have not been immune to harassment.

Chinese companies have begun to move away from employing foreigners. *The Financial Post* ended its statement saying that electronic attacks were also launched against some embassies and foreign institutions.

I have lived in China for many years, and have travelled to almost all of its regions, from north to south, and east to west. Everywhere I visited, I felt only kindness and cordiality from the Chinese people when dealing with foreigners. Whether in markets, restaurants or parks, I could feel the spirit of friendship, simplicity, and spontaneity with which the Chinese people generally treat foreigners. These are truly the sentiments of internationalism that we read about in communist literature.

However, the situation is entirely different when dealing with some official local authorities. I was once among a delegation of ambassadors on a visit to Guangzhou at the invitation of the local government. The authorities at the airport insisted that all ambassadors be searched—despite their diplomatic immunity. Some of the ambassadors rejected these measures, considering it an insult, so the airport authorities prevented them from travelling. All of us showed our solidarity with them and waited for hours until the Chinese Ministry of Foreign Affairs in Beijing was contacted, and the matter was resolved. The ambassadors received an apology and an explanation that the authorities at the local airport did not know the applicable rules. Objectively speaking, each ambassador has more or less experienced some kind of similar accidents during his stay of duty in China.

Some Syrian citizens were also detained in other cities for various reasons. The prison departments in those cities violated the existing legal procedures concerning prisoners and delayed submitting indictments because the charges were non-existent. And despite the active intervention of the Chinese Ministry of Foreign Affairs, these citizens remained in detention for months without trial. It eventually transpired that their detention was the result of false and vexatious accusations.

There have been many similar incidents, which give the impression that the local authorities in some Chinese cities are hostile to foreigners and do the opposite of what the central authorities instruct. While the above example took place years ago, I am now questioning things that are happening today. What is the point of shutting down the streets of foreign embassies in Beijing, as security forces recently did, and fencing off these embassies with barbed wire? This is something that did not happen even in those dark times a decade and a half ago, when North Korean refugees took advantage of the presence of foreign embassies in Beijing to seek asylum, when despite that crisis, the surroundings of the embassies remained normal. Moreover, opportunities for communication between foreign diplomats and Chinese society has become more and more difficult, much less people are talking to diplomats and foreign journalists. Sadly, this is happening today, at a time when the Chinese leadership has announced its commitment to opening up to the world and establishing better relations with its peoples.

Additional complications have recently been introduced to the procedures for obtaining a Chinese visa, and visitors to the Chinese consulates are often subjected to rude treatment, so much so that you feel as if the staff of these consulates are junior security personnel rather than professional diplomats!

Due to these measures, China lost a good portion of the support of the foreign business community, which has watched silently as Western parties called for a trade war against China. China's enemies took advantage of these Chinese measures to fuel hatred for China and warn of danger and the resurgence of Chinese racial nationalism. As this began to reflect on China's reputation in the world, interest decreased in the country and its culture. For instance, the number of German people wishing to study the Chinese language has decreased by about 20 per cent, and Chinese tourists feel that they are not as welcome as they have been before, not only in Europe but also in friendly countries like Russia.

Returning to a closed-door policy and building an iron fence to exclude the world will not serve China's ambition for a leadership position in the world. Moreover, these measures are entirely incompatible with China's adherence to globalization, and they strike at the very heart of the Belt and Road initiative. A nation wishing to open up to the world and expand global trade should not burn its bridges with the international community or close the door on human relations with the world.

Son: This topic is delicate, and there is no objective scientific method for evaluating it. China's treatment of foreigners still relies on the situation of each person individually, including their field of work, lifestyle, cultural background, etc. I can add an objective perspective here, and I think most foreign experts in Chinese affairs will probably agree with me.

The Chinese see themselves as one big family, and it is very difficult for a foreigner to enter such a closed circle. Looking at what Chinese students learn about foreigners, it is no more than a narrative of how China used to be a superpower and how it did not need anything from others, except silver. Importing this commodity left a negative impact on the memory of the Chinese people and taught them an unforgettable lesson. The story goes that in 1581, Zhang Juzheng, one of the ministers of the Chinese Emperor, noticed that the reliance of the existing financial and commercial systems on brass coins was complicating trading activities as the size and weight of the brass coins hindered Chinese Emperors from collecting taxes. So, the minister suggested replacing brass with silver, which is smaller and lighter. But China did not have enough silver mines.

Spain took advantage of the opportunity after discovering the legendary silver mines in Peru in Latin America. It fulfilled China's massive demand for silver and earned tremendous profits. This development energized the entire world trade at the time and amassed money in the vaults of the Spanish Empire. But in 1644, interruptions in the silver supply sparked turmoil in China and led to the collapse of the Ming dynasty. The unrest convinced China of the danger of relying on foreigners, so it returned once again to the closed-door policy and self-reliance. It took the Qing dynasty forty years to restore stability to the country.

In the eighteenth century, China became the main supplier of highly-sought-after tea to the British, which led to a boom in global commercial markets. Thus, despite the enormous power of the British empire, China played a leading role in world trade with its huge market.

The Chinese Emperor Qianlong even proclaimed in 1760 that if foreigners wanted to deal with China, they had to play by its rules! However, the Chinese Empire was later weakened, tempting Western powers to use force and wage the opium wars to open up the closed Chinese markets. Thus began a whole century of humiliation that the Chinese will never forget.

Only under Deng Xiaoping's rule in the 1980's did China once again open its doors, and foreigners flocked again to the resulting opportunities. In the late 80's and 90's, the Chinese regarded foreign visitors as millionaires coming from a civilized and advanced world and rolled out red carpets for them. When China began to create wealth at the beginning of the third millennium, its outlook towards foreigners changed. China's almost complete reliance on foreign investment was no longer necessary. Moreover, numerous areas in which foreigners had been working, such as investment institutions, technical engineering, and positions within the world's cross-border companies, were no longer needed. Most of the foreigners were replaced with local Chinese talent.

Walking in the streets of Beijing today, you will notice a decrease in the number of foreigners there; in fact, the majority of foreigners in China are either students, diplomats, or teachers of English. The first question people used to ask me in the past, at my meetings in Beijing, was if I worked at an embassy. When I answered no, the next question was whether I was an English teacher. Young Chinese view English teachers in China as people who could not succeed in their own country, so they decided to travel to China and teach English!

The Chinese government's efforts to raise and regulate Chinese laws at large involve complicated administrative procedures. Looking at the Chinese visa procedures and administrative transactions, we find that things are heading towards further complexity, rather than facilitation. China's community administration process allocates social credits for good behaviour, which makes foreigners feel continuously monitored, and as a result, uncomfortable. This is part of the government's efforts to replace as many foreigners as possible, create jobs for the Chinese, and work to empty China of foreign intruders who do not offer any added value to Chinese society.

For example, I find it amazing that there are no prominent Arab restaurants in Beijing, one of the most renowned capitals in the world, as there are in other countries. You might be surprised to learn that this is because China requires that every work visa applicant must be a holder of a university degree, but it is almost impossible to find a professional chef holding a university degree in the Arab world. As a result, no one can open a decent Arab restaurant in China. The general orientation behind this, as mentioned, is to improve the quality of the foreigners working in China, but while China succeeded in part by expelling foreigners of lower classes, it has failed to attract the quality people that it desires.

Because of the energy and efficiency of its youth, China does not need second-class experts today; it needs first-class and top-level experts at the international level. However, most foreigners are convinced that working in China has become extremely challenging and very few are willing to relocate. Chinese cities are among the most expensive cities in the world today, and the fees paid to Chinese international schools are among the highest worldwide, with average annual fees of $40,000 per child!

On the other hand, pollution in China limits people's daily choices, so you cannot go out or take your children outside most days of the year. Furthermore, YouTube, WhatsApp, Facebook, Twitter and Google are blocked in China. In other words, a foreigner in China is cut off from the means of communication used in other countries. Not being able to use Google and YouTube is a major disadvantage for foreign experts who are not fluent speakers of the Chinese language. Scientific research is almost entirely dependent on these websites. If you attempt to bypass the ban and use a VPN, you expose yourself to legal accountability in a country where the rule of law remains one of the old jokes.

On another note, China does not easily grant residency for more than one year and obtaining residency for five years remains almost impossible. To meet the requirements for permanent residency would require a miracle. The first thing that you read in the required conditions for PR is that you must be a Nobel Laureate or a high-rate taxpayer—the very people who will definitely not come to live in China for the reasons I mentioned earlier. As China does not grant citizenship to any foreigner, it is quite difficult for a foreigner residing in China to feel reassured, and this negatively affects their life and behaviour. A foreigner will be cautious in his investment plans and in giving his all, if he is not sure he can stay in China the following year. These are the factors that prevent China from attracting international talent.

State agencies treat the foreigner who has resided in China for thirty years the same as the person who has just arrived yesterday, so there is no difference if you were the first or the last; both obtain a one-year residency. I have heard a lot of stories of successful people who are good friends of China, but they were mistreated in a way that hurt their feelings, which led to an aversion to China as a country and government, although not to its people.

This is not a criticism of China, but a description of twenty years of daily experiences in this country. It is an objective examination of an undeniable reality, and it does not seek to offend the Chinese people. If you were to ask foreign experts from various walks of life about their opinion of the Chinese people, you would hear three common characteristics: 'great and nice people', 'smart people' with 'smart' here having a different interpretation, and 'unique and different people'. The Chinese are quite distinguished from the rest of the people of the world.

Father: I'd like to touch upon a commonly accepted concept in China, namely, whoever owns the technology owns the world. Some Chinese political factions believe that China's possession of advanced technology is essential for China to outperform other countries, including the United States. In general, this statement is correct, but incomplete. Japan can serve as an example here. Until a few years ago, Japan owned the most advanced technology, and its economy became second in the world, before being pushed down to third place by China. Due to its ageing society and its diminishing vitality Japan then suffered from successive crises, which affected the Japanese labour market by causing severe shortages and an economic downturn. In this regard, we notice a striking similarity between Japan and China; the latter is beginning to have the same problem as Japan because of the one-child policy. The ageing phenomenon in China is one of the obstacles that will hinder a leading role for China in the world.

Son: We have dealt with this topic elsewhere in the book, so I will not revisit it. But I will add that the ageing phenomenon which emerged as a result of the one-child policy will be one of the big problems that China will face in the coming years. The Chinese government has underestimated the effects of social factors on the desire of the new generation to have children, and those responsible for this issue remain captive to their research and theoretical estimates. The latest research indicates that the population of China will reach 1.5 billion people within 20 years. Thereafter it will decrease by half at the end of this century.

We all know how dangerous an ageing society is to any country in the world, but China will be the first developing country to enter old age. In other words, China will grow old before it becomes rich, which will undoubtedly restrain its international ambitions and impose new demands on it. Under the current patriarchal regime in China, the state is bound, as mentioned earlier, to the absolute welfare of the people. Elderly Chinese believe that the government is obliged to provide a decent life for them, and the ruling Communist regime will collapse if the authorities ignore this, just as happened in the Soviet Union in the final decade of the last century. It should be noted that the central pillar of Chinese society is founded on the principle of respect for seniors and the commitment of children to care for their parents. This principle places a lot of pressure on China's young people and limits their choices in life.

Moreover, the Chinese healthcare system is in a state of continuous development. It is set to become one of the most efficient healthcare systems in the world due to its central administration, the government's ability to get hold of Chinese people's data, China's superiority in artificial intelligence and data processing through supercomputers, and China's massive population. The improvement in health services will considerably extend the average life expectancy of the Chinese, which will place a heavy burden on China in all respects.

An example of the dangers of an ageing population to a nation's ambitions can be seen from Japan's experience. Despite Tokyo's technical and financial capabilities, military experts point out that Japan, China's main opponent in Asia, cannot match China in building aircraft carriers. Today, the Japanese navy complains of its inability to attract Japanese youth and to provide sufficient personnel for aircraft carriers. And this has forced it to adopt other strategies, such as making anti-aircraft missiles, strengthening its air force, and bolstering its strategic alliance with America. This scenario may be repeated in China. The significance of all this is that the aging factor has influenced and will affect countries' choices, development and strategic decisions.

In conclusion, there remains a question mark over the way the Communist Party addresses this threat. While initial data indicates that young Chinese couples do not want to have children, despite the encouragement of financial incentives and preferential policies, we should not underestimate the capabilities of the Chinese Communist Party of adopting radical solutions to this issue. After all, it's the same political system that came up with the one-child policy in the first place—an idea which stunned the world!

2: The Role of Research Centres and Intellectuals in ChinaPhobia

Research centres and intellectuals in America and China play a major role in developing or obstructing bilateral cooperation, thus spreading or curbing ChinaPhobia.

Father: If we look at history, we find that economic and even political differences can often be resolved through bargaining and mutual concessions. As for ideological conflicts, which are mainly fuelled by thinkers and researchers in research centres, they only end with the elimination of either side of the conflict. For example, only after the collapse of Germany under Hitler's rule did the ideological confrontation between Nazism and its enemies end. And this was repeated in the ideological struggle that flared up between the socialist and capitalist camps.

Unfortunately, today there are serious indications that the current trade confrontation between China and America is beginning to acquire an encompassingly ideological character. In other words, the clash extends to science, technology, military, media and other issues, which will influence the world in the future. It can be seen that thinkers, research centres and politicians in both America and China have become an essential part of fuelling the ideological clash, finding justification for an intellectual war between the two sides.

In this regard, several phenomena are emerging in the ideological differences between the two countries.

First, all American thinkers and researchers—regardless of how moderate they are toward China—are united in highlighting the danger that China's rise poses to America. Very few of them talk about the peaceful nature of the rise of China, while the absolute majority elaborate on the aggressiveness of this rise.

Secondly, there is a wave of deep hostility among the Chinese people toward America, which is the result of Communist political education practiced by the Communist Party of China, as well as America's attitudes towards Taiwan, the South China Sea, Hong Kong, Xinjiang and Tibet. This hostility has been reflected in the writings of Chinese thinkers and researchers over the past decade.

Only recently has the Chinese government realized the danger of stoking intellectual hostility to America, and therefore has taken measures to limit the spread of anti-American inflammatory material in Chinese mainstream media and social media, and such materials almost disappeared in China depending on the mood of the key holders. In the US, however, a similar wave of hostility is still strongly present because the media and social networks in America are not subject to government control; they exercise their activities freely without political interference.

On the other hand, the sudden disappearance of hostility to America from Chinese media that we noticed is a temporary tactical measure taken by the Chinese government to avoid further losses in its relationship with America. But that does not change the anti-American sentiments of the Chinese people. We have previously seen such temporary ebbs in Chinese media. When the wave of external hostility to the 'Made in China 2025' scheme intensified, Beijing was forced to reduce the media publication of articles supporting the plan. However, the scheme remained and is now being implemented. The Chinese Press has also suddenly stopped mentioning China's strength and the ability of the Chinese army to intervene decisively in Hong Kong.

Son: I want to discuss in some detail the current situation of American and Chinese specialist researchers, experts and consultants who advise the leaders of both countries. America surpasses China in terms of the quality of its experts in Chinese affairs and the depth of their knowledge of Chinese policy, for several reasons.

Firstly, the intellectual and research system in America interacts with state agencies, including Intelligence, the ministries, Congress and American command centres. In other words, American researchers have more tools, information and facts to help them in their work than their Chinese counterparts. By contrast, a lot of Chinese researchers rely on their own efforts through following the media, and the results of research centres and field visits. This explains why Beijing has been unable to understand the changes in the political climate in Washington in previous years towards China. As a result of weak advice, China's policies and decisions, as in the past decades, have remained unchanged.

Secondly, America relies heavily on the opinions and observations of its American citizens who live in China, especially those who are married to Chinese women. They are spread over crucial areas of the Chinese economy, and they are deeply involved in Chinese life. At the same time, they are woven into a natural web through their social relations with each other. The US administration is keen to periodically hear their opinions on conditions in China. This advantage is not available to China. From my own observation, most of the Chinese in America are married to women of Chinese origin, who do not mix or mingle significantly with the local American community, especially with the upper class. Moreover, China lacks influential Chinese businesspeople in American circles. Most of the rich Chinese in America are far removed from politics and keep out of the limelight. Many of them prefer to move as far away as possible from Beijing's policies.

Finally, most Chinese experts are employees of the Chinese government. Their behaviour and discussions stay within the narrow limitations of a formal discourse; therefore, it is difficult to separate the researcher from the government official in the lectures and discussions, and this leads to low credibility. Many of my American friends have told me that what is bothering them on the Chinese side is that many Chinese researchers and thinkers cannot admit the mistakes of Chinese government policies, even though they can clearly see them. They do not dare criticize any action taken by the Chinese government and are content with laying the blame on the American side, to the extent of painting China as an angel that does not err.

Chinese researchers are incapable of self-criticism or of admitting their mistakes. The inability to show vulnerability prevents them from establishing real human relations with America; therefore, they do not understand the true nature of the American personality and mentality. Their research depends mostly on books, the media, and other static sources, whereas sincere human communication is required to understand the truth of things. If you ask most Americans residing in China the question: 'Does China really understand America?' the majority will answer that China is a diligent student with regard to America's laws, constitution and history, and knows more than American citizens and specialists themselves. However, the Chinese government is not familiar with the mechanism of American decision-making, especially what goes on behind the scenes and in private sessions; does not appreciate the nature of the climate of American politics, and fails to feel the true sense of USA as a nation.

Therefore, China keeps falling into traps when dealing with the Western world. I can cite many examples here. For instance, when the Canadian authorities arrested the daughter of Huawei's founder, the Chinese government demanded that they release her immediately. Anybody familiar with Canadian affairs would understand that Canadian officials could not release the detainee because, despite their influence, they did not have the authority to do so. Only the independent Canadian judiciary could issue the release order. In other words, China was demanding the impossible. China's demanding tone impeded an acceptable solution to this issue. The Canadian public would not have accepted the submission of their country's jurisdiction, which is the pride of their country, to any foreign threats, especially those of a country which has—from their point of view—no independent judiciary.

Another example can be seen from the incident with the NBA. One of the NBA team managers Tweeted in support of Hong Kong's youth, but after several hours, this Tweet was taken down. Beijing's very strong response was the cancellation of the NBA's activities in China. Moreover, Chinese companies suspended the sponsorship contracts of these activities, and banned the broadcasting of US basketball games in China. Beijing took all these measures because it considered this Tweet an interference in its internal affairs; it demanded punishment for the director and the NBA's apology along with a pledge to prevent anything like that from happening again.

The regrets expressed by the officials of the NBA to their Chinese counterparts were of no help. Furthermore, the explanations they provided about their inability to apologize for the manager's actions, or to pledge not to do such things in the future were also futile. As the managers were not employed by the NBA, they could not tell any American citizen not to comment on what is happening in China, because US law guarantees the right of expression to everyone. China's actions against the American basketball team provoked the American public, who are determined not to bow to China's dictates!

These are some of many examples that indicate China's limited understanding of the nature of other countries. The problem in such cases is the absence of an expert or advisor, at Director or Deputy Minister level, who is able—or who dares—to explain the reasons for these incidents to the Chinese leadership, and who can provide advice to address matters in a friendly manner, especially in crises that violate Chinese national sovereignty. I can give many examples indicating the ineffectiveness of China's responses.

Father: Most foreign diplomats in Beijing realize that when such crises occur, they must prepare for a 'ferocious yet temporary thunderstorm' and be patient with Chinese officials. Time will take its course before things are back to normal. And this applies to China's relationships with countries throughout the world. Similar incidents took place during the US arms deal with Taiwan; the crises between Beijing and Japan, South Korea, most European countries, and Australia; and the crises with countries that have border disputes with China, such as India and Vietnam, as well as other countries that had problems affecting China's national sovereignty. The departing Ambassadors to Beijing of all these countries used to leave a single recommendation when they left office: be prepared to absorb China's first blow and to allow Chinese officials to vent their anger through media outlets, so they can appear as heroes protecting their country's best interests. In other words, the ambassadors should remain patient until the tension settles.

Son: I must point out that American experts generally outperform their Chinese counterparts in their professional work for the reasons that we have explained. However, Americans also lack a deep understanding of Chinese culture and people. Most of their opinions and analyses are based on tangible indications, while disregarding China's cultural and spiritual aspects. The data they absorb and analyze is usually via their own logic, standards and value systems, that's why the outcome and results are usually not accurate. The majority of these experts do not like the Chinese system of government, and therefore it is difficult for them to separate the Chinese regime from the Chinese culture. I cannot accept the statements of many foreign experts and officials when they say they love the Chinese people and culture and do not seek to be enemies with them, but they do have issues with the Chinese Communist Party, the ruling party of the country, by saying so. They attempt to divide the government, the party, and the Chinese people. If we look at the 100 million Communist Party members and add their family members and immediate relatives, we find that at least 700 million Chinese are directly connected to the Communist Party of China, which is the ultimate leader of China and the one in control of all areas of life. So how can anyone say that they are hostile to the Communist Party of China but not to China as a country?

Moreover, ties of friendship are lacking between the new generation of experts in both countries. The first generation, most of whom are retired, failed to pass on the bond that had been established between the two countries. There is a significant difference in the beliefs and policies of the two countries; however, when you thoroughly examine the feelings of experts from the first generation, you realize that they sincerely sought to advance the relationship and there were genuine connections between the two sides.

American and Chinese specialists were welcomed in research centres and officials' offices of the two countries, and homes on both sides were open to each other. One could sense a shared feeling between the two parties concerning their hard work to establish strong relations. Former experts managed to protect this relationship from slipping into the abyss during many historical moments and major crises, such as the Tiananmen Square incident in 1989, the Taiwan crises in 1996, the targeting of the Chinese embassy in Belgrade, the downing of an American plane, China's surprising readiness to cooperate with the US in the aftermath of the September 2001 attacks, and the 2008 financial crisis. The experts of the old generation took it upon themselves to clarify each country's circumstances and to persuade their respective governments of the importance of working together to overcome the crises.

While this led to a mutual appreciation of their accomplishments and successes, unfortunately such feelings are missing in the new generation of experts in the two countries. Young researchers in America see China as a threat to global American hegemony and leadership, and many think that America's lenient policies towards China are a huge part of the problem that China poses to the US today. They claim that the older generation of experts missed the golden opportunity to stop the rise of China!

Father: I think the situation is no better on the Chinese side. The new generation of Chinese researchers was born, studied and graduated in a powerful and prosperous country, which was able to work a miracle never seen in history. This generation is replete with confidence and does not recognize or accept that America's comprehensive openness to China was one of the most important reasons for this miracle. It is a generation which has grown up reading communist literature and the publications of Chinese research and media centres, which focus on America's attempts to contain and obstruct the rise of the Chinese nation. This generation firmly believes that America constitutes the biggest natural obstacle to China's restoration of its leading role among the peoples of the world. It is China's miracle generation, the generation of the one spoiled child—a young generation tired of the political heritage of China's godfather Deng Xiaoping's dictum of 'hide and bide' in relation to strength and patience.

This generation cannot understand or stomach a foreigner lecturing them on how things should be done, how they should manage their economy and different aspects of their lives, especially when they compare China's ascent with the West's relative decline. An understanding of this sociological factor is vital in order to explain the current situation.

Public and political moods in both countries tend to exude strength and toughness, backed by influential leaders who seek to mobilize people behind policies and slogans like 'China Dream' and 'America First'. As a result, calls for moderation and leniency in the two countries have been sidelined as both sides race to come up with new theories and ideas about the inevitability of the clash. Each is searching for tools to escalate the situation and exaggerate the dangers of the other side while looking for ways to punish and deter it, with the objective of obtaining personal glory in the research world, or to satisfy the leadership. We only need to take a quick look at the list of bestselling books in this field to see the popularity of authors who advocate militancy and confrontation.

The picture is the same when selecting advisers to the leaders in the two countries. Advocates of confrontation usually ascend like birds of prey from the pool of politicians and thinkers. In my view, this is a dangerous situation which does not necessarily reflect the nature of the relations between the two countries.

Son: In Europe and other countries interested in China, the quantity and quality of research and experts in Chinese affairs decreases significantly compared to America, and much of what we have explained regarding advisors on both the American and Chinese sides remain applicable for those other countries too. I think the reason for this decrease is the decline in the importance of the relationship with China. However, it is fair to say—and this is something Europeans themselves acknowledge—that China has a larger team of advisors with more expertise on European issues compared to European experts specializing in Chinese affairs.

And when it comes to researchers and sinologists in other parts of the world, especially the Arab region, Africa and even Latin America, the situation is even worse. China is the one drafting joint statements and cooperation agreements with these countries, such as the Arab–Chinese, Chinese–African, and Chinese–Latin Cooperation Forums, among others.

There is almost complete domination over Chinese research in these regions. The third world countries do not have teams of experts or advisors to discuss cooperation strategies with China, and even if these experts existed, the decision-makers would not seek their expertise or opinions. Moreover, in these countries, there is a severe shortage of essential data about China, such as Chinese trade volume and the nature of economic relations.

If we consider South Africa as an example, which is one of the most important and most developed countries in Africa, regarding China affairs, we find that the state of their research centres is quite weak. During my participation in an international conference in South Africa in 2019, I heard many complaints from officials, researchers, and specialists on Chinese affairs of how they are unable to obtain data from the state ministries on the details and nature of South Africa's trade and investments with China. It is difficult to find a specialist in Chinese affairs within the government sector and there are not enough studies on China. Therefore, South African researchers find themselves in an awkward position in meetings or discussions with the Chinese. This situation applies to many developing countries, and it is a weakness that Beijing naturally exploits in its favour.

Father: Now, we will discuss in detail the 'ideological' attitudes of some American thinkers and politicians. They sow doubt and tension, which leads to more hatred and mutual distrust, fuels ChinaPhobia, and creates more obstacles in the way of a constructive global role for Beijing. Two or three decades ago, the term 'partnership' could be used to describe the relationship between the United States and China; today, that has become impossible.

The status quo indicates that hostility, confrontation and containment dominate the discourse between Washington and Beijing. The majority of the political, research, and media circles in the United States now believe that China seeks to remove America from the position of world leadership and that China is no longer a partner but rather a threat to the future of America and to the world. Moreover, Washington is taking advantage of its global leadership role to pit the rest of the world against Beijing and warn against its growth. For example, Washington has succeeded in changing NATO's strategy, which was based on countering the Soviet Union, but now one of its tasks is to monitor China's military activities. The statement issued in December 2019 by the last NATO summit in London is proof of that.

For the first time since its formation seventy years ago, NATO regards China as a challenge and a possible adversary, and it stresses the need for a collective response to China's rise. This change was reflected in the statement made by Jens Stoltenberg, the NATO Secretary-General, in December 2019, when he said: 'China's growing military capabilities—including missiles that could hit Europe and the United States—mean the alliance had to tackle the issue together.' He added: 'China has the second largest defence budget in the world and has recently displayed a lot of new, modern capabilities including long-range missiles able to reach the whole of Europe and the United States,' and that 'China is coming closer to us in the Arctic, in Africa, investing heavily in our infrastructure in Europe, in cyberspace.' The head of the alliance concluded that the new NATO approach was 'not to create a new adversary but to analyze and understand and respond in a balanced way to the challenges China poses.'

Thus, China—in NATO's view—has become a potential adversary whose confrontation requires a collective response. This is the first collective Western stance towards China and an indication of the success of American efforts at the beginning of the globalization of the so-called Chinese threat.

Son: It's not an exaggeration to say that the current phobia about China in the USA is very similar to the one that took place in the 1950's against the Soviet Union, with one main distinction. Back then,

American circles focused on the threat of communist expansion and its ideology, while today, the focus in America is mainly on China's economic and technical threat and its military capabilities.

Unfortunately, the statements of some American officials and researchers regarding China these days remind me of the frenzied campaign that Republican Senator Joseph McCarthy led in 1950 against the Soviet Union. One remembers that dark moment when US Vice President Pence saw in China a grave threat to the United States in a speech at the Hudson Institute on 4 October 2018. Pence said:

'After the fall of the Soviet Union, we assumed that a free China was inevitable. Heady with optimism at the turn of the twenty-first century, America agreed to give Beijing open access to our economy, and we brought China into the World Trade Organization. Previous administrations made this choice in the hope that freedom in China would expand in all of its forms—not just economically, but politically, with a newfound respect for classical liberal principles, private property, personal liberty, religious freedom—the entire family of human rights. But that hope has gone unfulfilled.'

Pence accused China of many things like building its manufacturing base 'at the expense of its competitors—especially the United States of America,' forcing 'technology transfer' on American companies, stealing intellectual property, interfering in US elections against President Trump, and recruiting its researchers and students to spy on America. According to Pence, Beijing has 'turned plowshares into swords,' has stepped up its military harassment against America and the countries of Southeast Asia, has launched 'a new wave of persecution . . . crashing down on Chinese Christians, Buddhists, and Muslims,' and is 'seeking to dominate the world through loans and support for corrupt regimes in Africa, Asia, and Latin America.' Pence added: 'These are only a few of the ways that China has sought to advance its strategic interests across the world . . . Yet previous administrations all but ignored China's actions. And in many cases, they abetted them. But those days are over.'

Quite frankly, the US Vice President painted a bleak picture of China, displaying the intense hatred of the two countries and launching the most prominent campaign of new 'McCarthyism' in contemporary America. Translating the words of this American official into reality means that China has become a threat which has crept into America and begun to destroy elements of American power to weaken American leadership in the world!

Father: It is difficult to agree with the views of the American Vice President. We do not see Chinese battleships besieging American shores. We do not believe that Chinese missiles threaten the United States, nor are there any Chinese military bases surrounding it. What is baffling is that America, which considers itself the most powerful force on the planet, complains of and cautions about Chinese interference at a time when the two countries are still amid dialogue, partnership, and even cooperation in many fields. It is not fair for US Vice President to blame China for all of America's current difficulties. Reason and reality point to internal American causes for these problems that have accumulated over decades. However, it seems that it is easier to blame mistakes on others than to try to fix them.

Son: Unfortunately, Pence is not the only US official to talk about the Chinese threat. One year earlier, in 2017, the US National Security Council considered China to be an existential threat to America. Many researchers backed this attitude, including Michael Pillsbury, author of *The Hundred-Year Marathon*, which became the gospel of the American political circles regarding China. Pillsbury stressed that China has devised a 100-year plan to defeat America. He indicated that successive Chinese leaders have learned valuable lessons on America's weaknesses and strengths over the past decades. When American bombers shelled the Chinese embassy in Belgrade in 1999, Beijing concluded that its economic development alone was no longer useful in addressing American military hegemony.

After the 11 September attacks in 2001 and the continuing American wars in several countries, the leaders of China realized that American military domination had limits in terms of achieving its desired goals, and that America can lose. In 2008, China further realized that the American financial system had an existential crisis and significant weaknesses. Following Trump's election in 2016, Chinese leadership presumed that the political system in America was reeling, and on that basis began to set its long-term plans. According to the author of the book, these are the developments that opened the door to the arrival of President Xi; he is determined to challenge America, restore the glories of China, and maximize its role in the world.

Michael Pillsbury disputed some of the false opinions that prevailed in Western political circles, including the statement about how involving China in finding solutions to global problems could encourage moderation and cooperation with the West. However, Pillsbury is certain that time has proved this idea wrong.

Another statement in the book concerned Chinese economic success and how China would gradually shift from a closed communist regime to a more liberal system, and how with Western support, economic achievement would inevitably spread to the political arena and define the aspect of political change. But what happened was the exact opposite. To confront China, Michael Pillsbury advised America to seek to establish distinct boundaries for Beijing in the following stage, which China should not breach. These boundaries include:

First, America will not allow China to drive it out of the Pacific. Second, it will not allow China to export the ideology of the Communist Party to other countries, and third, America will not allow China to start an arms race with it.

In one of his lectures in the summer of 2019 in Oxford, UK, Pillsbury questioned China's ability to confront America: 'China has serious problems. The first is that after twenty-two years since Hong Kong was annexed, China has not been able to persuade the people of this island to integrate with it. And after seventy years of its founding, it has not been able to persuade the Tibetan, Uighur and Taiwanese people to be part of China. On the contrary, we see China struggling to maintain its territorial integrity. China also has deep economic problems due to domestic debt that will affect the development of the economy, as well as the factors of ageing, endemic corruption, and pollution.'

Father: John Mearsheimer asserts that China cannot grow peacefully and that America must escalate the confrontation with Beijing to set future rules for the world!

Graham T. Allison, Harvard University professor and a former assistant to the US Defence Secretary, analyzed the deeper causes of the US–China dispute in his book *Destined for War*, which was written in 2015. The book maintains that China views the century of American hegemony as the century of humiliation for China and that deep down the Chinese leadership feels that they are the creators of success. Therefore, pride, narcissism, and nationalism are what currently characterize the Chinese nature.

On the other hand, America—accustomed and addicted to world leadership—believes itself to be the creator of the Chinese Renaissance and will not allow China to compete with it. The author believes that disparity in the values system is the main difficulty in bilateral relations between the two countries. America calls for freedom, whereas China requires order. America views itself as the first in everything, and China considers itself the centre of the world. America believes that it has rights in Southeast Asia and the South China Sea, the part of the Pacific Ocean that starts in east Asia and ends in America, and which is essential for the maintenance of America's security. China, on the other hand, believes that the South and the East China Seas are part of Chinese territory.

Allison warned against falling into the 'Thucydides trap,' which refers to the theory that 'When one great power threatens to displace another, war is almost always the result'. The term 'Thucydides trap' appeared in a paid opinion announcement in the *New York Times* on 6 April 2017, on US President Donald Trump's meeting with Chinese President Xi Jinping. The Chinese President stated that 'both major players in the region share a moral obligation to stay away from the Thucydides trap'.

Son: According to several US and Western researchers, hostility towards China goes beyond the rivalry with America and the West over world leadership. As some of them put it, China has become a danger to humanity resembling the Nazi menace.

Gordon G. Chang, the author of *The Coming Collapse of China* and fellow at the Gatestone Institute, published a remarkable article on 11 April 2019 on the Institute's website, under the provocative title: 'China's Han Superstate: The New Third Reich'. In the article, he claims that there are common racial characteristics between China's

Han people and the Third Reich of Hitler. These include the endeavours of the Han to suppress the rest of the ethnic minorities, eliminate religions, suppress the believers, throw them into concentration camps—as is happening in Xinjiang and soon in Tibet—and insert Han officials to live with and control Uighurs in their own homes.

According to Chang, the Chinese consider themselves a distinct nation, distinguished from other peoples of the world, and descended from a unique line. The researcher continues that the Chinese government is also talking about the necessity of expanding the vital area of China—as Hitler did. Therefore, it occupied islands in the South China Sea, and it is now building a fleet with far more ships than owned by all of Europe, India and Japan combined. The writer adds that the Chinese media is promoting racism against the rest of humanity. For example, China Central Television broadcast a program that mocked Africans and likened them to monkeys, which recurred in 2017 in an exhibition held in a museum in Hubei Province under the title: *This is Africa*.

Another scholar used this racist accusation. Dr Fei-Ling Wang, the author of *The China Order: Centralia, World Empire, and the Nature of Chinese Power*, claims that Chinese officials believe they are distinctive from the rest of the human race and that they are, implicitly, superior.

Charles Horner, a scholar at the Hudson Institute, also wrote an article claiming that the Chinese leadership seeks to restore its legendary glories when the great emperors of China united the world under their banner. The world then lived under their splendid rule for some time, blessed with their generosity, which is a goal not so different from what the Japanese Empire tried to achieve.

Further accusing China of 'nationalist extremism and the pursuit to build the Han Empire to rule the world,' is a sharp escalation in the ChinaPhobia campaign and an attempt to burn bridges of understanding between America and China.

Father: This is on the American side. On the Chinese side, things are no easier. Some Chinese media outlets and social media sites have, over the years, continued to add fuel to the fire of hostility towards America. They mobilized public opinion with claims of an eminent American collapse, maintaining that China has grown stronger than America, which is now no more than a 'paper tiger' that can be easily overcome.

We understand that such statements seek to mobilize public opinion and fuel nationalist sentiments, but they end up hindering the possibility of an understanding between China and America, creating further causes for tension and mistrust between the two countries, and increasing China's enemies in the world.

In September 2019, a Chinese website published an interesting article by an anonymous author, titled: 'The Empire's Wooden Barrel', expressing the positions of many groups in China:

'Some of the staves of the American imperial wooden barrel have been broken, and the water is getting into the barrel. It will soon sink, and this is an irreversible course of events. This was the case with the Spanish Empire, the British Empire, and the Soviet Empire.' And the writer adds: 'Look, Trump is doing more than Gorbachev did when he broke the main barrel of the Soviet Empire. The result was the death of the Soviet Union.' The writer continues: 'Gorbachev broke the Soviet staves, piece by piece, but Trump uses a bulldozer to do the same thing,' he said. The article continues by saying: 'The first broken stave in the Spanish Empire was the stave of financial hegemony. In Britain, it was the stave of industrial hegemony, and in the Soviet Union, it was the stave of ideological dominance. In the US, the stave of industrial hegemony was irreversibly broken. Leadership moved to China, which now produces about 1.1 billion tons of steel, which equals the production of the whole world. This amount is enough to manufacture 6 million aircraft and 2.5 million tanks!'

The writer lists China's strengths in the government financial sector, which is focused entirely on real production and added value. As for the financial industry in America, it is a speculative sector hostile to production, and it will collapse. 'The Sino–American industrial dispute has been resolved. China prevailed!'

Until recently, Chinese media was rife with discussions about the possibility of a military clash with America. Some Chinese experts say that US air superiority ended with China's possession of strong defence and that American space domination ended when Beijing shot down a satellite in 2005 at an altitude higher than 800 kilometres. The effectiveness of US aircraft carriers further weakened in the age of missiles. These carriers do not dare approach the Chinese coast now, as they used to do in the Taiwan Strait in the nineties.

Son: We do not wish to escalate or complicate tensions with America by even discussing the validity of these popular opinions in China, but even if some of them were valid, publicly announcing them would hurt China before the USA.

Fortunately, high-ranking officials and strategists have a more reasonable attitude, calling for calm and efforts to resolve the current tension and find a new structure for the bilateral relationship. Henry Kissinger is one of them. He warned in October 2020 at an event organized by the National Committee on US China Relations in New York that: 'Conflict between US and China will be inevitable and result in a catastrophic outcome that will be worse than world wars unless the countries settle their differences,' he added: 'it's no longer possible to think that one side can dominate the other, they have to get used to the fact that they have that kind of a rivalry.'

There is also Wang Yi, a State Councillor, who delivered a speech at the America-China Chamber of Commerce in New York on 24 September 2019. The Chinese official refuted statements saying that China is the primary beneficiary of the partnership with America, and that China seeks to take its place. He said:

'The truth is that both countries have benefited dramatically from mutual cooperation in the past forty years. This cooperation, which is strengthened by our relative strengths, helped drive strong growth for the American economy, significantly reduced the cost of living for American families, and enabled American companies to reap huge profits.'

Wang Yi cited the following figures confirming America's benefit from this partnership: 'In the period from 2009 to 2018, US exports to China alone secured more than 1.1 million jobs in the United States. Also, most of the American companies made profits from their work in China, and trade with China saved $850 per American family annually.'

He further stressed that the trade war (or 'commercial friction' as he refers to it) costs consumers in the United States an additional

$52.2 billion. It also made at least 2 million American jobs disappear and reduced the growth potential in the United States by 1 per cent.

Wang Yi discussed popular American statements, such as how Washington was disappointed that it was unable to move China towards the liberal order. Yi commented on this by saying: 'In the modern era, China has made challenging explorations and repeated attempts in its pursuit of development and recovery, including the introduction of the Western system. But these efforts did not succeed because they did not fit China's national conditions and needs.'

The Chinese official stressed that his country could not export its social system or developmental model. China never intends to change the United States. Likewise, the Chinese official added: 'The United States should not seek to change China. The United States is working to make America great again and keep America great. Like the American people, the Chinese people have a right to live a better life.'

On the confrontation between the two countries, the Chinese official said: 'We hold responsibilities together towards history, and neither of our two countries can replace the other. Some people in the United States exaggerate the alleged shift of global power. They are concerned that China will challenge the United States and expel it from its global role. It's a strategic miscalculation about China and reflects a lack of self-confidence. China is still the largest developing country in the world. It is far behind the United States in terms of per capita national income, the human development index, and developments science, technology, and education.'

Father: Thus, if we want to summarize the points of disagreement between the two countries, they can be summed up in America as follows: The United States is worried about China for three reasons. Firstly, America failed to change the nature of the ruling regime in China towards the liberal Western direction, despite opening its technical and financial and administrative gates and all the assistance provided to China over three decades. Secondly, America is concerned about the growth of China's economic, technological and military strength, its increasing influence in the world, the high frequency of its military activities in the South China Sea, and its production of new types of weapons that threaten America. Washington is afraid of Chinese competition, especially after the tremendous technical progress that Beijing has achieved in recent years. Thirdly, having Xi Jinping as the new leader in China has strengthened the authority of the Communist Party and the socialist orientation in China and ended all American hopes of China's ability to adopt a more liberal approach in its governance.

China thinks that American concerns regarding China are exaggerated. Beijing's focus is to achieve the Chinese dream in building a modern, robust and advanced country that will enhance the spread of peace in the whole world. Beijing stresses that it does not interfere in America's internal affairs, nor does it seek to expand and export its system to the US. China is still a big developing country which has yet to catch up with the United States.

Son: We have previously pondered some of the measures the United States is resorting to in order to stifle China's growth and progress towards globalization, such as the trade war, the arms race, and the aiding of separatist movements. Washington has further resorted to exploiting the disagreement in Southeast Asia and pushing several countries in that region to form trade and military alliances against China.

Zbigniew Brzezinski, advisor to former US President Jimmy Carter on National Security, emphasizes in his book *Strategic Vision* that the situation of East and South Asia today is similar to that of Europe before the two world wars. He also predicts the same outcome: 'a devastating war similar to the two world wars.' His advice to the United States in the event of such war: 'The United States should follow the general principle that dictates avoiding any direct American military involvement in conflicts between Asian competing powers.' In practical terms, this means that Washington must stoke the differences between Asian countries and China and only play the administrator from behind.

This theory explains the efforts that Washington is now making to encourage the countries of the China Sea to stand up to China, take advantage of the disagreements between India and China in order to push themselves and Japan and India closer, and address Chinese projects in Southeast Asia.

Washington believes there are adequate grounds for this. There are border disputes between India and China which, in the 1960's, turned into a grinding war. India fears the expansion of China's influence around it. Delhi lost a round of influential battles with China in Myanmar, and the result was that China acquired a substantial commercial base in the Kyaukpyu Port on the Bay of Bengal in Arakan in the deep waters of the Indian Ocean. The scenario was repeated in China's acquisition of Gwadar Port in Pakistan, which was signed in 2015. Then China expanded its influence on Sri Lanka, signing in mid-2017 an agreement to develop Hambantota Port in southern Sri Lanka, taking 70 per cent of the port's shares.

In an interview with *Al-Araby Al-Jadeed* in November 2019, Indian diplomat G. Parthasarathy said: 'This is a strategy that Beijing is adopting to build military alliances and naval bases in Djibouti, Pakistan, Sri Lanka, Bangladesh and Myanmar, to encircle India and unify its enemies.'

Washington also recognizes Japan's grave concerns about China, given the historic hostility between Beijing and Tokyo and the dispute over the islands. It also realizes the Japanese concern about China's ambition to control the South China Sea, which threatens the lifeblood that feeds the Japanese economy.

These common Indian Japanese concerns led the two countries—with American encouragement—to announce in 2016 the establishment of the 'The Asia-Africa Growth Corridor (AAGC)' for maritime connectivity between the African continent, India and other countries in South Asia and Southeast Asia. This initiative came in response to the Chinese Belt and Road Initiative, to curb the growing Chinese influence in both Southeast Asia and Africa and guarantee safe shipping lines.

Japan has invested $40 billion in the project and is preparing to provide another $200 billion. India has also spent $20 billion and is preparing to provide more.

Father: Another manifestation of American pressure on China is its control of oil and gas resources in the countries of the Middle East and other regions of the world which provide China with two-thirds of its energy needs. It is interesting to note that all the countries supplying oil to China are suffering problems of unrest, or American sanctions. Let's start with a review of the facts.

Iran is a major oil country that sells a significant part of its oil to China. I believe that imposing UN strict sanctions led by USA on Iran was caused not only by the Iranian anti-Israel stance but also to create difficulties in the face of Iranian oil exports to China, and to hinder Chinese investment in Iranian oil fields. The sanctions forced China's national petroleum corporation CNPC to cancel major contracts worth billions of dollars to extract oil from Iran.

The second major oil supplier to China is the Kingdom of Saudi Arabia. Saudi Arabia has been implicated in Yemen through the so-called Operation Decisive Storm, which has been stagnant for several years. America has backed this Saudi war by providing intelligence to its bombers and fuel for its air force. Meanwhile, Washington is conducting confidential communication with the Houthis of Yemen. When Saudi oil fields and refineries were bombed recently in September 2019, a critical question surfaced: Why did the US Patriot missile system stationed near these oil refineries not counter the drones and missiles that bombed that area? The answer, I think, is that those fields and refineries, which are the largest in Saudi Arabia and the Middle East, were supplying oil to China.

Venezuela is the main source of oil to China from Latin America. In fact, China has invested tens of billions of dollars in Venezuelan oil fields. Suddenly, unrest and demonstrations erupted against the Maduro government; Washington rushed to recognize the Opposition leader as the country's legitimate president, and the US government decided to seize all Venezuelan assets in America.

As we follow the story, Russia has built pipelines to transport oil and gas to China, and it is now under severe US sanctions. Sanctions were even imposed on Russian companies which have sold advanced weapons to China, perhaps because of the Russian annexation of the Crimea, but the wish to pressure China accelerated these sanctions. Nigeria has also been supplying China with large quantities of oil for a long time, and it is now battling the Boko Haram terrorist movement, which is continuously attacking oilfields and other areas.

Also, several Chinese oil workers were killed in that region! There may be other causes for unrest and instability in these countries, but what is interesting is that these countries are all the major suppliers of oil to China.

We cannot ignore what Kissinger said on 11 December 2019, in an interview with the American newspaper *Daily Scape,* which is published in New York. He noted that decision-makers in the United States instructed the US armed forces to occupy seven Middle Eastern countries indirectly, in order to exploit their natural resources, especially oil and gas, indicating that controlling oil is the way to control the countries of the region. This statement relieves us of the need to provide further explanation.

Son: Honestly, I am not convinced about this conspiracy plan but attention must be drawn to the fact that the US authorities are leading the campaign against China and seeking to mobilize public opinion against it. However, wide ranging American public opinion is far less hostile towards China. The case is reversed in China. The Chinese leadership seeks dialogue to avoid a clash with America, while Chinese public opinion considers America an adversary and demands the Chinese government confront it and thwart its plans.

Thus, a quick look at the positions of the two parties shows their great disparity and lack of trust. They no longer view each other as partners, but as competitors and opponents. The persistent tension, mutual accusations and growing feelings of hatred and mistrust between the two countries portend the worst is yet to come in bilateral relations. They further confirm the deliberate American confrontation of China's global ambitions.

A number of politicians together with scholars in research centres, who are inciting hatred and sowing evil intentions, are adding fuel to the fire of divergence between China and America and exacerbating ChinaPhobia.

Chapter 4

Urgent Questions

1: Who are the Winners and Losers of ChinaPhobia?

The persistence of the ChinaPhobia campaign will have seriously negative effects on the economic development of the United States, China and the entire world.

Father: The persisting tension between the US and China will have repercussions not only on the relationship between these two countries, but on all the countries of the world and on all global organizations because China and America represent over 40 per cent of the global economy. In the current raging trade war, there are winners and losers, and both America and China stand to be the biggest losers.

The figures available indicate that the trade war between Beijing and Washington inflicts $1,000 damage on every American family annually. Trade war will result in a reduction in the American domestic product of about 1 per cent. Moreover, American companies with branches in China suffer losses of billions of dollars due to the flaws in production chains of their commodities, and the increase in the cost of raw materials resulting from the escalation of tariffs. These companies have also been victims of retaliatory measures by the Chinese government. According to a study conducted by the American Chinese Chamber of Commerce in Beijing and Shanghai in 2018, half of the American companies operating in China will be severely damaged, and a quarter will suffer lesser damage. The study suggests that these companies are expecting loss of profits, rising production costs, decline in demand for commodities, and a reduction in production levels.

Some American companies had to move their businesses outside China, which is also causing them heavy losses. For example, the executives of American garment manufacturers like Calvin Klein, Tommy Hilfiger, Crocs and Uniqlo have complained about the significant extra expenses they suffer because they were obliged to move their factories out of China to other countries. At the same time, American soybean farmers and meat importers are suffering more due to the raising of the Chinese tariff, despite the recent agreements that were made between Washington and Beijing concerning soybeans. American industries have also been affected by the limitations in production chains in China due to the trade war between the two countries.

Without a doubt, the effect of the trade war on China is severe. This is indicated by a statement of the Chinese Premier of the State Council, Li Keqiang, to journalists at the conclusion of the meeting of The National People's Congress of the People's Republic of China in Beijing. He expressed the impact of the crisis when he said: 'Government planners on all levels should turn the blade to inside and cut our wrists if this is required for implementing necessary sacrifices to maintain the economy on its feet.'

China's GDP is expected to decrease by 2 per cent due to the trade war, and global Chinese exports decreased by 3.2 per cent during the first months of 2019 in comparison to the same period in 2018. Imports declined by 8.5 per cent. Chinese GDP growth fell in the third quarter of 2019 to its lowest level in around thirty years at 6 per cent, in comparison to 6.2 per cent in the preceding three months of the same year. Trade with America declined by 14 per cent during the first months of 2019, which caused Chinese producers to suffer great losses due to the increase in American tariffs on Chinese commodities. Retail sales fell, and industrial production declined to its lowest level in seventeen years in August 2019. Residential property prices were affected due to the increase in customers' debts. This numbers are directly connected to the trade war and prove that any claim that China wasn't affected by trade war is false!

Son: The world is going to lose heavily because of ChinaPhobia, which—if it spreads—might lead to the split of international communities and the potential loss of time, effort and resources in confrontation, instead of building and raising the standards of living and quality of life for all people. The persistence and expansion of ChinaPhobia will undermine the great opportunities China is creating now for the development of the global economy. Vivid signs are evident when the Chinese leadership adopted a new development strategy under the name of 'dual circulation' which effectively prioritizes China's domestic market and production and adopts selective policies towards external markets. This is to be achieved by focusing on importing products that it most needs and investing globally in strategically important fields, overall a more inward policy, and this change came about because Beijing concluded that the coming years will be tough for China globally, and it needs to start preparing for a more hostile environment.

This is a lost opportunity for so many SMEs around the world that could have benefited from China's incredible market growth. Even more serious is the concern that ChinaPhobia might result in the rise of extremists in both countries, whose power would increase until they take full control. Consequently, any possibility of cooperation or dialogue would be destroyed.

You have indicated the losses suffered by some sectors of the Chinese economy, and I will add further details. The use of a high-tech prevention 'stick' by Trump's administration has severely twisted Beijing's arm. This happened, for example, in the decision of the US administration to ban US companies from dealing with ZTE, the iconic telecom corporation in China and one of the biggest in the world, and this meant the inevitable death of this huge Chinese state-owned company, and the possible loss of jobs for more than 50,000 of its skilled employees. This issue was resolved by forming an agreement between the American and Chinese governments, which includes degrading sanctions for China, like fining the company over

$1billion, and sending observers from USA (their expenses to be covered by ZTE) to monitor the operations of the company to ensure it meets US regulations. The responsibility of these observers will be to review the company's performance every year, and submit an annual evaluation report to the American authorities.

In fact, the aforementioned agreement has put ZTE, which is a Chinese government-owned company, and one of the most important Chinese tech companies, under the mercy of the American administration; even the Chinese army became very cautious dealing with the ZTE as all contracts signed will be reviewed by foreign agents! This agreement has reminded the Chinese of the taste of the dark days of the two centuries of humiliation.

Added to that is the issue of the Huawei company, which we mentioned earlier. American companies were prohibited from dealing with Huawei in order to suffocate this premier tech company, in addition to other sanctions imposed on China's largest tech companies.

Today most of the leading Chinese tech companies are on the American blacklist, and those are not preparing themselves to be on it sooner or later. Beijing's experts started exploring the possibility that some US circles are advocating cutting the direct internet cables to China, a move that will force China to use intermediate cables that will slow the Internet and will eventually devastate Chinese economy. These American actions led to a Chinese awakening, a 'Sputnik moment,' and to a firm conviction to work on preventing any future blackmailing.

Thus, despite the high cost of achieving this aim, China has decided to proceed with its efforts to manufacture semiconductors and electronic chips, which represent the most essential parts of electronic devices in the modern age. Experts estimate the cost might reach over $1.4 trillion, plus years of hard work. China has decided to work on mobile phone operating systems, so Chinese mobile phone manufacturing companies such as Huawei, Xiaomi, OPPO, Lenovo and others would have alternative operating systems for their phones to Android, which is owned by Google, and which the US government banned Huawei from using. These Chinese brands represents over 40 per cent of the global mobile phone market.

But at the same time, there are Chinese companies that will benefit from the clash with America. I have a few Chinese friends who work in the field of semiconductor production and their businesses have recovered during the past two years to an extent that surpassed all their expectations and dreams.

Undoubtedly, once Chinese companies achieve their targets in chip production, American companies will be the first losers. China was an important customer, purchasing around 40 per cent of US-made electronic chips. Those companies sell China at least one generation older product with high profit margins, and those high margins fuel the expensive RD to keep their leadership. This will strike a heavy blow to these leading American companies, which are the crown jewels of the USA's industry. Instead of harvesting taxes from these highly profitable companies, the US government will be obliged to provide financial assistance to rescue its companies and maintain their major global ranking.

At the same time, China has threatened to prohibit sales to America of the heavy rare earths that are used in manufacturing all electronic devices. China represents the main global source of this basic element, controlling more than 80 per cent of the world's production. This would ravage all American industries. As a result, several businessmen in America have started to seek this raw material from other areas within the US and around the world, at much higher prices, of course. With these examples, we can say that while the coming confrontation between the two countries might mutually benefit some local sectors, this will cost them a lot of additional energy and effort that could be better employed to benefit their citizens and consequently, all peoples of the world.

Father: Although there is no trade war between Europe and China due to absence of competition over global leadership between them, the European Union will be the main loser in the trade war between America and China for two reasons. Firstly, Europe has always thought of China as a huge economic opportunity and has developed the relationship to the extent that China is second only to the US in terms of commercial partnerships with Europe. Many of the tariff-affected products have a large proportion of EU-made parts. Aggravation of the economic disputes between China and the USA will have a negative impact on European trade with both countries. The second reason is that with the escalation of disputes between Washington and Beijing, America will pressurize European countries to join the US in boycotting Chinese companies.

The Huawei example emphasizes this, as America exerts strong pressure over European countries to abandon their cooperation with the aforementioned Chinese company. In 2019, after a comprehensive and detailed security check, London gave Huawei the green light, however the UK has changed its position on Huawei in 2020. After a decade of partnership Belgium decided to end its 5G plans with Huawei; many other Europeans countries will follow suit and chose less competitive and more expensive products which will cost the European people billions more euros every year. The politics will become clear to the Europeans when a deal is signed between Washington and Beijing and suddenly Huawei will no longer be seen as a security threat.

Inside the EU, the country that might be most concerned about the Chinese–American conflict is Germany, the largest of the EU economies and the biggest exporter in Europe. Germany produces almost the same value of exports as the US with no more than a quarter of the population. Additionally, one out of four German jobs depend on its export market, as the US is the largest consumer of German commodities. Decreased American demand resulting from trade conflicts will damage Germany. At the same time, China is considered a significant trading partner for Germany, and German exports to the Asian giant increased by more than 1,000 per cent in the past two decades.

The disturbances in Chinese–American relations, as well as the depreciation of the yuan, might result in Germany losing the large Chinese market. Thus, the Chancellor of Germany, Angela Merkel, declared that she considers that Germany is involved in the trade war between Beijing and Washington.

The negative impact of the trade war on EU exports to China and America is apparent as these exports decline. European companies have also been damaged by the increase in production costs in America and China. To avoid further losses, Europeans see the necessity of transforming the EU into a third power, independent of the American and Chinese masses. Significant voices in Europe call for the construction of a European security umbrella with a European army to protect it, no longer dependent upon the American military umbrella. French President Emmanuel Macron in February 2020 called for the establishment of a security nuclear umbrella and a new defence policy in Europe, in place of American protection. He expressed his readiness to provide a French nuclear umbrella to protect Europe.

Europe's calls to intensify economic cooperation and accelerate high-tech development have increased over the past few years. President Trump's protection strategy of inflicting additional American tariffs on European commodities has further encouraged Europe's calls for autonomy. Brexit forced European leaders to seek all means of maintaining the unity of European countries, protecting them, and strengthening their political and economic autonomy.

The EU has surprised everyone in the way it dealt with COVID-19 crisis; its swift and positive policies have reassured Europeans of the importance of the EU and catalyzed the ambitions to build a politically independent system.

Moreover, a number of countries in Southeast Asia are on the list of losers from the trade war, including Malaysia, Singapore and Taiwan, which Beijing considers part of China. Mahathir Mohamad, the ex-Prime Minister of Malaysia declared that his country is 'trapped between giants, and our voices will sink in the noise of trade war between America and China.' Definitely, that sinking does not only threaten the voice of Malaysia, but it will extend to its economic achievements as well.

There is a similar concern in Singapore which could end up the most damaged country in Southeast Asia. An analysis released by DBS Bank, which is one of the largest banks in the area, states that if China and America impose a tariff up to 25 per cent on all commodities they trade, Singapore will lose about 1.5 per cent of its domestic product for 2020. This is attributed to the fact that Singapore is the hub of transshipment for commodities required for final assembly in China, from countries like Malaysia and Indonesia.

It could be argued that petroleum-exporting countries in the Middle East, Africa and Latin America are also among the potential losers in the trade war. The slowdown of economic growth in China means a reduction in petroleum imports to provide for the Chinese economy. Raising the reciprocal tariffs between China and America will lead to an increase in the prices of commodities exported to markets in the Middle East, Africa and Latin America. Additionally, economic recession in America and China would lead to a decline in their large investments in Latin America and Africa.

Son: Let us comment now on the most notable winners of the trade war between China and the US. In the lead stands Vietnam and the countries of Southeast Asia and Mexico, which enjoy privileges that China lack, including the fact that 50 per cent of their populations are under thirty years of age. In addition, their ports and sea routes can transport goods cheaper than China's, local taxes are low, and foreign investment is encouraged much more so than in China. Their governments do not exert pressure on foreign companies for forced transformation of technology, as is the case in China. These countries have a cheaper labour force. According to the Ministry of Labour in Vietnam, the average salary of a Vietnamese worker is around $200, and in Myanmar and Cambodia it is around $100, which equals one-third to one-eighth of the comparable salary in China.

In general, areas of benefit for Vietnam can be summarized as follows:

- Increasing the exportation of cheap Vietnamese commodities to America to replace Chinese exports whose prices increased due to the tariffs. Since the beginning of the trade war, Vietnamese export volume to America exceeded $80 billion by 2021. Sales to America now form 16 per cent of Vietnam's external trade.
- Relocating a large number of American companies from China into Vietnam. A number of American textile and

apparel companies announced plans to move some of their production out of China into Vietnam, in order to utilize the cheap labour force and low taxes. The American Nike company also relocated to Vietnam where it accounts for half of the global production of Nike sports footwear. Global electronic companies Samsung and LG moved their factories out of China into Vietnam, with Samsung becoming the largest foreign company in Vietnam. It spent billions of dollars establishing its basic laboratories for technical development in Vietnam.

To avoid high American tariffs, some Chinese companies have resorted to using Vietnamese ports in order to re-export their commodities to the US as Vietnamese goods. This has increased the trade deficit with America in favour of Vietnam, which reached $40 billion in 2018. The American administration has issued a warning to the Vietnamese government to end these practices, and Washington has ordered Hanoi to look for other ways to reduce the deficit.

Indonesia, Myanmar, and the Philippines have become new destinations for foreign companies which are increasingly moving out of China. However, it is worth mentioning that China's neighbouring countries in Southeast Asia will find themselves in a relatively difficult situation due to the following reasons:

First of all, their cheap labour pools have relatively limited possibilities of expanding. In Vietnam, the labour force is about 10 million, in comparison to hundreds of millions in China.

Secondly, there are a lot of administrative complications, from different laws in different provinces and areas, to a lack of integrated production and supply chains like those in China where most production chains are combined in the same industrial areas. For example, when a bicycle manufacturer starts working in one area, government officials ensure they attract mostly bicycle parts manufacturing companies to that area. Hence, the bicycle manufacturing company does not have to leave its industrial zone to buy any parts or spares. This method of production is difficult to imitate in a country other than China for a single reason. The Chinese government, in its endeavour to achieve integration of manufacturing production chains, does not stop at giving preferential policies and tax exemptions to the companies that supplement the work of the bicycle manufacturers, but it also builds free factories and warehouses for them. The production chain companies are also offered sufficient bank loans.

When Foxconn decided to build a factory in a Chinese city with investment of $10 billion, the local government invested about $27 billion to prepare the infrastructure to receive such an investment. The Chinese administrative mentality always views matters from the perspective that the chicken brings the egg, i.e., large companies will not come to the region without the existence of other production chains that supplement their work.

Thirdly, the leaders of China's neighbouring countries are strongly orientated to refuse to take sides in the confrontation between China and the US. These countries realize that practicing this policy of neutrality is not easy, and it might cost them, however they know that standing in between is the wisest choice in order to survive in the long term.

Father: India has also appeared as a major competitor of China, and as a relocation destination for these foreign companies. Apple has announced that it will move a large part of the facilities of its affiliated Taiwanese company Foxconn out of China into India, following a pattern of other large companies who manufactured foreign cars in China and garment companies, etc. Such companies face problems in India, including the lack of developed infrastructure, difficulties with land acquisition, unavailability of permanent power, and lack of powerful supply chains. However, Indian government officials have announced that they will work to solve these problems in order to attract more foreign companies to India.

The existence of a limitless supply of an English-speaking cheap labour force is one of the features of India that attracts foreign companies. Its local market also represents the dream market of all companies, second only to the Chinese market. This explains the decision of many companies to move their industries and factories out of China and into India, even if only gradually. However, in my opinion, this 'honeymoon' for India will not last long. With the progressive growth and accelerating advancement of India, this country will represent a significant problem to America. Tensions, similar to those in the Chinese–American relations, will appear between India and the superpowers like America, and maybe China. One might as well come up with a book entitled 'India Phobia' in the coming forty years.

Son: Russia will be one of the countries that benefit relatively from the confrontation between China and America. Both sides of the conflict—especially Beijing—need Russia to lean in their direction. Convergence between China and Russia would be a great birthday present for President Putin because this would alleviate the burdens of American sanctions imposed on him. Moreover, for Russia to have on its side a neighbour like China, an economic giant with enormous capacities, would greatly mitigate the burden of Western pressure and weaken its impact.

Through my relationship with some Russian academic communities, I sense their deep concern regarding this convergence, from Russia's side. Their neighbour China is ten times larger than Russia in terms of population, with a 4,300 km border; a neighbour which historically had—and to some extent still has—territorial ambitions on parts of Russia, specifically Siberia, and whose economy is thirteen times bigger—this will always be a nightmare for the residents of the Kremlin in the future. Consequently, significant political currents are emerging in Russia, expressing their fears concerning excessive convergence with China. My attention was drawn to the statement of a Russian university professor during his lecture in Beijing University in October 2019. He said that the entity which collaborates the best in the Chinese–Russian convergence is the White House and decision-makers in Washington. The prize for Russian Chinese friendship should be awarded to the Beltway Street in Washington.

Concerning the Arabs, we mentioned that most Arab petroleum-producing countries will lose due to the Chinese–American conflict because of the decline in demand for petroleum by China and America. However, and generally speaking, most Arab countries will benefit from the Chinese–American conflict.

Rich Arab countries have actually begun to increase their investments in China and to strengthen relationships. This tendency has started to irritate Washington which, in the past, would have ignored such an issue. There are indicators that Washington has started to exercise pressure on its Arab partners in order to reduce their cooperation with China, and this pressure will intensify with time. Previously, Washington's stance was that it did not oppose the Arabs selling petroleum to Beijing, and it did not mind them having good economic relations with China. (America no longer needs to buy Arab petroleum, and it has a strategic interest in China becoming addicted to it, as the keys to its wells are in Washington's hands). Nevertheless, Washington recently started to notice the slow, but steady, efforts of Arab countries—those that fall into the sphere of American influence—to create strategic relations with Beijing. Americans were not happy to see senior Arab officials on TV, hastening to announce strategic partnerships with China.

By the way, Beijing highly appreciates the word 'strategic' and seeks to include it in almost of its international bilateral treaties, to the extent that China has made 'strategic relations' with more than 120 countries in the world, much to the derision of foreign diplomats in Beijing. When one has strategic relations with such a large number of countries, this means in fact, that one has no strategic relations with anyone at all.

I have started observing Washington's different attitude to the word 'strategic' in Chinese agreements with Arab countries, as follows:

- Washington watched The Emir of Kuwait's visit to Beijing and his consent to link what is called 'Kuwait Vision 2035' with the Belt and Road Initiative, awarding contracts worth tens of billions of dollars to Chinese companies.
- The announcement in Tiananmen square of Mohammed bin Zayed, the strong Emirati Governor and arguably the most influential leader in the Middle East, that China is the country of the future.
- The last visit of the Prime Minister of Iraq to Beijing in September 2019, accompanied by 95 per cent of his ministers,

and similarly Iraqi governors, who signed agreements with China worth around $20 billion for the reconstruction of Iraq in exchange for Iraqi petroleum.

• When Mohammad Bin Salman, the actual ruler of Saudi Arabia, came to Beijing in the middle of 2019, and linked his country's plan, known as 'Vision 2030' with the Belt and Road initiative, and gave his blessing to Beijing's policy in Xinjiang.

'Strategical Partnership' become a phrase that started to raise concerns in the White House. Through my interaction with the majority of Arab ambassadors in China, I am of the impression that America has actually started to exercise strong pressure to stop the strategic convergence between the Arabs and China, and to return to commercial and petroleum exchanges, which formed the basis of Chinese–Arab cooperation during the past two decades.

Father: Moreover, Africa can be considered in the lead among winners of the Chinese–American confrontation. African countries seek to use the rivalry of superpowers in the twenty-first century, including China and America, in order to win more good deals with these countries.

Son: I visited some African countries at the end of 2019 and participated in international conferences there, where I met a number of African officials and strategists. The notable issue about these meetings was that most of those who talk to the media about the importance of relations with China, are in fact hiding different attitudes, which I can summarize as follows:

African leaders are extremely sensitive to being lectured to or advised by any foreign visitor, regardless of the colour of his skin. This can be attributed to the heavy impact that foreign colonizers left on the African psychology, and the current persistence of forms of racial discrimination in many countries. The interesting thing is that Africa is progressing rapidly and countries like Ethiopia, Rwanda, Kenya and others, are successful examples of development which the rest of African countries seek to imitate, especially in improving living conditions and enhancing democratic choices. Having begun to feel this change, the African ruling class has started learning from its neighbours and imitating their successful methods of development, particularly in reducing and regulating pervasive corruption, and assigning only successful, experienced and honest figures to ministries and technocracy.

As we mentioned, Africa is no longer isolated from international rivalry, especially the Chinese–American conflict, which has intensified during the past few years due to the spread of the Chinese influence. I think that African leadership should summon all possible wisdom and intelligence to transform this rivalry into a driving force for the advancement of the continent. African countries can make this happen, by refusing to take sides with either of the superpowers, and maintaining the same distance from all other major strengths.

I believe that Africa is on the right track in this regard. If we examine the feelings of the international superpowers concerning their influence in Africa, we find that frustration is probably predominant. Lamenting its lost glory in Africa, Europe is worried and frustrated to observe the emergence there of the role of other great countries—like China—in Europe's place.

On top of that, the EU is worried about the expansion of the activities of Indian companies on the Dark Continent, in addition to Japan and Russia's efforts to establish cooperation forums with African countries, imitating China's strategies in Africa. America is also concerned about its situation in Africa, the major feature of which is restricting China's influence and blocking its expansion.

In its turn, China is living in a state of great frustration. Despite the bright history of Chinese–African cooperation on the journey of Africa's struggle for independence, and despite the hundreds of mega projects executed by Chinese companies in Africa accompanied by loud agreements, one realizes that in reality China does not represent a major element in the formation of African policies. China remains on the side lines and does not have the same influence on this continent as Europe and America. African–Chinese relations can be summarized as follows:

At the official level, a lot is heard about friendship and traditional partnership between China and African countries, and about the growth of commercial exchange, the large number of Chinese companies in Africa, the increase of African students in China, and other aspects of strategic partnership between the two sides.

However, moving a little bit away from the official level, we hear another story from each side. African leaders are not satisfied with China's economic engagement in Africa, especially the actions of Chinese companies in Africa and the behaviour of their employees. Chinese investments, most of which have come with government guarantees that were registered as debt within the African countries, are not being optimally used. The Chinese are commonly known in Africa as difficult people to deal with, as their investment system is complex and non-transparent.

China's investments and efforts in Africa have been unable to win the minds and hearts of Africa's people. Upon investigating the opinions of many simple African people about the presence of China in Africa, all agreed that China is not very different from its predecessors and other great countries: it covets the wealth of Africa, although it uses different tools to achieve its ambitions. The popular view about Chinese investments is that they did not come as free assistance or charity, and there is no great love for the Chinese presence there. Rather, African peoples will pay many times as much in bribes to the ruling classes on both sides, as the resources China invested.

What I mean is that people of Africa don't necessarily feel grateful to China, a feeling that is expected by the Chinese, while the Chinese perspective towards Africa is that it is a continent of great complexity. Plus, a cooperation with the Africans is hard to achieve, as in addition to being financially poor, Africa is still taking its first steps in human development. It is also a continent prematurely inflicted with democracy; African leaders, especially in the past decade, change constantly because of elections, and each new leader eliminates the work of the previously elected office.

Newly elected leaders in many African countries, and other allies of China, may not have a positive attitude towards China. The problem with China is that it prefers dealing with authorities and current ruling parties, and it does not attach importance to people's diplomacy, or care about communicating with all parties, particularly the Opposition. This always gives the impression that China is biased towards the existing power, and this is what takes it back to the starting point after every change in power.

Additionally, China believes that the complex African political regimes have tribal, ethnical and religious complications that make it very difficult for officials from a country with one predominant ethnicity and one ruling party to understand, that's why many Chinese people think that Africans are difficult to work with. Without government guarantees, many of the Chinese companies which are now obliged to use the local labour force, are not going to take the risk of signing local contracts for construction works which have a fixed delivery or deadline date. This is because the general perception is that African labourers do not work with the same efficiency and speed as the Chinese. Moreover, Chinese companies will get lost in the administrative corruption and the complexities of tribes and clans which create a huge risk for their investment and could cost them serious losses.

In their turn, ordinary Chinese people consider Africa a poor continent, but one that is rich in natural resources, which are misused by the government due to corruption. It is also a becoming a popular tourist destination for a growing number of tourism fanatics in China, who like to post exciting photos on Chinese WeChat. The Chinese think that their government is wasting a lot of money in Africa, and that the important contracts it signs benefit corrupt groups on both sides. They also think that it would have been better to spend this money inside China to improve the living conditions of the millions of Chinese who are still facing difficult conditions that are not much better than their African brothers!

The conclusion is that official efforts from both sides to improve the image of Chinese–African relations have failed to impart the positivity that was created in past decades, following the independence of both nations.

Father: The countries of Latin America are among those which have gained considerable benefit from their relationship with China, and from the Chinese–American dispute in general. There are several factors that strengthened China's presence in Latin America. During the last two decades, Washington neglected its own 'back yard' i.e., the countries of Latin America, and during that time devoted its utmost attention to the Middle East and Southeast Asia.

America's absence made it easier for Beijing to access Latin America. Subsequently, at the beginning of the twenty-first century, Leftist regimes were ruling a large number of countries in Latin America, declaring their animosity to the American 'imperialist' policy, and welcoming cooperation with the socialist regime that rules the People's Republic of China. Additionally, because of the nature of the political system in the USA, the American government does not have the power to force its States into economic partnerships with foreign countries. Furthermore, American law prohibits the government from intervening in the affairs of private sector companies. In this regard, the role of the government is limited to counselling, and it needs to exert greater efforts to convince the States and private companies to invest in other countries—efforts which might not even work. These problems have complicated American government efforts to strengthen its investments in Latin America. In contrast the Chinese government, due to the extreme centralization of authority, can give immediate instructions to its companies, and even to the private sector, to move quickly to invest abroad, whether in Latin America or elsewhere.

Finally, during this period, Beijing achieved remarkable growth and was able to lift hundreds of millions Chinese people out of poverty. This economic success encouraged the leaders of Latin America to request China's assistance to eradicate their own poverty and underdevelopment. The majority of the population in Latin America suffer from poverty, 60 per cent of the roads are not asphalted, 70 per cent of wastewater is not processed, and the old energy grids cost serious electricity losses. Latin American countries saw the Chinese development story as the perfect textbook case study.

Son: I want to point out something very important in the relationship between China and Latin America, which is that China's presence there is very recent and is not aimed at competing with or replacing America. Chinese interest is primarily directed at strengthening the influence of China in Southeast Asia because what happens there, affects the national security and China's strong interests in that area. I agree with one of the current ambassadors of a Latin American country in China, who wishes to remain anonymous, who said that America is mistaken in thinking that an expansion of the Chinese presence in Latin America will be aimed against American interests. According to the Ambassador, the Chinese presence there is primarily commercial. No matter how much Beijing tries, it is unable to compete with Washington in that area because of the similarity in political regimes, and because of the historical, cultural and economic links between countries of Latin America and the US. Added to that is the existence of political relations that amount to alliances between Washington and some countries in the area. To quote the Ambassador:

'We hope that the commercial Chinese presence there will lead to an American awakening and more American openness on the countries and peoples of the Latin continent. Washington has neglected that continent, and the White House, in the era of Trump, is practicing a policy that harms the historical relations and social links that exist between peoples of Latin America and the people in the USA. Just look at commercial pressure and treatment of emigrants, what's happening on the borders of Mexico, the wall story will over last Trump and will leave long term side-effects.'

As usual, Beijing sought to institutionalize its relations with the Latin continent through establishing the China–Latin American and Caribbean States Cooperation Forum (China–CELAC Forum). The Forum consists of twenty-three countries from Latin America, and it aims at strengthening economic and political cooperation between both sides, with its first conference held on 8 January 2015 in Beijing. Establishing the Forum opened the doors of the countries of Latin America to Chinese influence. The volume of Chinese trade to countries of Latin America increased from $17 billion in 2000 to $315 billion in

2020. President Xi Jinping declared that Beijing aims to increase this figure to $500 billion by 2025.

China has also granted loans of $148 billion to countries of Latin America, and the volume of Chinese investments there reached $109 billion. What is worth mentioning is that most of these loans were spent on energy and infrastructure projects, and these are the two domains in which the Chinese companies surpass their Western counterparts. $96.9 billion (i.e., 68.5 per cent of the loans) were allocated to fund energy projects, and $25.9 billion (18.3 per cent) were spent developing infrastructure, while $2.1 billion (1.5 per cent) was allocated for mining projects, and $16.2 billion (11 per cent) for other projects (including government bonds, commercial finance, developing businesses, and others).

China was also able to obtain significant political gains. In August 2018, El Salvador declared it was terminating its relations with Taiwan and establishing diplomatic relations with China. Other countries in Latin America followed suit, namely The Dominican Republic and Panama.

On the occasion of the fifth anniversary of establishing the Forum on 27 September 2019, through Wang Yi the Foreign Minister, Beijing made four ambitious suggestions to develop cooperation with the countries of the Forum. The suggestions are:

- Firstly, to participate in building the Belt and Road in a high-quality manner, giving priority to cooperation under 'The Digital Silk Road'.
- Secondly, to expand cooperation into the areas of poverty alleviation and pollution prevention.
- Third, to support cooperation in the frame of diverse mechanisms, and then protect the shared interests and the development space that is available for developing countries.
- Fourth, to strengthen the mechanisms of building the Forum, alongside China's readiness to work with countries of Latin America and the Caribbean in order to surmount obstacles and achieve common development.

Father: As a matter of fact, China has hastened to build the Digital Silk Road with Latin America as can be seen from their constructing a number of Chinese technical projects there, among the most important being the renewal of telecommunication networks in the countries of the continent. China has also invested heavily in projects to establish space stations in Latin American countries. China has built a space station with a sixteen-storey antenna in the Argentinian region of Patagonian. Beijing has also introduced their facial recognition system to a number of South American countries, commencing with Venezuela. This step irritated opposition forces there because facial recognition is used to monitor those who criticize the government.

In the military domain, China has signed contracts with Latin American countries, yet there is no confirmed information about the volume of cooperation between them. However, in a ceremony on 6 May 2019 in the American Embassy in Honduras, Navy Admiral Craig Faller, Commander of US Southern Command, mentioned that the sales of Chinese arms to the area reached about $615 million over the past five years. Faller added:

'China is a relatively new member in the arms market in Latin America. Chinese arms constitute only 3 per cent of the arms imports for those countries. Chinese arms are usually less expensive than those available in the US or Russia. Sales of the Chinese Defence to the region expanded from small arms to more advanced systems, including radars, armoured personnel carriers, combat aircraft, and military vessels. Venezuela has become the major buyer in the region of Chinese arms, in addition to other countries like Bolivia, Ecuador, and Peru which represent important clients for Chinese arms. What distinguishes China are the military gifts like trucks and small speed boats.'

Son: But cooperation between China and Latin American countries was not problem-free. Ecuador obtained a Chinese loan of $18.4 billion and experienced what they call the scandal of the Coca Codo Sinclair Dam. Costing about $2 billion to construct, the dam cracked after it was completed, because of inadequate hydrological engineering research. The dam was built in a very seismologically active area, close to a volcano that has been active since the sixteenth century. An independent review of the dam design conducted in 2010 warned that the amount of water in the operating area had not been studied for about thirty years. These issues led to a serious technical problem with the dam, which had a negative impact on the reputation of China and its companies.

In Venezuela, the largest commercial partner to China in Latin America, violent internal conflicts broke out between the government and the Opposition party, which is supported by Washington. Venezuela obtained Chinese loans of more than $60 billion, giving a life-saving injection to the local authorities in Venezuela.

On 10 November 2019, a coup d'état took place in Bolivia which deposed China's friend, the Leftist president Morales. Relations between America and the communist Cuba once again became tense. Washington imposed another set of sanctions against Havana. A close look will notice that most close friends of China in Latin America are facing pressure from the USA.

There is a wide conviction among people in some Latin American countries that Chinese companies are the cause of the problems in the Amazon rainforests; their actions have led to a deterioration of the environment, the spread of corruption, and an enhancement of the big-stick policy practiced by ruling regimes, who have realized that they are no longer internationally isolated because of their friendly relations with Beijing.

These negative developments, however, did not largely affect the economic and political gains that Beijing has obtained in Latin America. The proof is that most of the countries in Latin America support China in international organizations. On the economic side, many countries on the continent refused to join the American trade war against China, and they did not adhere to the American sanctions against the Huawei company.

This is similar to what happened in Brazil. Despite the ascent of a Rightist president, who is a friend to America, the Brazilian government allowed Huawei to establish a $800 millon factory there, for the manufacture of mobile phones. It also accepted Huawei 5G network. The Chinese company DiDi (China's Uber) was warmly welcomed and invested billions of dollars there; Uruguay also signed a cooperation agreement with Huawei for the use of the fifth generation.

However, the American military expert, Faller, thinks that China is conducting a process of strategic consuming for Latin America by manipulating its space and telecommunications, and imposing its standards on infrastructure projects in that continent. This threatens the security of the US. That is why we are now hearing voices in Washington warning against China's increased presence in 'America's backyard', while what they are actually calling for is a revival of the 1823 Monroe Doctrine, to be used to weaken China's presence in Latin America.

2: How Does China Think?

In order to achieve a better insight into China, it is imperative to understand how the Chinese think, and how they perceive themselves, America, and the rest of the world.

Father: The answer to this question is the cornerstone of efforts to solve the problems between China and America. Without deep perception of the Chinese attitude, there cannot be a way to settle the pending issues between the two countries, or to find a common ground for understanding and mutual trust in order to resolve the tension and animosity that dominates their relationship.

From the outset, we should indicate that the success achieved by China in the past forty years has enhanced the feelings of pride and national fervour in the Chinese personality. These feelings were fuelled especially in the past five years due to the aggressive intrusive policy led by President Xi Jinping. His key word was 'confidence', confidence in their leadership, confidence in their culture, confidence in themselves and in their bright future. Chinese leaders have ambitious plans to realize the historical Chinese dream, according to Chinese officials. These plans are aimed at restructuring the Chinese economy, addressing the remaining internal problems, strengthening the armed forces and dealing with corruption, flaming national fervour and

Chinese popularism and paving the way for a bright future for the Chinese nation.

The initial success of the Belt and Road Initiative—China's first global initiative—demonstrated China's leading role in the growth engines of the new world i.e., in AI, quantum computing, robotics and other fields. The Communist Party of China presented these achievements as the end of the age of historical humiliation from which China suffered, and the end of a series of defeats with which China was inflicted due to foreign interventions during the centuries prior to the establishment of the People's Republic of China. The Party used these achievements to convince the Chinese of the validity of Communist ideology, and the safety of the approach followed by the Communist Party of China.

Herein lie the reasons that made the current Chinese leadership give up some of the liberal reforms that took place in Deng Xiaoping era. State-owned enterprise support was enhanced, and private companies were restricted, including foreign enterprises. The censorship of the Communist Party was imposed on these companies through trade-union committees, in addition to augmenting the role of the Party on boards of directors. This also explains the return of the Communist Party of China's comprehensive education campaigns that are now organized all over China. The Communist Party aims to enhance its ideological control over the Chinese community, in the face of the liberal ideas which spread especially during the era of Hu Jintao.

Son: I would like to talk in greater detail about this important topic. Distinction should be made between two mentalities that exist in China today: how the majority of Chinese people think, and secondly how the Chinese leadership thinks. Distinction in this regard does not indicate a separation between the two groups or their lack of connection. As we mentioned earlier, the state of mind of the Chinese people, their overriding interests, and their opinions of their leadership have always been the compass of Beijing rulers and the determining factor for the course of events in China.

Naturally, the mentality of the Chinese lower class is different to that of the leaders, because of the inability of ordinary Chinese people to acquaint themselves with real facts and information. As we all know, a free flow of information, especially from outside, is not available; the decision-makers in China control resources and quality of information. There is a weakness within the objective political education of the public.

This Chinese regime is not based on the foundations of democracy as it is globally understood, which is the predominantly Western-based meaning, and China's leaders are not chosen by people through direct elections. In addition, and due to the nature of the Chinese culture, the level of transparency is very weak in China and the majority of the Chinese remain almost completely separated from government-related affairs, and from what happens around the Forbidden City. Thus, due to my observations living in China, and because of my constant encounters with the different social classes there, I can confidently say that the ordinary Chinese person considers America to be at the heart of the world's problems, as well as believing in conspiracy theories plotted by external enemies against China.

Nevertheless, and even at a time when the Chinese have a negative attitude towards Western policies, they welcome and tolerate the West's culture, and many of them still aspire to send their children to study there.

In fact, the Western cultural invasion has penetrated the Chinese community in a systematic and radical way that has not been witnessed in Russia or Japan or any of the other countries worldwide that lost out in their confrontations with the West. If we examine the financial establishment and first-tier leaders in China, we find that most of them have sent their children to study in Western universities, especially America. England, on the other hand, has received only a small number of the children of the ruling class, and many, if not the majority, of the big business families have acquired foreign nationalities or permanent residency.

Furthermore, Hollywood-style education dominates the imagination of China's children. Western consumerism has also spread in China in a way that surpassed even Western countries themselves. At the same time, the ancient cultural heritage of China was not bequeathed to the new generation. Thus, reverence for all that is foreign spread in the Chinese community, causing it to almost lose its identity.

The Chinese leadership realized the seriousness of the situation, and about ten years ago, it started taking measures to increase the level of Chinese identity. Among them is restoring the position of Confucianism and Taoism that were neglected for decades. It also allowed Buddhism to spread again in China in order to become a subordinate and assistant for atheist Chinese communists to strengthen their control over the country. Chinese history, which was ignored for decades, has been restored in order to remind the Chinese people of their ancient history and the central role of China in human civilization.

The Chinese nation is distinguished as the only one that survived for thousands of years and whose civilization continued without interruption throughout history despite all the difficulties and catastrophes it witnessed. This is the dominant and acknowledged theory in China today.

Father: With the flow of funds to its treasury and the increase in its military force, new feelings started to engulf the Chinese leadership. As one of the previous leaders told me: 'In the past, we were used to need and economization; for example, using ten dollars to solve a problem that requires a hundred dollars in the light of a difficult and unstable global political atmosphere. However, at the beginning of the new millennium, the treasuries of China and the Party were filling, and China became a destination or a "Mecca" for international companies whose "pilgrims" with golden keys court the Chinese. These feelings were culminated when the American leadership resorted to asking our assistance to overcome the difficulties of the financial crisis that inflicted America in 2007.'

At that critical moment in the history of China, a deep discussion was held within the Chinese leadership, and a comprehensive self-assessment was conducted, reviewing the result of forty years of diligence and hard work since the opening and reforms were launched. The outcomes achieved were impressive by all criteria. The Chinese leadership viewed the situation abroad and observed the floundering of the global superpowers. New vocabulary started to appear in the morals of the Communist Party as official Chinese discourse began to highlight pride in their accomplishments, and trust in the methods of the Communist Party. This orientation was crowned with the ascent of Xi Jinping to the leadership because he was the right person for this new era which expresses the feelings arising in the Communist Party of China. In other words, the new sense of confidence in China's approach, and its need for a new burst of energy in the same pathway, led the leaders of China to choose Xi Jinping and put him in charge of the country, the Party, and the army, in addition to granting him full powers to overcome centres of powers which were impeding the rise of China.

China's engines ran on full power because this suitable golden era will not last forever, and China had to take a great leap forward to seize this golden opportunity. Here we can understand the reasons why Beijing resorted to an aggressive intrusive policy, or overreach— as described by experts in the Chinese affairs—because the period of international tolerance for such a policy will not be sustainable forever.

Son: It seems that affairs are going in this direction. Beijing realizes that the policy of 'turning a blind eye' towards China practised by the West in general, and America in particular, is about to end. Thus, the Chinese leadership is accelerating its procedures to create new realities on the ground concerning its controversial files with other countries. This can be seen in Beijing's behaviour towards Japan, for example.

Previously, in relation to the border dispute between the two countries, reactions were limited to restoring the status quo before raising the matter of the disputed islands. Now however, we can see Beijing's persistence in creating a new status quo as a reaction to the Japanese government's occupation of the disputed Diaoyu (Senkaku) Islands. Beijing has taken vigorous measures, including imposing a self-identifying flying zone system over the majority of the East China Sea, and increasing the presence of Chinese military vessels there. These measures have put Japan in a critical situation and imposed a new status quo upon it.

The same behaviour is repeated in the South China Sea. Previously, China used to face its neighbours' expansion policies with denunciation and warnings only. Considering the aggressive policy adopted by Beijing, their response to some expansion works conducted by the Philippines and Vietnam in the disputed islands exceeded everyone's imagination. It was manifested by building new artificial islands, in addition to expanding and building military bases on them. Three years of work by the Chinese surpassed by three thousand times the amount of work of its neighbours in building, expansion and reclaiming these islands during the past thirty years. Thus, China has imposed a new status quo in the region. Everybody knows that China will not withdraw from these islands, and will never, under any circumstances, hand over their ownership to any other country. China considers itself as a winner in the salami-slicing strategy it followed in this issue, and the new status quo it imposed, which everybody has to deal with.

It is important to look at the situation in Xinjiang with this in mind. Chinese leadership resorted to decisiveness in that situation, and the same view was taken in the Belt and Road initiative, as well as the issues of Hong Kong and Taiwan. Despite the fact that China did not succeed on all the fronts it started simultaneously, we can say it has created a new status quo in favour of Beijing regarding issues that had been bothering its leaders for a long time. Today, the observer will see that the golden period of tolerance with China has practically ended with America and Europe losing patience with Beijing's policies. This book presents the greatest proof that the international 'honeymoon' with China is almost over. It is fair to say that Beijing was right in its intrusive and overreaching policy, because in the world of political realism, golden opportunities are only offered once, and it will be impossible for China to do in the coming ten years what it did in the past decade.

Father: I would like to highlight the Chinese peoples' attitudes to the policies of President Xi Jinping. There are voices on the inside—mainly from other political power houses and businessmen whose companies were damaged—that criticize the orientation of the current Chinese policy, and think that such policies have produced international reactions that cost China serious losses. Had it not been for these policies of Xi Jinping—they believe—the phenomenon of ChinaPhobia would not have emerged in the first place.

They refer particularly to the Belt and Road Initiative, which the West sees as a systematic Chinese expansion in the world, and to the approach of 'imposing new status quo' in the South China Sea, which represents one of the most important drivers of international trade. Introducing 'Made in China 2025' scared most of the Fortune 500 companies. In addition, cancelling the maximum presidential term of office eliminated any hope of change in China, the hope that had helped with the strategic patience of countries towards Beijing, whose feeling was that strategic patience and waiting for new blood in the Forbidden City every ten years is less costly than a confrontation with the rising dragon. The world is anticipating the next decade or two with Xi Jinping characteristics.

Neither do they welcome the full control of the Communist Party of China in the Chinese economy through strengthening the dominance of government companies on the Chinese market, instead of the private sector in China. The pretext being that government companies represent the basic pillars of reliability in critical times, specifically in the possible confrontation with America in particular and with the West in general. The advocates of this government orientation are of the opinion that a lot of businessmen hold foreign passports, and with the first bullet, they will be the first to leave, especially now that they have transferred the major part of their money outside China, and they have moved their families to live in Western countries that represent the tip of spear against China's rise.

Thus, we can say that Beijing's economic policies of prioritizing the state-owned enterprises, accompanied by the de-leveraging policies of past years did not enjoy great public support because the private sector—which is suffering now—employs around 80 per cent of the labour force in China. The public system has also been greatly affected by the anti-corruption campaign. This was manifested in the behaviour of many officials in this sector, who—out of fear of committing mistakes and the resultant severe accountability—refrained from adopting creative initiatives, thus limiting the motivation of many officials to undertake bold new steps which affected the efficiency of the public sector.

While Beijing's campaign was relatively successful in reducing and limiting the spread of pervasive corruption in all aspects of life in China, it did not succeed in treating the repercussions of this campaign which points to the core weaknesses of the governmental administrative body. As we mentioned, Chinese officials avoid making real and useful initiatives at work, as there is a huge margin for error, for which they will be held accountable. For this reason, decision-making at the provincial level and below was greatly affected and it seemed that officials at that level lost the motivation and vibrancy that had been their biggest feature. Instead, they turned to studying the decisions of the Party and enrolling in its educational courses and memorizing the speeches of its Secretary-General. However, the bureaucratic administration does not admit that, instead attributing the economic difficulties that China is undergoing to the external pressures resulting from applying its strong policies aimed at the rise of China, and to the globally weak economic atmosphere.

Son: Aside from the economy, Xi Jinping's policies have generally satisfied the people because they touch the heart of the Chinese nation and its desire to regain its role in humanity. When you talk to masses of Chinese people, there's a genuine support for what Xi Jinping is doing. When he was appointed, he promised to double the income of families in the next ten years. My seventy-year-old mother is law is my criterion in this, she is a good representative of an ordinary Chinese citizen who sees her retirement pension increasing according to Xi's promise. I see for myself how vividly her quality of life is increasing from the quality of gifts she gives my children and the superior food she is buying. This also explain 'The Ipsos Poll' which announced in October 2020 that China is the happiest nation on Earth; a staggering 93 per cent of Chinese who took part of the massive poll (19,516 adults in 27 countries) said they are happy. The analysis notes: 'The only country showing a significant increase in happiness since 2011 is China.' Netherlands is ranked second at 87 per cent and the US ranked 11th on the list with 70 per cent of respondents indicating they are happy.

This approval of Chinese leadership also gives some political power to Beijing's external policies, which had always been criticized and condemned by the people. By the way, the basic criticism was always directed against the performance of the Chinese Ministry of Foreign Affairs, and this situation has a historical background. China is still relatively new in the domain of foreign diplomacy because for many centuries Chinese emperors were convinced that 'Tian Xia', which is the name of old China, translates as not only the centre of the world, but also the centre between heaven and earth, and anyone who desires to have dealings with China, must come to China.

This explains the non-existence of Chinese diplomatic missions abroad before the twentieth century. The Chinese Ministry of Foreign Affairs was only established in 1901 due to pressure from foreign countries. Interestingly, Chinese authorities at the time could not find a suitable person among its citizens to head the first Chinese diplomatic missions to America and Europe. The reason major Chinese officials declined to accept this position was due to the commonly held opinion that foreign work is a punishment because it means leaving the paradise of China and going to work in hell. So, Beijing had to appoint the previous American consul to this position for three years. His name was Anson Burlingame, and he was accompanied by two low-ranking Chinese officials as a translator and a secretary.

The Chinese refer to the Ministry of Foreign Affairs as 'Ministry of Translators' and this is true to some extent. A lot of the major officials in this Ministry are foreign language graduates, since mastering a foreign language is one of the most important requirements for Chinese ambassadors and diplomats in different countries. The Ministry of Foreign Affairs is also called the 'Ministry of Trade' because Chinese embassies abroad attach great importance to commercial affairs and prefer them to political issues.

In addition, the lack of creative initiatives by this ministry has put Chinese diplomacy in a defensive position and transformed it into a reactionary tactic. This makes the position of the spokesman of the Ministry of Foreign Affairs one of the most difficult in China because he always receives local criticism. They even call him 'Mr Denouncer' in reference to the fact that all Beijing can do in the face of provocations by other countries is have their frowning spokesman condemn them in the strongest possible terms. It's well-known among experts in China's affairs that during the last decades, the Chinese foreign ministry received many packs of calcium supplements from ordinary people as a subtle hint that Chinese diplomacy needed to toughen up!

As a joke, I tell my foreign friends, especially those in the Western world, that their best friend in China is the Communist Party because it is the only power that can restrain the Chinese people's aspirations and their mood and keep China from the brink of war. If the Chinese leadership assented to the internal popular state of mind, the danger of a Third World War would be just around the corner. The Chinese public eagerly desires to settle their account with Japan for refusing to apologize for what it did to their country during its occupation.

They are also keen to teach America a lesson and prevent it from intervening in China's affairs, including Taiwan and Hong Kong. They look with great astonishment on how small countries can dare and challenge China within their claimed borders. Thus, having a strong party that restrains the local state of mind is a strong guarantee of maintaining the peaceful nature of Chinese external policy, and in preventing the deterioration of Chinese international relations towards conflict and war.

I end with the conclusion that the policies undertaken by Xi Jinping have accelerated a change in the state of mind of the ruling circles in the West, especially in Washington, against Beijing. They have also strengthened Western conviction that China is a threat to its dominance and role in the world. Nowadays, the controversial question which lurks in the minds of Chinese experts is: Have Xi Jinping's impulsive policies shortened the timeframe to achieve the Chinese dream, or have they delayed it? While I tend to conclude that they have shortened that period, we will have to wait for the final answer—only time will tell!

Father: Despite all that, the Chinese leadership believes in the clear and definite plan which thousands of scientists and experts worked on for many years. For example, the 'Made in China 2025' plan, which ends in 2049, defines precisely the role of each ministry and establishment in building China's industrial future. Having initially received opposition from the outside, this plan was theoretically withdrawn. However, China proceeded, and recently implemented a new strategy of 'dual circulation,' which is an important element and definitive DNA of 'Made in China 2025'. China's dependence on foreign advanced technology can in principle only be relieved by executing the Made in China 2025 plan. Huge projects that will change the face of China over the coming fifty years include plans for reorganizing China's land areas as follows:

- Allocating Chinese Coastal areas to be primarily productive areas,
- Transforming areas in the middle of China into administrative, educational, and health centres,
- Transforming the borders into national protected areas and reserves.

Considering government and private investment in renewables, pollution control, provision of fresh water/wastewater, climate transition, nature protection, housing renovation, etc. Chinese President announced at the UN inaugural meeting in September 2020, China's goal to be carbon neutral by 2060. According to Chinese officials (Xie Zheng Hua Research Centre, 12 October 2020) achieving that goal will require new investments of over $10 trillion between 2020–2050. By that time, China will be a global leader in new energy and environmental industries.

In light of such ambitious plans, the Chinese realize that a bright future is not far away, and that their dream of living in a strong, advanced and flourishing country, which regains its rights and unity, is near at hand. This also explains the currently overwhelming feelings of pride and national glory. Chinese people understand that they are living one of their best times in the 7,000 thousand years of recorded history of their nation.

Son: I would like to add that the Chinese take pride in the fact that the special philosophy they created for scientific research and inventions is what led them to this impressive economic success. They also have a philosophy they call the 'Chinese scientific miracle', consisting of the following elements:

- Accustoming their young bureaucrats from an early age to serious productive work, allowing them to express their creative and innovative ideas, especially in areas of economic development. These ideas and inventions are received by technocrats at the middle level, people who know the problems that the government is facing and know the reasons for the leadership's sleepless nights. Those ideas will be packaged as options that the political kitchen in China at the highest level will examine.

- The useful ideas will be chosen and sent back to the advisory level where thousands of experts study all angles before these proposals can be sent back to the leadership in the right political language with a ready-to-go executive plan to be implemented immediately, with close monitoring and follow-up.

- If we examine in detail many decisions that have changed the face of China, we find that most of them evolved through this process. This means that a lot of decisions come from the bottom to the top; unlike many other countries where the majority of ideas come from the top downwards.

- In practice, the scientific Chinese mind depends on principles of pragmatism and application, linking the viability of any project with the visibility of commercial implementation and its financial return. Thus, Chinese scientists do not seek international fame or Noble Prizes. Their actual reward lies in seeing their innovations applied in projects and gaining financial profits.

- That is why many, or even most scientists in China, are involved in commercial businesses and profitable projects. Success is measured by the level of practical application of the ideas of these scientists, and by how many of them are adopted by the government or the market and eventually become a reality. This approach does not exist in the mentality of American scientists who care about scientific and technical aspects at the expense of practicalities.

- The Chinese are distinguished by their creative style of imitating and copying foreign inventions. They do not just imitate and transform them quickly to reality, but they also modify to suit the Chinese environment and mentality.

These additional applications can sometimes be more important than the original invention itself. The WeChat application is an impressive example of the use of this characteristically Chinese skill.

- The Chinese have developed WeChat—which was a messaging program based on Israeli technology in the first place—and within ten years, they transformed it from a mere means of communication to the most important part of daily life in China. Via WeChat, you can now pay bills, book flight tickets, access online hospital, run your company via different working groups, buy your cinema tickets, pay utilities, donate to charity, and even get bank loans in seconds, based on your digital social record. During the pandemic it was converted into a health checking system.

- The Chinese are proud that they moved from the role of students and imitators in the domain of inventions, to the role of international standard-makers, and that they switched from the policy of buying resources to one of buying knowledge and adapting it to fit Chinese requirements. If we continue the topic of telecommunication networks, China bought 2G from the West and made necessary modifications to upgrade to 3G. Having also participated in the research to establish the standards for the introduction of 4G, China is now the standards maker for 5G systems worldwide.

- China is way ahead of its closest competitors in the world in nuclear energy and renewable technology such as wind and solar energy.

- Successive Chinese leaderships are characterized by allowing the immediate implementation of new inventions in small, limited pilot areas. If these inventions succeed, they are spread throughout China. This unique government approach, which takes inventions into consideration to improve living standards, has consequently resulted in strengthening the control of the Party over China.

The best example is the story I was told by a friend—the founder of one of the most important electronic payment companies in China—who explained how the authorities dealt with electronic payment companies. He said: 'We started working in impossible circumstances. Our projects commenced without an official license, but we were expanding under the eyes of the government. Our offices were only hundreds of meters away from the relevant ministries, who had even assigned some officials to conduct regular meetings with us and discuss ways of solving our problems. These officials knew that we were breaking the law, and we realized that we were liable to imprisonment at any time.' The founder electronic payment company added, 'After the spread of electronic payments in China, the government undertook the regulating work and granting of licenses for the stronger large companies that benefitted, at the same time terminating the work of smaller companies which could have endangered the financial stability in China.'

I don't believe that such practices exist in any other place in the world, where the authorities tolerate, in such manner, illegal activities in such a sensitive and strategically important sector as finance.

This is why WhatsApp was and still is years behind WeChat in adopting online payment, as they needed to lobby to get the licenses and approvals before starting this service.

Father: There is another feature that characterizes the Chinese governmental system. It does not wait for inventions to happen; rather it plans and assigns scientists and experts to conduct them. Then, it encourages the private sector to invest, by offering financial assistance, rewards and a full set of subsidies. This means that the invention process in China is planned and does not leave space for scientific coincidence. One example is what happened in the sector of conventional car manufacturing, and specifically, electric cars.

The Chinese government opened their market to establishing joint ventures between Chinese companies and the most important car manufacturers in the world, with the aim of transferring technology to China. Foreign companies investing in China at that time made enormous profits, and China has become the most important market for these companies borne out by the fact that they now have a 70 per cent share of the Chinese automobile market.

Initially, this official policy was faced with strong internal opposition—to the extent that officials were accused of treason—because it led to the bankruptcy and disappearance of China's local brand car manufacturing companies like Tianma and others. Later on, the Chinese realized that this orientation ultimately led to transforming the foreign technology of car manufacturing to the Chinese market. When the Chinese authorities realized that local companies could not compete with foreign car manufacturers or establish their own internationally recognized Chinese automobile brand, the Chinese government provided huge financial support for their strongest local car company, Geely, in order for it to expand globally. On this basis, Geely bought the Swedish Volvo and the Malaysian Proton brands, as well as the British Lotus sports car manufacturer, and tens of other international companies. Thus, Geely has become a magnate that represents China in the world of international cars. China also concluded that its local companies would not be able to compete in the domain of conventional engines. It identified the production of electric engines as the fulcrum for breaking foreign dominance, and allocated hundreds of billions of dollars in loans and assistance to Chinese electric car manufacturers.

In this regard it is worth mentioning that the Chinese government offered financial assistance of up to $10,000 for each Chinese electric car sold. The authorities undertook the establishment of the infrastructure for fuelling stations to provide electrical energy for these cars in all Chinese cities. In addition, numerous Chinese provinces hastened to grant financial aid to those Chinese companies emerging in the electric car market, by giving them free land and loans. Elon Musk was granted an exception enabling Tesla to have its 100 per cent foreign owned factory in Shanghai, a factory that was built in quality and speed that astonished even a dreamer like Elon, Government even arranged for billions of US Dollars for Tesla, a factory that saved Tesla by enabling it to produce over million cars and made Elon one of the richest men, as a result, China got what it needed, the technology of

EV got localized. The number of Chinese companies manufacturing electric cars has reached over 200, with strong competition between them and the outcome of this rivalry will soon yield strong companies which will be regarded as local champions. When that happens, the Chinese government will support the winners and help them to move their brand to foreign markets to become 'international champions'. Li Auto and Xpeng already export to Europe.

Son: I want to add that in China, there is a deep conviction that autonomy of political decision is one of the most important reasons for the current rise of the Chinese. Here in Beijing, comparisons are always drawn with the previous competitors of America. Japan has been tamed by political pressure since it depends on America for its defensive policy. Germany, housing the largest American military base in Europe, is unable to emerge from Washington's shadow. The USA succeeded in manipulating the leaders of the Soviet Union and catalyzed their conviction that they needed to dismantle their political structure and system in order to survive. However, the Chinese leadership insists on having political autonomy, presenting its independent political system as the one that has always inspired the national interests of the country, and expressed the aspirations of the people of China. The Chinese people themselves brag about this feature of their successful Chinese external policy.

These are the current feelings of the Chinese people, and in light of this national fervour and populist mobilization, it would be impossible for any Chinese leader to make substantial concessions for America or to make a strategic retreat in front of it. These circumstances challenge the possibility of finding compromises for ongoing major problems which rely on the principle of reciprocal strategic concessions. For example, China declared that the disputed islands in the South and East China Seas are Chinese property. Chinese public opinion passionately supported this claim, and it is therefore impossible now for Chinese negotiators to make any concessions regarding these islands.

Let me give another example. During the trade war between China and America, it was agreed that the Chinese government would make some concessions regarding America's demands to implement structural reforms in its economy, relating in particular to the policies of state-owned enterprises. When this news broke, the Chinese public—especially the extremist groups—opposed these concessions. They considered them an abuse of the basic principles on which China is based, and an attack against Chinese sovereignty. The Chinese government found itself obliged to withdraw from the commitments it had made.

Father: The Chinese of today are very aware and proud of their history; they consider themselves to be the children of a 5,000-year-old civilization—the only ancient society that still persists to this day. The Chinese word for China 'Zhōngguó' does not imply so much a geographical sense as a political one, and it means 'the Central State' or 'Centre of the World' or even 'the Celestial Empire'. Previously, China had another name 'Tian Xia' which translates as 'the land under paradise, between heaven and earth'. Present-day Chinese are still very aware of the meanings of these names and see that China was, and remains the largest country in the world, even the centre of the world, and other countries are on the sidelines. Thus, according to the Chinese, it is natural for China to regain the lead in the world.

This long history affects the thinking of Chinese officials who are used to seeing time as their ally rather than an enemy. Thorny issues are left to time; in time solutions will be found to every problem. Deep in the minds of the Chinese, there are no final solutions to any problem. Problems—according to the Chinese—do not disappear completely, but every problem leaves traces that might in time interact again, they know that China has a proven record of being one of the few if not the only civilization that were able to revive and thrive after long period of dark times, all of the Chinese learn this in school and back home. Thus, it is difficult to get a clear and final attitude towards problems with other countries from the Chinese.

Furthermore, Chinese development programmes are adopted and determined according to temporal phases that might take 100 years each. During past centuries, China experienced a hundred years of weakness, surrender and humiliation. With the arrival of the Communist Party of China in 1921, a new 100-year phase of national liberation, unity and building the basis of a socialist country began.

The coming hundred years, due to begin in 2021, will be a phase of the comprehensive rising of China, regaining its glories and achieving its historical dreams.

Son: We move on now to answering the following question: How do the Chinese people view America today? In China, there are many points of view regarding America. To the Chinese who lived, studied, or have relatives in America, who mingled with the American community, and internalized a lot of the American traditions, America is characterised by moderation, and to some extent, admiration. The dominant public position of the majority of the Chinese community is affected by what is promoted on social networking websites, in centres of research and cultural and intellectual activities, and through the internal propaganda of the Communist Party of China. They explicitly express a negative, and sometimes aggressive, attitude towards America as a state but not necessarily towards American people, despite the admiration of some of them of the American lifestyle and the American dream. It is a classic love–hate relationship. Finally, the Chinese government's official position is characterized by being conservative, cautious and careful, in order to maintain open bridges with America.

We are reviewing the prevailing opinion among the majority of the Chinese community because at the end of the day, public opinion is what exerts pressure on the official policy, driving it to take more extreme attitudes from America and not yield to it. The general public say that China is the future and not America. China is growing and developing, while America is shrinking and becoming isolated. They promote the following numbers.

Every ten years, the volume of the Chinese economy multiplies. During the era of President Clinton, the volume of the Chinese economy was equal to one-eighth of America's. During the Bush era, this rate increased to a quarter, and at the time of Obama to a half, while during the reign of Trump, the Chinese economy equals two-thirds of the American one. They are completely positive that this escalation, though difficult, is stable and achievable.

There are now plenty of areas wherein China surpasses America. To put it more clearly, over the past thirty years, the Chinese economy multiplied ten times, built the biggest middle class in the world, ended objective poverty and generated $4 trillion of reserves of hard currency. At the same time, the quality of life of most Americans deteriorated in most aspects while government spending exceeded $4 trillion on wars in the Middle East and Afghanistan.

They add that China is strengthening its global influence, and its openness to the world is increasing, citing as an example the Belt and Road Initiative, which more than 170 countries have joined. On the other hand, America is becoming more isolated, is losing its allies, while its enemies are multiplying throughout the world. Even among the international organizations on which America used to rely for implementing its dominance such as WTO, World Health Organization (WHO), United Nations Educational, Scientific and Cultural Organization (UNESCO), and others, despite Biden's reverse policy, the general mood in the USA is that going inward demonstrates a serious American retreat.

NATO, which strengthened America's military dominance, has had its very existence threatened by the crisis that took place between Turkey and America, Turkey and Greece and other internal problems. Many European members of NATO do not approve of America's positions towards China and Russia.

In Southeast Asia, America is soliciting its previous allies to form an international alliance against China, but most countries in the region prefer non-enmity to China. G7 is currently struggling with internal issues, and is declining in size in the international economy, some of the G7 members economy are even less than some provinces in China! In comparison with the increased influence of the new Group of Seven, which are China, Russia, India, Indonesia, Brazil, Turkey and Mexico. In 1995, the volume of the economy of these countries combined was equal to half of the economy of the G7. In 2015, the economy of the two groups became equal. In 2040, the economy of BRICS will be twice the size of the G7.

At the same time, America is minimizing its presence within the UN, the organization that was designed by the USA, while China is growing in strength and occupying more high-ranking positions within these organizations through UN Peacekeeping Forces.

Due to the decline in the size of the American economy's share in global markets, and the abuse and continued weaponizing of the US Dollar, America's financial dominance in the world through the Dollar and the international SWIFT is facing serious problems and attempts are being made to change this situation. Russia, the world's largest petroleum producer, has terminated the relationship between its petroleum and the US dollar, as did many large petroleum-producing countries like Iran and Venezuela.

The EU has also developed a SWIFT alternative for the Euro, while China, which is the largest trade country in the world, has signed agreements with a number of countries that use local currency instead of the dollar. Additionally, China already started the commercial use of the digital RMB, which will create its own ecosystem by leveraging the size and strength of the growing Chinese economy which will create a new status quo.

The majority of public opinion concludes that time is the ally of China. In the coming forty years, China's economy will become twice the size of the American economy. When that time comes, dialogue between the two countries will be totally different from its current situation. There will no longer be American dominance or monopoly in international decision-making. The world will be totally different, and the Chinese–American relationship will be characterized by equality.

3: Could ChinaPhobia Become an International Phenomenon?

The global wave of ChinaPhobia is influenced by the relationship between China and the rest of the world, and by the occurrence of economic and intellectual developments. Countries friendly towards, benefitting from, or who have strong economic relations with China, will find it difficult, and maybe will not even dare, to be hostile towards China. This means that not all of America's allies are ready to adopt America's position against Beijing.

Father: We will begin this explanation using the example of the relationship of Arab countries with China and America and looking at how the Arabs view both America and China.

Regarding America, obstacles hinder the possibility of a public and diplomatic improvement in Arab–American relations. The primary drawback is America's total bias towards Israeli policy in the Middle East, particularly under Trump's administration. Washington has taken a set of measures in this regard, the first of which is their recognition of occupied Jerusalem as the capital of Israel, and the recognition of the Syrian-occupied Golan Heights as a part of Israel. Both measures contradict the Security Council resolutions which America had previously agreed upon, especially resolution (S/RES/242) which considers both Jerusalem and Golan Heights to be occupied lands. Moreover, Washington backed Israel in the 'deal of the century' plan to resolve conflict in the Middle East, which declines the basic rights of the Palestinians, and it is this that undermined US credibility and terminated its role as a sponsor of the Middle East peace process.

Washington's linking of terrorism to Arab and Muslim countries forms the second obstacle. The resulting travel ban to America for citizens of a number of Arab countries has contributed to the spread of Islamophobia and Arabophobia. These obstacles fuel the typical hostility of the Arabs towards America, and make it difficult for Arab-ruling regimes to adopt American policy. Above all lies the catastrophic mistake committed by America in Iraq, the tragic consequences of which are very much evident today.

On the other hand, it can be said that China has a positive image among Arabs in general. China did not invade the Arabs, or occupy their lands, nor does it support Israeli policy against them. Certainly, Beijing does not determine its policy with other countries based on mere emotional considerations and historical events alone. Instead, Arab countries desirous of benefitting from the rise of China must agree to three conditions: to recognize the One-China policy, not to intervene with Chinese internal affairs, and that their relations with other countries are not to be at the expense of China's international relations. We will talk about this in greater detail.

In 2001, Arab countries started discussions with China to establish the China–Arab States Cooperation Forum. At one point, I headed the negotiating delegation of Arab ambassadors in Beijing. During negotiations, Beijing insisted on the following three conditions: All Arab countries must admit that Taiwan is part of China, and Arab capitals must cut all their economic, cultural, and sporting relations with Taipei. The second condition is that Arab countries must not support opposition movements or organizations established by Muslims of China, whether internal or external. The third condition is that the development of Chinese–Arab relations must not be at the expense of Beijing's relations with both Israel and Iran. The head of the Chinese delegation back then, Zhai Jun, who later became Vice Foreign Minister, told me that violating any of these conditions would undermine the mere thought of establishing this Forum.

Difficult negotiations were held for three years, and the Arab delegation insisted on abiding by an article they wanted added to the political manifesto, stating that the three islands that Iran has been occupying since 1971 in the Gulf (which are Greater and Lesser Tunbs and Abu Musa) belong to the UAE, not to Iran. Negotiations stopped and almost failed because of the Arabs' insistence on this amendment, while China refused any prejudice against Iran. However, we were surprised when the Emirati government—which had previously committed itself strongly to this point—later mitigated its attitude and retreated, following high-ranking Chinese communications. Only then progress was made—in accordance with Chinese conditions—in the procedures of establishing the Forum, which saw the light in 2004.

Son: This Forum, through ten designated platforms, has become the main engine to move Chinese–Arab relations forward and to strengthen Chinese influence in the Arab region. Cooperation between the two sides witnessed a quantum leap after the emergence of the Belt and Road Initiative. The Chinese–Arab commercial exchange increased from $36.7 billion in 2004, to over $300 billion in 2021. China imports over $150 billion and exports goods of over $140 billion. There are now thousands of Chinese companies implementing infrastructure projects in most of the Arab countries. In 2019, China invested over $30 billion in non-financial sectors, which counted as 31.9 per cent of FDI in the Arab world, with $1.5 billion as direct investment, and undertook contracts valued at over $32.5 billion in 2019.

Moreover, China has trained 6,000 Arab experts, and enrolled about 10,000 Arab students into its universities. An intensive cultural cooperation between both sides resulted in translating hundreds of literary and political books and organizing historical and intellectual symposiums about the role of the Arab and Chinese civilizations in human development. A plan was also put in place to regulate the exchange of 10,000 Arab and Chinese artists, and cooperation agreements were signed between 200 Arab and Chinese cultural establishments. China has invested about $60 billion in Arab countries, and imported 157 million tons of Arab petroleum in 2017, forming 37.5 per cent of China's overall petroleum imports.

President Xi Jinping announced the allocation of $20 billion for Arab countries in need of post-war construction, alongside the establishment of a China–Arab Banks Association. China will fund this association with $3 billion. Added to that is a long list of cooperation in the areas of health, agriculture, education, computer industry and nuclear energy. Currently, there are discussions between China and countries of the Gulf Cooperation Council to create a free-trade zone between themselves; this would be the largest such zone in the Middle East and Africa. This economic expansion of Chinese–Arab relations explains why ChinaPhobia did not spread in the Arab region, and why Arab countries did not join America's efforts against China.

Father: This is true. This orientation was promoted after the Initiative of the Belt and Road in 2013, which opened new horizons for Chinese–Arabian economic cooperation. On 28 March 2015, China published its vision of the 'Belt and Road' which connects China with the Arabian Gulf and the Mediterranean Sea through Central Asia and Western Asia. The Maritime Silk Road was designed to begin at the Chinese Coast and journey to Europe, through the South China Sea and the Indian Ocean. This means that the Arab region is not only a significant part of the project, but it plays an essential role as it is also the axis of the BRI and sea routes. Since its official announcement in 2013, all twenty-one Arab countries have declared their participation in the BRI. Since 2016, the majority of Arab countries have joined the 'Asian Infrastructure Investment Bank' (AIIB) which Beijing established as a multilateral financial institution. It is considered by some as a rival to the US-dominated International Monetary Fund and the World Bank.

Egypt put the Suez Canal Economic Zone at the disposal of the BRI project. The Chinese Company 'TIDA' is in charge of an expansion process for the first phase of the economic zone in the Suez Gulf project, and has finished the development and investment of

7.3 sqkm in the Egyptian area of Ain Sokhna. It succeeded in attracting sixty-eight Chinese companies and factories to invest a first phase total of $1 billion in the area. Now, there are 1,500 Chinese companies working in Egypt. The electric train project 'Al-Salam—Administrative Capital—10th of Ramadan' in Cairo was implemented at a cost of $1.2 billion. It was funded by the Export–Import Bank of China, and it is to be repaid within twenty years, with an interest rate of 1.8 per cent.

Large BRI projects were conducted in the United Arab Emirates, the most of important of which is the China–UAE Industrial Zone. It made noticeable progress after one year of planning, marketing and construction. China–Oman Industrial Park in Duqm in the Sultanate of Oman represents a successful example of Gulf–China cooperation under the Belt and Road.

Kuwait has also announced it is unifying its comprehensive development plan for 2035 with the BRI. The biggest Arab economy Saudi has also announced its 2030 vision integration with BRI. Morocco has made up its mind and decided to move strategically towards China.

These facts assert that the majority of Arab countries have great economic interests with China despite the strong American influence there.

Son: Among the Arab countries, America has many old friends in the area, primarily Gulf countries which host the biggest US Army bases out of the USA, Morocco and Egypt. Although this alliance between Washington and some of these countries was strengthened militarily in the past on the grounds of disputes between Iran and some Gulf countries, this did not have a negative impact on the wider cooperation between them and China. The irony is that China has become the first commercial partner for America's traditional allies in the region like Saudi Arabia, UAE, Qatar and others. Its biggest ally in the area, Israel, is opening its doors widely to China, Haifa Port is operated by the Chinese, which right next to a US naval base; Chinese love this spot!

Chinese companies are the first to benefit from the petroleum of the Arabian countries that produced 33,786,000 barrels in 2019 representing 35.5 per cent of global production, which is an area of American influence. Here, the growth of military cooperation between

China and America's allies is worth mentioning. Saudi Arabia and UAE have purchased billions of dollars' worth of Chinese arms, and there are hundreds of Chinese military experts in these countries. We have also to keep in mind that UAE—one of America's allies in the Middle East—has transformed into a central station (Port of Jebel Ali) in the import and distribution of Chinese commodities throughout the Arab region.

Thus, the Gulf countries that are practically under America's sphere of influence are considered China's premier trade partners among Arab countries. China has also established its first military base abroad in an Arabic country, Djibouti.

Father: I want to clarify a few things regarding the relationship between the Gulf countries and America. In their private talks, a lot of leaders in Gulf countries express their worry concerning America's reckless and fickle Middle East policy. They also have a deep conviction that Washington is an unreliable ally. It failed them at the time of Obama when it converged with Iran and signed the nuclear agreement with it, and when it surrendered Iraq to Iran. Washington supported the removal of its ally Hosni Mubarak from power in Egypt, and withdrew its alliance with Turkey in favour of the Kurds. Later, it—partially—abandoned the Kurds in Syria in favour of Turkey.

Moreover, Washington evaluates the behaviour of its Arab allies based on their position towards Israel. It does not understand that the normalization of relations between Gulf countries and Israel could cause friction in all these countries. The most annoying issue for Gulf countries, particularly Saudi Arabia, is that America views them as mere moneybags—they always have to pay for America. While not expressed explicitly by Gulf rulers, these feelings are an additional element for their convergence with China; the constant instability in that area, and the ambiguity and hesitance of American policy, drive these countries to look for alliances with other fast-growing countries, including China.

In this regard, I will give the following example. Despite America's threats in relation to banning cooperation with the Chinese Huawei company in the 5G domain, Saudi Arabia, UAE, Bahrain and Qatar, which are America's largest allies among the Arab states, allowed the use of Huawei 5G, and they did not concede to American pressure.

Everything we have mentioned above explains the positive image that Arabs look at China despite the COVID-19 crisis and the intensive anti-China sentiment of the global media towards Beijing, especially post COVID-19 era. 'The Arab Opinion Index', which is regarded as the main index in the Arab world has shown that more than half (55 per cent) of the 28,000 respondents in thirteen Arab countries feel positively towards China foreign policy, against 81 per cent who felt that US policy in the Middle East presents a threat to the security and stability in the region.

Son: China directed its efforts to the other Muslim countries. It formed strong relations with Pakistan and invested around $60 billion there, including establishing Gwadar Port. China is also consistent in buying petroleum from Iran despite American sanctions, and a large number of Chinese companies work in the Iranian economy.

Beijing has also built large economic partnerships with Indonesia, Malaysia, and even Turkey, in spite of the conflict between them about the Uighur issue. Through the fast growth of cooperation and partnership, China guaranteed for itself the support of the main Arab and Muslim countries on the two issues of Taiwan and the Uighurs, as these countries have cut all relations with Taiwan. As regards the Uighurs issue, on 8 July 2019, twenty-two countries, including Germany, France, Switzerland, Britain, Japan and Canada, sent a letter to the Human Rights Council, criticizing China for its policies in Xinjiang territory, and requesting it to stop mass arrests. Beijing considered this as intervention in its internal affairs and responded by 'rebuking' the countries that signed. Not only that, Beijing demanded the Muslim countries with whom it has good relations to sign a 'counter' letter to the UN Human Rights Council. Most Muslim and Arab countries supported Beijing in this issue. This was manifested in a 'counter' letter to the Human Rights Council published on 12 July 2019, and signed by thirty-seven Muslim countries, including Saudi Arabia, UAE, Qatar, Algeria and Syria.

The letter confirmed these countries' support of the procedures undertaken by the Chinese authorities in Xinjiang. The signees of the letter congratulated China for its impressive human rights achievements, and declared that they 'were acquainted with the massive damages caused by terrorism, separatism, and religious extremism of all ethnic groups in Xinjiang.' It continued: 'In the face of the dangerous challenge of terrorism and extremism, China has taken a series of measurements to fight terrorism and extremism in Xinjiang, especially through establishing vocational education and training centres, *to ensure the area is secure again.'* The letter advised that China invited a number of diplomats and journalists to Xinjiang, and what they witnessed and heard completely contradicted what was conveyed by the media. It demanded the international community not to make accusations based on *'uncertain information before visiting Xinjiang.'* Consequently, these Muslim countries adopted the attitude of the Chinese government in Xinjiang.

Father: It would be useful to touch upon the attitudes of Central Asian countries concerning the Uighurs issue. The Chinese Uighurs are ethnically related to the peoples of these countries. There are around 1.5 million Kazakhs living in the Chinese area of Xinjiang, where the Uighurs live, in addition to a large number of Uzbeks and Tajiks and others; all of whom are Muslim peoples. For this reason, attention was turned to possible reactions from these countries concerning events in Xinjiang. There is definite public discontent regarding what happens in the 'education' camps in Xinjiang, and approximately 2,000 Kazakhs left China for Kazakhstan. There were a few demonstrations in Kazakhstan against these camps. However, Kazakhstani official authorities friendly with Beijing responded to these demonstrations strongly and decisively, and described participants as terrorists. In fact, Kazakhstan is considered among the countries where China has invested the most heavily in Central Asia (around $20 billion). There are also thousands of Chinese companies working in Kazakhstani territories. This country provides China with petroleum, gas and other minerals. This is another example whereby governments which are economically connected with China will not allow ChinaPhobia or enmity to spread over their territories.

Son: In relation to Africa, China could also build a strong base on this continent, manifested by the establishment of the 'Forum on China-Africa Cooperation' in 2000 which has become the major engine to expand China's influence in Africa.

On 27 February 2018, Al Jazeera reported on its website information about the Chinese presence in Africa, mainly:

'China has a strong influence in 63 per cent of Africa, and it has highly cooperative relations with thirty-six African countries. Beijing took special care of training the African parties' leaders. It organized 200 training courses in China, and 139 courses to train high-ranking officials in African governments. It also announced about 1,000 courses it ran for leaders of African youth organizations. In relation to loans, China offered about $100 billion for African governments, in addition to a wide military cooperation between China and African countries whether in providing arms with Chinese loans, or training African military personnel.'

These advanced Chinese relations with Africa preclude the spread of ChinaPhobia in most countries of the Dark Continent. Thus, China's success in strengthening its influence in Africa led the West to exert great efforts to cast doubts on China's presence in Africa, and attempt to damage China's cooperation with African countries. This appeared in many forms: through highlighting the risk of Chinese loans offered to Africa and labelling them a Chinese trap, spreading information about the negative aspects in the practices of some Chinese companies in African territory, and in general tainting the assistance offered by China to Africa.

A perfect example of this was published by the French newspaper *Le Monde* in January 2017 about the existence of espionage systems in the building offered by the Chinese government as a gift to the African Union in Addis Ababa 2012, and which is considered as a symbol of China–Africa cooperation. To summarize the story that was published by the French newspaper, one of the African employees discovered—by accident!—that the servers of Chinese computers in the African Union building got busy with data activities between midnight and 2 a.m. every day, although there was nobody in the building at that late time. His enthusiasm drove him to follow the origin of what he saw as a flaw. So, he discovered that daily accessible data and all internal secrets of the Union stored on almost all devices in the building were being transmitted to and stored in other mysterious servers in unknown units that were not in Addis Ababa. They were in fact 8,000 km away from the Ethiopian capital, in the Chinese city of Shanghai.

According to *Le Monde* all Chinese engineers who worked in the building were removed, and all Chinese electronic servers were replaced. All correspondence exchanged daily between the officials of the Union was encoded and transmitted through a route other than Ethio Telecom that cooperates with China, and which is the general operator of Ethiopia's telecommunications network. However, the newspaper did not stop there in its investigation. It also narrated a scene that could have come straight out of a cold war of Intelligence, or from a Hollywood movie. An Algerian cybersecurity team, called in by the Union to scan the whole building, discovered mini microphones that the Chinese had installed in different places in the building.

China hastened, through the words of Kuang Weilin, Beijing's Ambassador in the African Union, to officially deny the feature story in Le Monde, describing it as 'preposterous, and incomprehensible.' He was supported by the new Chair of the African Union, the Rwandan President Paul Kagame, who announced that nobody was spying. He was preceded by Moussa Faki, the Chairperson of the African Union Commission, who made a similar declaration, denying the feature story altogether. Ethiopia's resigned Prime Minister Hailemariam Desalegn followed suit and confirmed that China–Africa relations are 'strategic and totally comprehensive'.

In brief, such developed relations between Africa and China guarantee that Beijing will have the support of about fifty countries for China's external policy. Logically, these countries will preclude the spread of ChinaPhobia over their territories.

Father: It has recently become apparent that China is using the issue of debt to limit the outbreak of ChinaPhobia among the governments of small and developing countries. In this regard, I want to clarify a few points. Some Western entities describe the loans offered by China to developing countries as traps that Beijing set for them. Some American experts and politicians expand by talking about the inability of these countries to pay back these loans, and that Beijing controls some ports of these countries, something they described as neo-colonization.

I would like to highlight the following points:

Firstly, if any entity must bear responsibility, it is definitely the governments of the countries receiving these loans. China did not force these loans on any country, and those sovereign countries that availed of them were completely free to choose their channels of funding. China did not impose conditions like economy restructuring and liberalization of prices and adherence to human rights—as the World Bank does—before granting these loans. These governments should have considered their capacities and abilities to repay the loans before accepting them. For example, if with my abilities I can only handle the consequences of a $500 million loan, why should I ask for $5 billion? This applies to Sri Lanka, Bangladesh and Myanmar among others, and is a result of mismanagement, if not corruption.

Secondly, the topic of Chinese loans has entered the heart of electoral processes in developing countries whenever exchange of power is taking place. The Opposition accuses the government of abusing national sovereignty through mortgaging some vital sights and resources to China, because of their inability to pay back the loans. They pledge, should they win, to 'liberate the country of what is called "Chinese colonization",'—the purpose being to defame the election opponent and gain more votes from electorates.

Third of all, China realizes only too well that it takes serious risks in offering large loans to politically unstable countries. More than 70 per cent of BRI countries are high-risk countries, and taking this step involves the possibility of losing this funding. The perfect example for that is Venezuela. China invested billions of dollars in this country which suffers external blockade and internal tensions. These Chinese investments are now exposed to risk because of the severe internal crisis in the country. It is noticeable that the US and the International Monetary Fund refrained many times from giving loans to politically unstable countries due to the high risks of non-payment.

Most of China's critics forget to mention that the absolute majority of Chinese investments are in the infrastructure sector, grids, roads, bridges and schools, things that are cannot be moved out of the country, so if anyone is taking a risk, it is China. Another forgotten fact is that China has very limited tools to force those countries to pay back; this is actually why China is trying to involve international and regional financial institutes in the funding of BRI operations internationally, including AIIB and Shanghai Organization Development Bank. Loans are much easier for an international institute to collect, versus bilateral agreements.

Finally, the term 'Chinese loan-traps' first appeared in the US and spread through the international mass media. It is used in order to cause offence to China and damage its reputation, and it is very difficult not to agree with the view presented by the Spanish magazine *Esglobal* in September 2018: 'The West depicts Chinese investments and loans that Beijing grants to developing countries as an economic tyrant that devours its victims. At the same time, it turns a blind eye to a clear point that is not mentioned frequently, which is: the purpose of these loans is to address poverty and underdevelopment that these countries suffer.' In spite of that, these loans created big problems between China and the benefitting countries.

A problem concerning Hambantota Port in Sri Lanka is the main example of criticism of China's external economic policy towards developing countries. The President of Sri Lanka acquired large loans from China in the period between 2010 and 2015, estimated at $5 billion, to develop infrastructure. After implementing these projects, the Sri Lankan government could not find the money to pay back the minimum level of interest on the Chinese loans, and had to mortgage about 70 per cent of the port to China. When the Opposition won under the slogan of 'liberating the country from Chinese control' and a new government was formed, it started to reclaim control over Hambantota Port. This has created a problem in the relationship between the two countries, despite official statements to the contrary.

The same thing happened in Malaysia—although in a different form—when Mahathir Mohamad, during his electoral campaign to evoke nationalism against China in Malaysia, accused the former

Prime Minister Najib Razak of taking suspicious loans from China. When Mahathir succeeded, he cancelled some of these loans and re-negotiated some contracts that had previously been signed with China. In a rare case of success, Malaysia was able to decrease by one-third the cost of rail projects that China is implementing for $15.7 billion. Beijing has also agreed to make another concession, by using Malaysians for 70 per cent of the labour force working on the project, and allowing contractors 40 per cent of the project implementation works.

On 21 February 2020, Eric McGlinchey from George Mason University published a study saying that China has 45 per cent of the external debts of Kyrgyzstan, 40 per cent of the external debts of Tajikistan, and 21 per cent of the external debts of Uzbekistan. As with the rest of developing countries, the governments of these countries declared their inability to pay back these loans, and expressed their readiness to put some of their establishments at the disposal of Chinese companies. In 2018, the government of Rahmon in Tajikistan declared that it was unable to pay back $332 million loan from China to rehabilitate Dushanbe energy station. Consequently, the Chinese company TBEA Electric received control over the gold mine in Garmo Heights. Due to the failure of the Tajik government to pay back the Chinese loan, another Chinese company hastened to capture a large share of an aluminium melting factory in Tajikistan, in addition to large tax exemptions enjoyed by the Chinese companies. This had a negative impact on the financial resources of the country, and added new problems to the already unstable Tajik economy.

In Kyrgyzstan, the government took a Chinese loan of $386 million to rehabilitate an energy station in the capital city Bishkek. In January 2018, an examination of the region revealed that the rehabilitation was not implemented due to corruption, and the inhabitants remained without heating. In January 2018, six officials were brought to trial, including two former Prime Ministers, and charged with misusing the Chinese loan. Whether Beijing is right or wrong, the scandals that surrounded these loans tainted the positive image that China wanted to convey.

The Centre for Global Development, headquartered in Washington, warned last year against this Chinese orientation when it indicated that twenty-three out of sixty-eight countries who benefitted from 'Belt and Road' loans have become greatly exposed to debt stress. The Centre added: 'Eight countries, Tajikistan, the Maldives, Pakistan, Djibouti, Laos, Mongolia, Montenegro, have become exposed to the risks resulting from Chinese debts.' The Centre went on: 'There are concerns that Chinese debts problems will create an inappropriate degree of dependence on China as a creditor. The increase in debts and the growth of China's role in managing bilateral problems led to the aggravation of internal and bilateral tensions.'

Son: It seems that China has been aware of these things in its relationship with Pakistan, the largest beneficiary of Chinese loans. Beijing decided to transform its financial standing with Pakistan into a success story for its investments under the Belt and Road. The new Pakistani government, headed by Imran Khan, expressed concern over Chinese loans, and demanded a reconsideration of their conditions. Beijing responded to these demands by freezing the funding of tens of intended projects in Pakistan. The new Pakistani government withdrew some of its demands, and some Chinese projects were implemented in Pakistan. There is an indication that China, in the first place, is betting on the relationship with the Pakistani army rather than with its political parties. This was borne out through its appointing a retired Pakistani general for the Chinese–Pakistani economic path, which includes most of the Chinese projects under 'Belt and Road in Pakistan'.

Beijing is keen to reveal the bright side of the loans offered under the Belt and Road Initiative, and not talk about problems arising from these loans.

Despite that, some important questions arise, such as: Why did relevant Chinese authorities offer loans of billions of dollars to poor countries like Sri Lanka, Bangladesh, Tajikistan, and others, while—supposedly—knowing that these countries will be unable to pay back those debts in the future?

Why did Chinese banks and planning bodies—supposedly among the best in the world—fail to research the economic viability of the two Sri Lankan projects, the airport and seaport, and warn the Sri Lankan government of the consequences of these loans?

I will try to answer these two questions, using my knowledge of the situation from my twenty years of living in China. China does not have extensive experience in the domain of foreign investments, and the Chinese institutions responsible for economic viability studies are still relatively weak, or at least lagging behind China's capacity for project construction. Government attention in international investment has been focused on two areas, firstly using the fiscal surplus that was created by the massive export operations. The second one is the search for external projects for Chinese construction companies after the internal infrastructure project market reached saturation point, in addition to sourcing natural resources like petroleum, gas, and the various minerals on which China depends for turning the wheel of its economy. Chinese government departments found that the best method for these ventures is to provide finance to the targeted projects, guaranteed by the foreign governments. These foreign government offer list of priority projects in which they want China to invest. The relative government entities in China conduct a perfunctory viability study, for which the most important step is to have the national insurance company SINOSURE to agree to enlist in the project and provide the insurance that guarantees payment to the Chinese companies and banks. This acceptance depends, in the first place, on the financial situation of the recipient state. Alternatively, the Chinese leadership may instruct SINOSURE to give consent based on China's national interests. Examples of this are Pakistan, Venezuela and even Egypt, countries whose financial situations could not match the minimum requirements for the financial guarantee.

There is fierce competition among Chinese companies themselves to get these projects with the main purpose of putting their labourers and suspended machinery to work. They don't worry themselves about the profitability of the overseas projects as the majority of them are engineering, procurement, construction (EPC) projects, the ownership and management of which are handed back to the client upon completion. I don't believe that economic viability of the projects was a priority as long as there was an acceptable guarantee to return the loans. The problem in Sri Lanka emerged because the decision-maker chose the airport and the seaport next to his base, a remote area that lacked basic infrastructure, an area that was important for the next elections!

Father: This does not relieve the Chinese government from responsibility. It should have, first of all, checked the ability of the governments of Sri Lanka and Bangladesh, for example, to pay back the large loans they received from China. I do not rule out the existence of pervasive corruption behind these projects.

Son: In this regard, I would like to point out something I have always noticed, which is the sensitivity of China regarding issues of sovereignty. Many former Chinese officials told me: 'China does not allow any party to lecture us or teach us how to manage our country. We do not intervene with issues of other countries, nor do we teach them how to manage the government and the projects.'

This has always been one of China's problems because there is a very thin line between respecting the sovereignty of others and indifference! I would like to go back to the topic of the impact of loans on the attitudes of other countries towards China. It is natural for China to expect that countries which receive its loans and assistance would not participate in ChinaPhobia. It would also be illogical for the government of any country to participate in campaigns against China and adopt Chinese separatist movements, and then seek assistance from China. The Chinese government, after all, is not a charity that provides for others without economic and political returns. Earlier on, we indicated some of the conditions China requires from those who desire to receive its economic benefits.

This is the method used by all superpowers that give assistance and loans. We have never heard of America or other superpowers giving their assistance to any entity that opposes them or criticizes their policy. In other words, Beijing receives large political benefits, gaining not only economically from the loans it grants others. In fact, China has used its financial influence to encourage Cambodia, Laos, Myanmar, and Thailand to mitigate the attitude of the ASEAN against China's policy in the South China Sea. Even the Philippines, which is the main party in the South China Sea islands dispute, and which won a ruling from the International Court of Justice against China, has softened its position after the ascent of its new President, and started convergence with China and divergence from America, in the hope of receiving economic benefits from China. The same thing happened with Bangladesh and Indonesia regarding the Uighurs issue.

Father: We notice this transformation in the attitude of most Muslim countries towards China, as they are not willing to sacrifice the larger economic interests that connect them with Beijing. In the same way, Arab countries would prevent any of their parties from promoting or adopting the ChinaPhobia policy.

The other issue that Beijing insists upon in its relations with countries it invests in, or with whom it has diplomatic dealings, is the recognition of Beijing's government as the representative of the Chinese people, and the recognition that Taiwan is part of China. Up to the end of 2019, the last country to cut its relationship with Taiwan in order to obtain Chinese investments was Kiribati, which is an archipelago in the Pacific Ocean. This happened in September 2019, with the result that the number of countries that still have diplomatic relations with Taiwan has decreased to fifteen. Beijing exerted intense pressure on the five African countries that still recognise Taiwan, to make them cut their links with Taipei. China has given large economic inducements for these countries to succeed in its endeavour. Four of the African countries have ceased relations with Taiwan and acknowledged the One-China policy. Swaziland still recognizes Taiwan and continues to be subjected to Chinese inducements and pressure to change its position.

Finally, one factor that remains to be mentioned is that the transformation of China to the largest global consumer market has become one of the most important deterrents against ChinaPhobia in the Third World. Nowadays, China has begun linking countries of the developing world with Chinese markets. Commercial data indicates that China is the number one importer of raw materials and agricultural products in a large number of third world countries. In addition, Chinese companies lead in providing consumer goods for third world markets. The fact that China today is the biggest trade partner of more than 130 countries is a really powerful tool for Beijing, and the

Chinese officials are getting better and better in exploring methods of leveraging this fact.

In short, the growth of China's economic power, and the augmentation of its financial relations, especially with developing countries, is one of the most important reasons for the spread of Chinese influence in Africa, Asia and Latin America, and is also one of the factors that prevent the spread of ChinaPhobia there.

Son: In a previous chapter, we mentioned that one of the reasons ChinaPhobia emerged lies in China's exponential growth, which enabled it to become a rival to America. As a matter of fact, this growth has generated a new factor that augments the problems between China and other countries, especially developing nations. An increased arrogance and disdain is apparent now in the behaviour of Chinese youths, especially the rich, towards third world peoples and countries. This will have a negative impact on China's reputation and influence in developing countries, and it will activate ChinaPhobia there.

The majority of Chinese youths consider themselves as extremely more advanced than Arabs, Africans and Latins. Through my acquaintance with this group, I conclude that one of the reasons for this attitude is their conviction that China, whose growth was way below that of these countries thirty years ago, has now attained a significant level of wealth and development, while the Arabs, Africans and Latin peoples have remained the same, or become even more miserable. The problem is that this view does not stop at contempt for developing countries, but it has become the base on which China's youth build their view and understanding of life. The main criterion for success according to these young people is the ability to accumulate fortunes. Thus, Jack Ma, the founder of Alibaba Group, Lei Jun the founder of Xiaomi, and Ma Huateng the founder of Tencent are the heroes of this era because they succeeded and became billionaires. The youth of today no longer consider an excellent scientist, researcher, a hardworking teacher or an honest employee as idols for the new generation.

Hence, the fast material development in China was offset by the under development of moral and spiritual virtues in the new Chinese generation, and it is reflected in their condescending and arrogant attitude towards the citizens of developing countries. For example, you can find many important businessmen in China, mostly the younger generation, refuse to meet leaders of developing countries due to the low economic value of these countries.

In their report to the *Harvard Business Review*, professors Stewart Black and Allen Morrison—with thirty years' experience of working with major Chinese companies—shed light on the most important international problem for Chinese companies.

The main issue is the lack of respect for others and their different cultures, and the arrogance of the managers of these companies. They summarized this problem with the words of a government official in a country where a number of large Chinese companies operate, as he said: 'The reason for the arrogance of the Chinese, their lack of respect for others and their local communities, their extortion of local companies by taking a large amount of interest themselves, and their indifference towards the environment unlike their behaviour at home, is because China is a large country, and it grew very quickly and for a long time.' When Chinese youths return from their travels to developing countries, their favourite topics of conversation are the poverty and underdevelopment of their infrastructure in comparison to China, the superiority of the Chinese cuisine compared with foreign food, and the inability of these countries to rehabilitate their historical sites, ruins and archaeological monuments. Such discussions strengthen racism in the minds of young Chinese, and reinforce their final conviction of the excellence of the Chinese civilization over third world countries that are sinking in underdevelopment, debt and political instability. The view of the global tourist sector view is not positive towards the behaviour of Chinese tourists, a problem that is well-recognized in China. Tourist guides accompanying large Chinese groups have many stories to tell about the offensive behaviour of some Chinese tourists, who are mostly young, and about their lack of interest in the cultures of other countries. The first question they ask when visiting any foreign tourist attraction is about its age, which they compare with China's—usually more ancient—ruins. When the Chinese visit foreign museums, their attention is directed to the existence of Chinese antiques and exhibits in one museum or another. When it comes to food, Chinese tourists prefer their own food above all others, especially after their third day abroad when most probably, discussion will turn to the richness of the Chinese cuisine. Of course, generalization is always dangerous but what we are talking about is a general feeling that comes from daily interaction, including among our own family.

Certainly, in the global tourist sector, all countries are competing to attract Chinese tourists who are the first-class shoppers of the world. In 2019 over 160 million travelled the world spending over $220 billion on luxury goods; this number will grow over the years and is expected to reach 300 million travellers within twenty years. How they conduct themselves will be one of the most important factors in shaping the world's view of China, either negatively or positively.

Father: I believe that the root of ChinaPhobia, which started to spread in different countries around the world, is the failure of China to create an appropriate and convincing mechanism with which to address the world. Current Chinese international political dialogue is unable to convey a clear and transparent understanding of China's objectives, and the core of its policy to achieve these objectives. I have met many leaders from around the world, and the impression they give is that they do not comprehend China's actual policies towards their countries, and they do not know precisely how Chinese leaders anticipate achieving their international plans. This incomprehension creates a feeling of caution, concern and sometimes fear, towards China.

Usually, a visiting foreign leader will hear nice things from the Chinese leaders, but when he or she returns home and asks his or her administration to follow up and revert on the progress, the leader finally realizes that most of what they were told in Beijing does not correspond to actual reality. Here lies the problem, ambiguity and precaution and big slogans are features of China's external policies.

'It's sometimes easier to understand America's direction than China's direction because of the open nature of the debate and the openness of the debate, while America's direction is something you can glean from various readings, conferences and discussions, understanding China's direction is more opaque,' said Anwar Mohammed Gargash, ex-Minister of UAE foreign affairs, and current diplomatic advisor to the UAE President, at the World Policy Conference in Abu Dhabi in October 2021.

Not disclosing details and avoiding explicit expression is a cultural legacy in China that can be felt during meals and in their private sessions. Secrecy, manipulation, hinting and non-verbal communication are authentic Chinese arts, and extensive knowledge and experience are needed to decode these indirect messages and assemble the pieces of the puzzle.

In other words, the Chinese official practices these methods as soon as he steps on the career ladder. This can be attributed to the following reasons:

Firstly, the Chinese think that words that are open to multiple interpretations and understanding that will provide an escape route for the speaker and provide him with a defence against humiliation when the desired outcome is not achieved. Second, the political legacy put in place by Deng Xiaoping was based on the policy of 'hide and bide', precaution, pondering, and pre-meditation, keeping a low profile internationally, avoiding direct conflicts. These are things that the current leadership has abandoned, believing that this policy is redundant and no longer suits the needs and aspirations of China.

The third reason is that China is not yet able to formulate cohesive international policies and agendas. Beijing lacks the presence of deep-rooted establishments and teams of experts skilled in implementing its leaders' international aspirations. Many might question the validity of this claim, given China's impeccable record of achieving goals and public dissemination of long-term plans. My answer to these questions is the following.

These accomplishments have occurred inside China, within its national framework, in an environment that falls under the control of the Party and the State. However, the international field is not the same as China's homeground, and it contains a lot of unexpected and variable elements and orientations. As we mentioned, China does not have establishments that can be consulted to interpret complex international situations. Internationally, influential countries like

America, Russia, and the major European countries have considerable expertise in addressing international crises, and have appropriate weight to influence situations. This has not happened in China which was confined to itself throughout history, and did not play any international leading role over the past three centuries. The relations of the Chinese Empire with foreigners were managed by the same administration responsible for managing the internal affairs of citizens of China, and countries under the Empire. Moreover, as we hinted, the mentality of the Empire was based on the opinion that China is the centre, and other countries are either marginal or under the Emperor's court.

Son: There is another issue that we should address, which has a negative impact on China's reputation, and augments its problems with the world. That is the gradual abandonment of the Chinese of one of their most important historical traits, which is modesty. If you ask representatives of foreign missions in Beijing what they think is different about China's external policy, the answer will be that China is speaking in an arrogant and loud voice, and Chinese ambassadors all over the world, particularly in developed countries, have appointed themselves as lecturers on good behaviour, and as guardians for the implementation of international law, according to China's interpretation. In my opinion, this change has occurred due to the governmental bureaucracy that currently prevails in China. It is known that Xi Jinping when he took up his role was not satisfied with the performance of Chinese diplomacy in general. The administrative circles failed to correctly execute the Chinese President's call for self-confidence.

Adoption of an effective external policy was actually realized through perfunctory and objectionable methods, aimed at proving loyalty. While the highest leadership still speaks in a calm and objective language, China's foreign ambassadors competed at raising their tone and conveying messages of implicit threat to whoever offends China. In my opinion, this happens because the lower circles in authority try to rigidly implement instructions from the senior levels, resulting sometimes in an opposite outcome to the original instruction. For example, the Chinese President's call for confidence and effectivity resulted in the unprecedented use of a language of condescension and indelicacy, contradicting what the Chinese leader called for. The reason for this sudden unfavourable behaviour on the part of Chinese diplomats could be in response to the intervention of foreign governments in matters concerning China's internal affairs. However, this diplomatic conduct reflected negatively on China's image and further damaged Beijing's relations with many countries. Chinese diplomats protested loudly when:

- Canada arrested Meng Wan Zhou, the daughter of the Huawei founder,
- Germany's Foreign Minister received one of Hong Kong's youth,
- Czechia's Mayor made statements about Taiwan,
- Australia accused Beijing of espionage in Australia,
- Norway awarded the Nobel Prize to Chinese opposition figures, the manager of the NBA basketball team in America made statements in support of the opposition in Hong Kong,
- Turkish leaders made statements concerning the Xinjiang issue.

The list of relevant examples goes on, and the interesting thing is that loud Chinese protestations did not resolve any of the issues, nor did they lead the other parties to change their behaviour. Instead, they augmented the tension with other countries, and increased the level of ChinaPhobia.

This behaviour reduces the positive impact of the growth of the Chinese economic giant and sways international trust in China.

Father: In this regard, I remember certain experiences during my term of duty as an ambassador in China, which indicate that Chinese diplomacy then was in fact quieter, more patient and less noisy.

At the beginning of the third millennium, the Chinese authorities made a firm decision to get rid of the Falun Gong spiritual movement, which had become very popular in China. Its headquarters were removed, and many of its members were imprisoned, with claims from the American Press that they were tortured. The interesting thing is that this movement had proponents all over the world, including in the

US. Massive protests China were organized in America. In the middle of this anti-China atmosphere, President Hu Jintao paid an official visit to Washington in 2006. Diplomatic circles in Beijing believed that anti-China movements on the streets of America, in Congress and in American mass media would negatively impact on the visit. In fact, the protests augmented and American demonstrators organized noisy marches in front of the residence of the Chinese President in Blair House in Washington, where they shouted anti-China slogans, heard by President Hu Jintao. American journalists who supported Falun Gong sneaked into the White House during a joint press conference with the American President at that time. They showered the Chinese President with provocative and intolerable questions and shouted at him for several minutes. The foreign diplomatic compound in Beijing was astounded when it became aware that none of those anti-China protests affected the results of this visit. The Chinese embassy in Washington did not rush to protest, and Hu Jintao did not interrupt or shorten his visit. The Chinese government did not take any measures against American interest in China, and the visit, which ended peacefully, in fact developed Chinese–American cooperation.

The second incident is related to the Dalai Lama. In 2007, American legislators decided to bestow on the Dalai Lama the Congressional Gold Medal. This irritated China, which organized a media campaign in opposition. Things became aggravated when America's President Bush attended the ceremony to award the medal. This happened at a time when Beijing was inviting presidents of the world to attend the opening ceremony of the Olympic Games in 2008. Many foreign ambassadors in China expected that China would not invite the American President due to his participation in the aforementioned ceremony and his reception of the Dalai Lama. However, the opposite happened. The invitation was sent, and the attendance of the American President at the Olympic Games opening ceremony in Beijing was announced in advance. Articles condemning America and its president published in China did not deter the Chinese government from sending an invitation to the American President.

4: Could ChinaPhobia be Mitigated?

ChinaPhobia did not appear because of an existing ideological contradiction between the USA and China, as was the situation between Moscow and Washington. It arose as a result of clashing interests and mutual concerns. Such enmity can be overcome and mitigated before it grows, without necessarily leading to the dissolution of ruling regimes in either China or America.

Father: This truth opens the door to the possibility of finding a mechanism of coexistence and problem-solving. To achieve that, both China and America have to take an imaginative and innovative approach with specific procedures and steps in order to consider mutual concerns, and to decrease the causes of tension that appeared in their bilateral relations. I will start with China.

In the minds of peoples of the world, the image of China invokes the Orient's charm, beauty, and mystery of its legends. The achievements of the Chinese civilization, including culture, inventions, and lifestyle, have spread all over the world. Confucianism and Taoism, with their wisdom and teachings, have invaded the minds of the world. Throughout history, Chinese civilization was characterized by two basic features: tolerance among races, religions and sects, and advocacy of peace and cooperation among peoples.

In ancient history, the Chinese Empire did not wage great external wars. Rather, it attracted the rest of civilizations through cooperation, trade, partnership and benefit-sharing. The lamp of trade was the lighthouse that illuminated paths of this cooperation. Understanding between Chinese, Muslim, Arab and Indian civilizations grew, and close cooperation at that time enabled the interchange of scientific achievements and cultural and spiritual morals. The four inventions of China spread in the ancient world and European, Arab, Muslim and Indian markets were filled with ceramics, tea and silk coming from China. On the other hand, this understanding built strong bridges of cultural and spiritual cooperation among these cultures. Arab and Indian architectural arts, and later European skills, were brought into China by major Arab, Indian, and European engineers and craftsmen who built entire cities, including Beijing. Many foreigners worked as high officials at the imperial palace. In addition, Islam, Buddhism and Christianity spread in China. These religions were considered a part of the sublime spiritual construction of China rather than strange trends.

Ibn Battuta and then Marco Polo and other explorers wrote about the charm of China and the tenderness and tolerance of Chinese people. ChinaPhobia did not exist at that time, although China was among the largest and most advanced countries.

Examining the causes that triggered the current ChinaPhobia, and to which we referred in a previous chapter, indicates mutual responsibility for the appearance of this state of enmity. China has taken procedures and made decisions. Misunderstanding of these Chinese steps and biased interpretations led to the augmentation of feelings of ChinaPhobia.

Giving up some of the liberal principles declared by Deng Xiaoping, becoming inhospitable to foreigners, the economic plans that deprived foreign companies of their previous privileges, the new strict approach to religions, strengthening the domination of communism over economic and cultural life, the events that took place in Hong Kong and Xinjiang, and the penetrative policy in the South China Sea.

All these developments have awakened caution and worry among China's neighbours and Western circles which had based their attitudes on the possibility of China transforming into a liberal country, like the West.

Son: I want to expand on two points. First, throughout history, flexibility had always characterized the mentality and politics of the Chinese. The present generation should always remember what Laozi, the founder of Taoism, said, that flexibility wins over brutal and harsh forces. Flexibility was one of the reasons for China's power and continuity for 5,000 years. Trading flexibility for coarse politics was never going to work in favour of Chinese development. It is not possible for innovation and creativity to flourish in an atmosphere of limitation and harshness where freedom of information is denied.

Secondly, China, over decades, has bragged about its peaceful rise and its adoption of an external peace and development policy. However, fear has been stirred among China's neighbours by the exacerbation of the situation in the South China Sea concerning disputed islands, and the increasing Chinese military presence there, in addition to discussions about the augmentation of China's strategic military power including building Chinese aircraft carriers, satellites, a military stealth bomber, and new generations of rockets, as well as the change in Chinese military doctrine and the establishment of military bases abroad. They have also given a new justification for the American military build-up in Southeast Asia. These actions have attracted strong propaganda aimed at spreading ChinaPhobia. They also provided fuel for American entities to talk about risk and threat from China, and about China's 'big stick' policy in Southeast Asia. These entities have organized a broad campaign to defame the expression of China's peaceful rise.

It is true that America's attempts to contain China, to weaken it and stop its progress, are mainly attributed to ChinaPhobia. However, it is also true that certain procedures followed by the Chinese government, which might be justified from the perspective of Chinese interests, have further fuelled this campaign. The result was a decrease in the international appeal of China, and a worldwide dimming of popular feelings of empathy and admiration for China. This has paved the way for an expansion of ChinaPhobia to new locations. There are some popular anti-China movements in countries of Central Asia (such as

Kirghizia and Kazakhstan) where a number of protests took place against the Chinese presence, and also in some African countries.

We all remember how the biased media described the ascent to presidency of populist politician Michael Sata in Zambia in 2011 as the first African President against China. The main motive for such movements is not mistakes committed by Chinese individuals or companies, but there are also local and international forces who have a political interest in augmenting the danger from China, and inflaming ChinaPhobia.

Thus, the errors of some Chinese companies become the subject of constant attention by certain media who magnify them, focus on the negative aspects, and publish them on a wider level to incite against China. It is notable that the phenomenon of ChinaPhobia was transferred to countries like Russia that are friends of China. Despite the good relations between the governments and presidents of both countries, surveys reflected an increase in the number of criticizers of China in Russia. On 18 September 2019, results of a survey that was conducted by the Russian Levada Centre were published, and they indicated an increase in the rate of anti-China mentality in Russia from 15 per cent to 39 per cent during the past two years. This is happening in Russia despite the great openness between the two countries and the growth of trade and unprecedented coordination between them on the international field, especially in the Security Council.

We also witnessed the spread of biased Coronavirus news and how it was described by the international press as the 'China virus', or the 'virus coming from China'. On the other hand, the H1N1 virus that spread in America many years earlier was not linked to America, despite its manifold risks in comparison to the dangers of the coronavirus that spread in China. This indicates that international empathy with China could not stop such biased and unfair treatment.

China must not stop at simply looking at itself in the mirror and defining its external and internal policy on that basis, but must also realize how the world sees it today. Unfortunately, the positive international view of China has started to change for the worse. The Chinese have to realize that countries around the world are no longer convinced by the pretexts that China used in the past forty years to advertise itself as a vehicle of global development and growth. In many aspects, China no longer belongs among the developing countries—a motto that won Beijing many international economic advantages and much international empathy. Moreover, Chinese leaders have to quieten down and stop talking about China's success in lifting its people out of poverty and transforming their lives as the biggest Chinese contribution to humanity. How are peoples of the world connected to this issue? The average Arab suffering from the continued crisis gets irritated by these slogans. When China brags about its absolute success in handling COVID-19, announcing that life and the economy is back to normal, while an average Irish farmer is still deeply affected by the pandemic, he will not fall in love with China nor he will embrace the glory of China's story.

The great advancements that China achieved during the past decades, and the selfish behaviour of Chinese companies, have changed the view of the leaders of developing countries towards Beijing. It has become difficult now for those leaders to comprehend the statement that China is a developing country and that it represents the Third World in the Security Council, and expect other developing countries to support China's affairs and its external policy! The West in general no longer considers China as the world's factory. Rather it considers it as a fierce rival threatening to weaken and replace the West. Major economic forces in the world no longer see the ambitious programmes adopted by the Chinese government as beneficial job opportunities, but rather as a source of fear and limitation for their companies. This negative view does not only concern China, but it also includes all countries that ascend to the position of 'superpower'. It is the tax of success.

Furthermore, the requisites of China's soft power have been exhausted and are no longer convincing. Nobody still believes that an enormous country like China with large foreign-exchange reserves and an advanced technical base, is unable to multiply its external assistance to aid, to facilitate and support its many ultra-billionaires in launching global charity programs that help people outside of China. On top of that the Chinese government's serious mistake of politicizing their cultural institutions abroad, and seeking to mobilize overseas Chinese to support China's external policy has sowed doubt and distrust in the relationships of overseas Chinese with their local communities in other countries. The same thing applies to China's external mass media which utilizes objectionable direct advertising styles. Chinese companies operating overseas suffer from the negative image that has also been formed about most of them, that they exist as a means for gaining quick profits, plundering local wealth and polluting the environment.

Father: To avoid more global tension, the US must reconsider much of the basis of its current international policy. The Americans, who have been used during the past quarter-century, to behaving like winners, the leaders of the world, the strongest and most efficient, must change and stop behaving like international policeman and the absolute ruler image that resides in their minds.

America was previously the strongest economic and military power on earth, and this fact was strengthened after the dissolution of the Soviet Union. America has the capacities and financial institutions to exercise financial control over the world. American power did not change; it increased. What changed however was the global situation that predicts the emergence of a new rising force, headed by China, which started to introduce itself in all domains, and required a share in the international economy and influence that were previously exclusive to America. According to many indicators, the Chinese economy has become a strong rival for its American counterpart; in fact China's economy has surpassed the US economy when measured by the more refined yardstick that both IMF and CIA now judge to be the single best metric for comparing national economies. Graham Allison has argued in his provocative article in *The National Interest* that the IMF report reveals that China's economy is one-sixth larger than America's. Graham Allison rightly asked: 'Why can't we admit the reality?'

India and Russia started to accumulate factors of power, and now they are important international military and economic powers. Thus, the level of America's contribution to the global economy has dropped to its current 25 per cent and will continue going south. The American military was also a victim of the same relative decline. In the 90's, the US Army budget was bigger than the remaining twenty countries behind it, today even with the continued unsustainable increase in the Pentagon's budget, those twenty have shrunk to eight!

The Americans have to admit these facts and deal with them, and descend quietly from the top of the tree to the ground. Using violence and rough methods to hinder advancement, especially with China, results in adverse consequences. I will give an example of the futility of this method. The US imposed sanctions on China's arms exports, especially strategic missiles including rockets, bombers, and drones, in addition to space equipment. The result was that China now possesses all of this arsenal, and competes with the US in cyber arms and AI. Today the USA is weaponizing its high-tech dominance by threatening China with stopping sales of the semiconductors and commercial aircraft for which China pays $400 billion annually. I bet that within twenty years, China will be the biggest headache in these fields for American companies! America also resorted to imposing economic and military sanctions against Moscow, but Russia proved its resilience, and was able to manufacture new generations of arms that pose a real threat to the US. The 'big stick' policy adopted by America against China and Russia led these two countries to convergence on the grounds of enmity to America.

I conclude that the policy of blockades, sanctions, containment, and threats against China did not stop the rise of China, nor did it weaken the power and influence of Russia. These methods have instead pushed China and Russia and other rising forces to adopt aggressive and extreme attitudes towards the US.

America created globalization, and it stood against trade protectionism and advocated the freedom of transporting people, money, and commodities through borders, and respect of human rights. Ironically, the current American administration stands against all these values that Washington initially launched and implemented for managing the world.

We do not want to judge and convict American policy, but we are pointing out that certain facts relevant to China - especially now that US foreign policy has become ChinaPhobic—will not force China to retreat, but will have adverse consequences. In short, I believe that the Chinese are not worried about the future, and they continue to work to achieve their dream of building a strong and flourishing China. Competition and cooperation between China and America facilitate the solution of any problem in the world, and the opposite is also true: conflict between Washington and Beijing will complicate and aggravate the problems of the world.

Regardless of the feelings of Americans towards the Chinese, the concerns of China's competitors, or regrets for having helped China—what is required from Washington now is to be realistic and pragmatic, and to admit the bitter reality. That reality says that it would be difficult, even impossible, to shrink the Chinese dragon to the size America has designed for it. It has grown and started to demand some privileges that were exclusive to America. It no longer accepts the position of employee or even a highly paid CEO on the Global Board of Directors. The Chinese dragon needs recognition as a stakeholder and an important position on the Global Board of Directors.

Today, the Chinese refuse to adhere to international rules and laws that were formed by the USA in its own interests, and imposed on others, at the prime of its victory. The Chinese want to change these rules to serve their interests, in line with their new status on military and economic levels. The Chinese consider themselves as the children of a continuous success for the seventy years of the 'People's Republic of China'. They have never lost a war, and during the past forty years, they did not suffer any major disasters that would hinder their progress. They have built a strong nation that competes with America on all fronts, and they have a strict and cohesive leadership. The Chinese are proud because their military in its weakest times, forced the largest military force in the world, i.e., America, to accept a tie and withdraw its plans to invade North Korea. This pride increases with the current economic equality. Why should we, the strong ones, the Chinese, adhere to America's orders, when its closest allies have rebelled against it and countries in its orbit started to drift away?

Son: Despite the existence of such feelings among the Chinese, in general, the main orientation I see now while I am in China is a preference for dialogue over a confrontation with America, a favouring of cooperation over conflict, a search for common ground, a denouncement of threat, domination and monopolizing decisions and a return to dialogue and negotiation to solve problems between the two countries, in order to arrive at a vision for building future relations on new bases of equality and mutual benefit.

Through my conversations with the Chinese in private sessions, I formed the conviction that can be summarized as follows. The Chinese do not seek to eliminate America and replace it on the throne of the world. They are not ready to pay the price of being number one. Basically, as we mentioned earlier, even if some Chinese entities advocated or sought global leadership, the reality indicates that China does not have the capacity to handle being number one in the world. Neither the culture nor the geographical location allows it, and neither the global climate nor the financial and emotional abilities make it possible for China to eliminate America and ascend the international throne. They know that if China was to become the first power in the world, its enemies would exceed its allies. Thus, the intelligence of the Chinese and their continuous wisdom over thousands of years prevents them from thinking in this manner! They want an influential regional role in Asia, and a voice that can be heard in international affairs, as well as a portion of the returns on their investment in the world's company, instead of an employee's salary.

Naturally, China will proceed in its growth and development, and it is not accountable for America's retreat. China does not assume responsibility for the USA's political and economic problems, and it is not ready to stop its progress and wait for America to solve its problems. The Chinese logic states that if America is now suffering from many crises, they alone have to bear the responsibility for solving their problems themselves, without holding others responsible. I do not think that America's interest lies in weakening China's influence or seeking the collapse of its regime! As we mentioned earlier, the dispute here is not a zero equation, but a confrontation over who will be the strongest at the end of this century. It is a race based on being able to reform and self-reinvent, it's a race of knowledge and it's about possessing the technical advantage. Petroleum, mines, heavy rockets, and aircraft carriers will not settle the battle because knowledge and technology is the power of the future and the basis of nations' strength.

Conclusion

'Change' is one reason for the emergence of ChinaPhobia. China has changed, and America is changing as well. The change that occurred in China was comprehensive, and Beijing now aspires to play a bigger role in international politics following its economic and financial growth. Moreover, Chinese leadership has gradually abandoned the liberal approach of the West, strengthened the role of the Communist Party, and established an assertive external policy based on not having a truce with America especially in areas of national core interest. The principle of group leadership was also downgraded, while the authority of the current President was augmented with his term of office being made unrestricted, giving a great deal of power to President Xi.

In America, the ascent of President Trump from non-traditional political circles reflects the beginning of this change. Trump adopted the 'America First' slogan reflect a change in the mood in the USA. It is changing to become 'America first versus China first', the American Dream is at a crossroads with the Chinese Dream.

It was inevitable that winds of change in both countries would intersect, and the resulting political storm shook not only them, but the whole world. Change in China was difficult and was achieved over a great number of years. Likewise, the birth of change in America will not be easy because the elite and those benefitting from the present situation are still strong. They refuse to surrender America's sole leading world position.

On the other hand, Beijing refuses to adhere to the rules established by Washington in the past fifty years, and it wants to instigate a new international system reflecting new power relationships in the world and taking China's interests into consideration. However, two problems in America currently aggravate the situation. The first one is the determination of the ruling class not to recognize the rise of China and its transformation into a rival superpower. The second problem is the fact that none of the politicians in the Republican and Democratic Parties dare to confront the American people and tell them the truth about the change in power relationships in the world.

We understand the difficulty of this situation, which can amount to political suicide. Furthermore, American society will not surrender to this new reality before exhausting all means of destroying the Chinese giant and eliminating it from global leadership. This idea is enhanced by the previous record of the Americans in subjugating their old competitors, like the Soviet Union, Germany and Japan. Here lies the danger of transforming ChinaPhobia into fierce confrontations, whether directly or through proxies, that will split the world anew and exhaust all its material and human resources.

To avoid that, we emphasize the necessity for deep and creative dialogue between China and America, on the basis of mutual concessions. This method might lead to a quiet rise of China and a relatively smooth descent of America; hence, the world will avoid more tremors and disasters. This sounds impossible, but it is essential that in this transitional stage leadership must be in the hands of rational persons and intellectuals who are capable of influencing public opinion, of controlling and calming the strong feelings of populism and nationalism, and of dispelling the illusions that veil today's reality.

The rise of China is a fact now, and America cannot return the Chinese Dragon back to its bottle; not only because China has the strength of all of America's previous competitors combined, as we mentioned earlier, but also because the international community no longer accepts that one country dominates the world and controls its destiny.

Moreover, the youth of the twenty-first century are now indifferent about inheriting the rules of the past century. Young Westerners do not believe in the justice of their countries' dominance over the world, nor do the young people of the Third World understand why they should adhere to the legacy of their ancestors' erroneous policies. The world today is heading towards multipolarity, and America and China are between these poles. The rise of China as the world's largest economy does not mean that America will become weaker economically, or that the standard of life of the majority of Americans will be affected. However, if Washington cares about maintaining the current standard of living for its population, it must look for new ways to fund itself instead of relying on the Dollar's dominance and exploiting the world economy.

We realize that the mere suggestion of these ideas could cause serious turmoil among American officials, but their persistence in ignoring the changes that have taken place in the past years, and in failing to acknowledge the new power relations, will further augment the situation. This could also lead to enormous destruction in the world because neither China nor the accompanying emerging powers like Russia, India, Indonesia, Turkey, and Brazil will accept the remnants of international influence that they are used to receiving from global forces in the past century.

The proof is that the G7 which led the world for many decades have—to all extents and purposes—come from the past, and they do not represent the current or future reality. At the same time, the BRICS group do not represent the future of the world either, nor do they replace the Group of Seven. Nevertheless, with the increasing power of the emerging forces, their contribution to the world economy will rise, along with an expansion of their role in formulating a new reality and future for the world.

In this transition period, we believe that it will be wise not to start conflicts with the American elite and the behind-door power circles; instead, they should be given some time to find a solution and a means for preserving their existence and interests to reinvent themselves within the upcoming new power structure.

History has shown that change is the way of the world and no situation can endure forever. We think that the moment of truth, that is, the moment of change in international relationships, has arrived. What is happening now in Chinese–American relations is a transitional stage where the ruling classes in both countries try to adapt and deal with inevitable changes. Attempts to hinder China's progress will not pay back over the long term because the rise of China relies more on internal Chinese elements and sources, than on external forces. Rational thinking predicts that China, despite all obstacles, will only get stronger in the present and in the future.

But unfortunately, attempts to stop China's progress will continue more frequently and more fiercely in the coming years. The commercial and political bickering between Beijing and Washington will persevere until both sides understand that their objectives cannot be achieved through confrontation, and until America becomes convinced that it is unable to stop the rise of China. Till then, the vanguard in both countries should not further incite the dispute, instead it should encourage building bridges of cooperation instead of conflict between China and America. We do not think that ChinaPhobia will definitely transform into a cold war because the volume of commercial, cultural, scientific, educational and human exchange, and the mutual dependence between China and America, cannot be compared to the past situation between America and the Soviet Union.

Despite the current tension in Chinese–American relations, the facts indicate that a total separation and decoupling of the two giants is impossible. The common links that were woven between the two countries over the past forty years are too strong for either the Chinese or the American leadership to cut. There are American investments in China of about quarter of a trillion dollars. There are also $5 trillion of Chinese financial holdings in American government bonds and the American stock exchange. Despite the trade war and historic hostility between China and USA, business between both nations is booming, with more trade, more deficit and more US investment in China and more Chinese companies going public in the US. These are the facts on the ground that will prevail eventually.

The general conviction is that it is impossible for either China or America to overcome the risks of climate change, because between them both countries produce 40 per cent of global greenhouse gases. We cannot solve climate change without both the USA and China reducing their emissions. Moreover, displacing the production chains that were established during the past decades between the two countries will lead to an economic crisis that will not only affect China and America, but also the economy of the entire world.

We realize that it would be wise to activate constructive forces between the two countries in order to prevent their relations from declining into conflict and tension. Fortunately, and as we mentioned earlier, problems between China and America are not of an ideological nature, rather they are political and economic disputes which can be solved by making agreements and mutual concessions, not necessarily resulting in the dissolution of either party. At the same time, we cannot forget that strong bonds and interdependence among European countries were unable to prevent devastating wars that killed tens of millions and were catastrophic for human civilization.

We must caution against two dangerous phenomena that have started to emerge. Firstly, the race in areas of technology and future sciences in both countries is being directed towards dishonourable and dangerous ends and has deviated from serving progress, development, and the good of humanity.

The second dangerous phenomenon lies in the unity of Americans to fight the rise of China. Even the more moderate and tolerant Americans demand that America must stop helping China, as it did in the past when it assisted China's rise from poverty to a middle-income nation. They also say that Beijing has to depend on itself if it wants to become a rich country. Americans think that they provided China with two basic elements that helped it grow. First, the American fleets in Southeast Asia created a peaceful environment for the rise of China, and secondly, America opened its technical, financial and economic doors to the Chinese.

There is consensus in America today that those doors should now be closed in China's face, particularly in the technological and financial domains, in order for America to maintain its global status. This process has begun already with procedures taken by the American administration to ban dealings with Chinese technology giants, and to impose pressure on Washington's allies to do the same and stop injecting technology and money into the Chinese economy. Washington will not allow Western companies to replace American firms in dealings with China.

America leaves little choice for its allies; for example, they either choose to use WhatsApp and deal with the CIA, or they depend on the Chinese WeChat and fall victim to Chinese security authorities. In this case, the West prefers the CIA over the Chinese security authority.

This has actually started to happen with a number of entities such as Israeli tech companies who are under pressure to move away from China, and with Kuwait and the Gulf countries, Britain and others being coerced to terminate contracts with the Chinese Huawei company. These are just harbingers of the full-blown confrontation, and it must be said that this conflict is inflicting serious damage on American companies themselves due to losing the largest consumer market in the world, i.e., China. Since money is ruling America now, American firms will not keep paying the price solely for the decisions of the White House.

Another issue that inflames ChinaPhobia is Beijing's hesitation in taking seriously its obligations as a great power. China is demanding the rights of a great power, but it procrastinates and evades paying the price, on the pretext that it is still the largest developing country in the world. However, the question is: how can a country like China become the world's largest economy, and at the same time, keep introducing itself as a developing country? This is an incomprehensible Chinese riddle.

The reason China tries to abstain from acting like an international superpower is to attempt to escape paying the price of full membership, but it blames others, saying that the Global Board of Directors does not want it to join, so why should it pay the price?

We believe that China does indeed desire to be an important influential member of the Global Board of Directors, but at the same time, it avoids paying the price. Through the Shanghai Corporation Organization, BRICS and AIIB, Beijing tried to establish a new Global Board of Directors, with new members including Russia, countries of Central Asia, India, Brazil and others. However, China has realized it cannot afford the cost. Despite the great achievements made by Beijing, some obstacles still slow its movement towards world leadership.

The first obstacle is its ageing society, as China will be the first country in history that ages before reaching world leadership. The second obstacle appears in the excessively local nature of the Chinese political mentality. Many Chinese officials still think that what happens in China is an internal affair of sovereignty, and that their internal policy is a matter that exclusively concerns their Communist Party. These officials do not want to realize that China's internal affairs have rapidly become the concern of the whole world. When China coughs today, the UAE trembles, and when China gets sick—as happened with the corona epidemic—half of global tourism becomes paralyzed, and half of the commodity markets in the world suffer from recession.

Moreover, Nigeria will refrain from commencing its developmental projects in the Boko Haram areas of influence because the price of petroleum decreased to less than $60 due to the decline in Chinese demand. Thus, suffering and problems will continue in the largest African country which will constitute the base for Africa's rise in this century. It should not be forgotten that farmers in Brazil are directly affected by the decision of Xi Jinping to increase the purchases of soybeans from America, and that three months of Coronavirus epidemic in China were enough for Australia to lose about 2 per cent of its GDP.

It will take some time before Chinese leaders realize that their decisions have serious international impact, affecting regions unknown to them, and that the excessive attachment to sovereignty is no more than a populist illusion. Until then, Chinese leaders have no other option than to get involved in the existing structures of the international system, fulfil their obligations as a superpower, and stop using the pretext of being a 'developing country'.

As China is a new prospective member on the old Global Board of Directors, it must inject a positive atmosphere by transferring its experiences to achieve developmental miracles for this Board. It also has to abandon economic egotism and national fanaticism, and implement the principles it advocates such as state equality and respect for smaller nations. Beijing says that it is the largest developing country; thus, it is required to represent the developing world on the Board, and to work on changing its internal regulations in a way that serves all humanity, not just the golden 1.4 billion people. Beijing must also mimic its experiences in investment and development, hence putting the chicken before the egg. So, China must implement its obligations before it enjoys the rights and privileges as a member of the Board of Directors. We know that for Beijing this is difficult to digest, but it seems now that it's the only way.

Internally, China should apply a valid open policy to the world, and abandon the ideological wall with which it currently surrounds itself. It also has to become more flexible in integrating foreigners and allowing them to be woven into the fabric of Chinese society, as well as offering them fair and unbiased opportunities to work and reside in China. There's no doubt that the absolute majority of Chinese population love their country and are proud of what it has achieved under the leadership of the CCP. Success acts like a magnet, it attracts people and creates a once-in-a-lifetime momentum. Therefore, it's in China's interest to trust its peoples' judgment by allowing the free flow of information. We believe that the more open China becomes, the prouder Chinese people will be of their leadership. We see this in the 160 million Chinese who travel around the world every year; each one of them comes back with more love for their country and a better understanding of China's achievements.

On the other hand, the leaders of this current Global Board of Directors should open the doors patiently to the new Chinese member, giving it opportunity and time, without overwhelming it with hostile pressures and sanctions.

It does not serve the interests of the Global Board of Directors to close their doors in China's face. International efforts would be futile if one of the strongest nations in the world did not join them. It is essential to include China in the existing frames of world management, otherwise the result will be an augmentation of the leadership conflict between two lions in a burning jungle. China has grown and developed to the extent that financial inducements and ceremonial positions do not tempt it anymore, even if it was given the position of CEO of the Board with a high salary. We believe that Beijing's interim objective now is to gain recognition as a full-fledged member of the Global Board of Directors, with all its accompanying rights and obligations.

Much more important than confronting China are the current emerging issues. The world today is threatened by the terrifying outbreak of the coronavirus, in addition to the great recession in the world economy, and the shameful problems of the augmentation of pollution and global warming and famines that today severely affect more than a billion people. In order to save the world, it is essential to unify efforts, especially between America and China.

We hope that this book will stimulate all parties to deep consideration aimed at finding creative solutions to avoid the confrontation of the century. While it is the starting point for new and bold thinking; this book does not offer final answers or solutions for the problems that affect the future of the world.

We end with an invitation for meditation and learning, with a poem that was recited during Dr Karim's Aspen Institute action forum, a poem that sparked the idea of this book and catalyzed a pledge to work hard to prevent 'ChinaPhobia'.

'Look again at that dot. That's here. That's home. That's us. On it everyone you love, everyone you know, everyone you ever heard of, every human being who ever was, lived out their lives. The aggregate of our joy and suffering, thousands of confident religions, ideologies, and economic doctrines, every hunter and forager, every hero and coward, every creator and destroyer of civilization, every king and peasant, every young couple in love, every mother and father, hopeful child, inventor and explorer, every teacher of morals, every corrupt politician, every 'superstar,' every 'supreme leader,' every saint and sinner in the history of our species lived there—on a mote of dust suspended in a sunbeam.

The Earth is a very small stage in a vast cosmic arena. Think of the rivers of blood spilled by all those generals and emperors so that, in glory and triumph, they could become the momentary masters of a fraction of a dot. Think of the endless cruelties visited by the inhabitants of one corner of this pixel on the scarcely distinguishable inhabitants of some other corner, how frequent their misunderstandings, how eager they are to kill one another, how fervent their hatreds.

Our posturings, our imagined self-importance, the delusion that we have some privileged position in the Universe, are challenged by this point of pale light. Our planet is a lonely speck in the great enveloping cosmic dark. In our obscurity, in all this vastness, there is no hint that help will come from elsewhere to save us from ourselves.

The Earth is the only world known so far to harbor life. There is nowhere else, at least in the near future, to which our species could migrate. Visit, yes. Settle, not yet. Like it or not, for the moment the Earth is where we make our stand.

It has been said that astronomy is a humbling and character-building experience. There is perhaps no better demonstration of the folly of human conceits than this distant image of our tiny world. To me, it underscores our responsibility to deal more kindly with one another, and to preserve and cherish the pale blue dot, the only home we've ever known.'

— Carl Sagan, 'Pale Blue Dot', 1994